El Pulpo

IRREGULAR SCHOOL REPORT OF
THE DDDEPARTMENT OF SCIENCE FICTION & ECONOMICS
Winter 2006/7

EDITORIAL (1)

by G.K. Chesterton

I cannot understand the people who take literature seriously; but I can love them, and I do. Out of my love I warn them to keep clear of this book. It is a collection of crude and shapeless papers upon current or rather flying subjects; and they must be published pretty much as they stand. They were written, as a rule, at the last moment; they were handed in the moment before it was too late, and I do not think that our commonwealth would have been shaken to its foundations if they had been handed in the moment after. They must go out now, with all their imperfections on their head, or rather on mine; for their vices are too vital to be improved with a blue pencil, or with anything I can think of, except dynamite.

Their chief vice is that so many of them are very serious; because I had no time to make them flippant. It is so easy to be solemn; it is so hard to be frivolous. Let any honest reader shut his eyes for a few moments, and approaching the secret tribunal of his soul, ask himself whether he would really rather be asked in the next two hours to write the front page of the *Times*, which is full of long leading articles, or the front page of *Tit-Bits*, which is full of short jokes. If the reader is the fine conscientious fellow I take him for, he will at once reply that he would rather on the spur of the moment write ten *Times* articles than one *Tit-Bits* joke. Responsibility, a heavy and cautious responsibility of speech, is the easiest thing in the world; anybody can do it. That is why so many tired, elderly, and wealthy men go in for politics. They are responsible, because they have not the strength of mind left to be irresponsible. It is more dignified to sit still than to dance the Barn Dance. It is also easier. So in these easy pages I keep myself on the whole on the level of the *Times*: it is only occasionally that I leap upwards almost to the level of *Tit-Bits*.

I resume the defence of this indefensible book. These articles have another disadvantage arising from the scurry in which they were written; they are too long-winded and elaborate. One of the great disadvantages of hurry is that it takes such a long time. If I have to start for High-gate this day week, I may perhaps go the shortest way. If I have to start this minute, I shall almost certainly go the longest. In these essays (as I read them over) I feel frightfully annoyed with myself for not getting to the point more quickly; but I had not enough leisure to be quick. There are several maddening cases in which I took two or three pages in attempting to describe an attitude of which the essence could be expressed in an epigram; only there was no time for epigrams. I do not repent of one shade of opinion here expressed; but I feel that they might have been expressed so much more briefly and precisely. For instance, these pages contain a sort of recurring protest against the boast of certain writers that they are merely recent. They brag that their philosophy of the universe is the last philosophy or the new philosophy, or the advanced and progressive philosophy. I have said much against a mere modernism. When I use the word 'modernism', I am not alluding specially to the current quarrel in the Roman Catholic Church, though I am certainly astonished at any intellectual group accepting so weak and unphilosophical a name. It is incomprehensible to me that any thinker can calmly call himself a modernist; he might as well call himself a Thursdayite. But apart altogether from that particular disturbance, I am conscious of a general irritation expressed against the people who boast of their advancement and modernity in the discussion of religion. But I never succeeded in saying the quite clear and obvious thing that is really the matter with modernism. The real objection to modernism is simply that it is a form of snobbishness. It is an attempt to crush a rational opponent not by reason, but by some mystery of superiority, by hinting that one is specially up to date or particularly 'in the know'. To flaunt the fact that we have had all the last books from Germany is simply vulgar; like flaunting the fact that we have had all the last bonnets from Paris. To introduce into philosophical discussions a sneer at a creed's antiquity is like introducing a sneer at a lady's age. It is caddish because it is irrelevant. The pure modernist is merely a snob; he cannot bear to be a month behind the fashion. Similarly I find that I have tried in these pages to express the real objection to philanthropists and have not succeeded. I have not seen the quite simple objection to the causes advocated by certain wealthy idealists; causes of which the cause called teetotalism is the strongest case. I have used many abusive terms about the thing, calling it Puritanism, or superciliousness, or aristocracy; but I have not seen and stated the quite simple objection to philanthropy; which is that it is religious persecution. Religious persecution does not consist in thumbscrews or fires of Smithfield; the essence of religious persecution is this: that the man who happens to have material power in the State, either by wealth or by official position, should govern his fellow-citizens not according to their religion or philosophy, but according to his own. If, for instance, there is such a thing as a vegetarian nation; if there is a great united mass of men who wish to live by the vegetarian morality, then I say in the emphatic words of the arrogant French marquis before the French Revolution, 'Let them eat grass'. Perhaps that French oligarch was a humanitarian; most oligarchs are. Perhaps when he told the peasants to eat grass he was recommending to them the hygienic simplicity of a vegetarian restaurant. But that is an irrelevant, though most fascinating, speculation. The point here is that if a nation is really vegetarian let its government force upon it the whole horrible weight of vegetarianism. Let its government give the national guests a State vegetarian banquet. Let its government, in the most literal and awful sense of the words, give them beans. That sort of tyranny is all very well; for it is the people tyrannising over all the persons. But 'temperance reformers' are like a small group of vegetarians who should silently and systematically act on an ethical assumption entirely unfamiliar to the mass of the people. They would always be giving peerages to greengrocers. They would always be appointing Parliamentary Commissions to enquire into the private life of butchers. Whenever they found a man quite at their mercy, as a pauper or a convict or a lunatic, they would force him to add the final touch to his inhuman isolation by becoming a vegetarian. All the meals for school children will be vegetarian meals. All the State public houses will be vegetarian public houses. There is a very strong case for vegetarianism as compared with teetotalism. Drinking one glass of beer cannot by any philosophy be drunkenness; but killing one animal can, by this philosophy, be murder. The objection to both processes is not that the two creeds, teetotal and vegetarian, are not admissible; it is simply that they are not admitted. The thing is religious persecution because it is not based on the existing religion of the democracy. These people ask the poor to accept in practice what they know perfectly well that the poor would not accept in theory. That is the very definition of religious persecution. I was against the Tory attempt to force upon ordinary Englishmen a Catholic theology in which they do not believe. I am even more against the attempt to force upon them a Mohamedan morality which they actively deny.

Again, in the case of anonymous journalism I seem to have said a great deal without getting out the point very clearly. Anonymous journalism is dangerous, and is poisonous in our existing life simply because it is so rapidly becoming an anonymous life. That is the horrible thing about our contemporary atmosphere. Society is becoming a secret society. The modern tyrant is evil because of his elusiveness. He is more nameless than his slave. He is not more of a bully than the tyrants of the past; but he is more of a coward. The rich publisher may treat the poor poet better or worse than the old master workman treated the old apprentice. But the apprentice ran away and the master ran after him. Nowadays it is the poet who pursues and tries in vain to fix the fact of responsibility. It is the publisher who runs away. The clerk of Mr Solomon gets the sack: the beautiful Greek slave of the Sultan Suliman also gets the sack; or the sack gets her. But though she is concealed under the black waves of the Bosphorus, at least her destroyer is not concealed. He goes behind golden trumpets riding on a white elephant. But in the case of the clerk it is almost as difficult to know where the dismissal comes from as to know where the clerk goes to. It may be Mr Solomon or Mr Solomon's manager, or Mr Solomon's rich aunt in Cheltenham, or Mr Soloman's rich creditor in Berlin. The elaborate machinery which was once used to make men responsible is now used solely in order to shift the responsibility. People talk about the pride of tyrants; but we in this age are not suffering from the pride of tyrants. We are suffering from the shyness of tyrants; from the shrinking modesty of tyrants. Therefore we must not encourage leader-writers to be shy; we must not inflame their already exaggerated modesty. Rather we must attempt to lure them to be vain and ostentatious; so that through ostentation they may at last find their way to honesty.

The last indictment against this book is the worst of all. It is simply this: that if all goes well this book will be unintelligible gibberish. For it is mostly concerned with attacking attitudes which are in their nature accidental and incapable of enduring. Brief as is the career of such a book as this, it may last just twenty minutes longer than most of the philosophies that it attacks. In the end it will not matter to us whether we wrote well or ill; whether we fought with flails or reeds. It will matter to us greatly on what side we fought.

Originally published as 'The Case for the Ephemeral' in G.K. Chesterton, *All Things Considered* (John Lane, New York, 1909)

EDITORIAL (2)

by Benjamin Franklin

[...]

Tho' I seldom attended any public worship, I had still an opinion of its propriety, and of its utility when rightly conducted, and I regularly paid my annual subscription for the support of the only Presbyterian minister or meeting we had in Philadelphia. He us'd to visit me sometimes as a friend, and admonish me to attend his administrations, and I was now and then prevail'd on to do so, once for five Sundays successively. Had he been in my opinion a good preacher, perhaps I might have continued, notwithstanding the occasion I had for the Sunday's leisure in my course of study; but his discourses were chiefly either polemic arguments, or explications of the peculiar doctrines of our sect, and were all to me very dry, uninteresting, and unedifying, since not a single moral principle was inculcated or enforc'd, their aim seeming to be rather to make us Presbyterians than good citizens.

At length he took for his text that verse of the fourth chapter of Philippians, *'Finally, brethren, whatsoever things are true, honest, just, pure, lovely, or of good report, if there be any virtue, or any praise, think on these things.'* And I imagin'd, in a sermon on such a text, we could not miss of having some morality. But he confin'd himself to five points only, as meant by the apostle, viz.: 1. Keeping holy the Sabbath day. 2. Being diligent in reading the holy Scriptures. 3. Attending duly the publick worship. 4. Partaking of the Sacrament. 5. Paying a due respect to God's ministers. These might be all good things; but, as they were not the kind of good things that I expected from that text, I despaired of ever meeting with them from any other, was disgusted, and attended his preaching no more.

I had some years before compos'd a little Liturgy, or form of prayer, for my own private use (viz., in 1728), entitled, *Articles of Belief* and *Acts of Religion*. I return'd to the use of this, and went no more to the public assemblies. My conduct might be blameable, but I leave it, without attempting further to excuse it; my present purpose being to relate facts, and not to make apologies for them.

It was about this time I conceiv'd the bold and arduous project of arriving at moral perfection. I wish'd to live without committing any fault at any time; I would conquer all that either natural inclination, custom, or company might lead me into. As I knew, or thought I knew, what was right and wrong, I did not see why I might not always do the one and avoid the other. But I soon found I had undertaken a task of more difficulty than I had imagined. While my care was employ'd in guarding against one fault, I was often sur-prized by another; habit took the advantage of inattention; inclination was sometimes too strong for reason. I concluded, at length, that the mere speculative conviction that it was our interest to be completely virtuous, was not sufficient to prevent our slipping; and that the contrary habits must be broken, and good ones acquired and established, before we can have any dependence on a steady, uniform rectitude of conduct. For this purpose I therefore contrived the following method.

In the various enumerations of the moral virtues I had met with in my reading, I found the catalogue more or less numerous, as different writers included more or fewer ideas under the same name. Temperance, for example, was by some confined to eating and drinking, while by others it was extended to mean the moderating every other pleasure, appetite, inclination, or passion, bodily or mental, even to our avarice and ambition. I propos'd to myself, for the sake of clearness, to use rather more names, with fewer ideas annex'd to each, than a few names with more ideas; and I included under thirteen names of virtues all that at that time occurr'd to me as necessary or desirable, and annexed to each a short precept, which fully express'd the extent I gave to its meaning. These names of virtues, with their precepts, were:

1. TEMPERANCE.
Eat not to dullness; drink not to elevation.

2. SILENCE.
Speak not but what may benefit others or yourself; avoid trifling conversation.

3. ORDER.
Let all your things have their places; let each part of your business have its time.

4. RESOLUTION.
Resolve to perform what you ought; perform without fail what you resolve.

5. FRUGALITY.
Make no expense but to do good to others or yourself; i.e., waste nothing.

6. INDUSTRY.
Lose no time; be always employ'd in something useful; cut off all unnecessary actions.

7. SINCERITY.
Use no hurtful deceit; think innocently and justly, and, if you speak, speak accordingly.

8. JUSTICE.
Wrong none by doing injuries, or omitting the benefits that are your duty.

9. MODERATION.
Avoid extreams; forbear resenting injuries so much as you think they deserve.

10. CLEANLINESS.
Tolerate no uncleanliness in body, cloaths, or habitation.

11. TRANQUILLITY.
Be not disturbed at trifles, or at accidents common or unavoidable.

12. CHASTITY.
Rarely use venery but for health or offspring, never to dullness, weakness, or the injury of your own or another's peace or reputation.

13. HUMILITY.
Imitate Jesus and Socrates.

My intention being to acquire the *habitude* of all these virtues, I judg'd it would be well not to distract my attention by attempting the whole at once, but to fix it on one of them at a time; and, when I should be master of that, then to proceed to another, and so on, till I should have gone thro' the thirteen; and, as the previous acquisition of some might facilitate the acquisition of certain others, I arrang'd them with that view, as they stand above. Temperance first, as it tends to procure that coolness and clearness of head, which is so necessary where constant vigilance was to be kept up, and guard maintained against the unremitting attraction of ancient habits, and the force of perpetual temptations. This being acquir'd and establish'd, Silence would be more easy; and my desire being to gain knowledge at the same time that I improv'd in virtue, and considering that in conversation it was obtain'd rather by the use of the ears than of the tongue, and therefore wishing to break a habit I was getting into of prattling, punning, and joking, which only made me acceptable to trifling company, I gave Silence the second place. This and the next, Order, I expected would allow me more time for attending to my project and my studies. Resolution, once become habitual, would keep me firm in my endeavors to obtain all the subsequent virtues; Frugality and Industry freeing me from my remaining debt, and producing affluence and independence, would make more easy the practice of Sincerity and Justice, etc., etc. Conceiving then, that, agreeably to the advice of Pythagoras in his Golden Verses, daily examination would be necessary, I contrived the following method for conducting that examination.

I made a little book, in which I allotted a page for each of the virtues. I rul'd each page with red ink, so as to have seven columns, one for each day of the week, marking each column with a letter for the day. I cross'd these columns with thirteen red lines, marking the beginning of each line with the first letter of one of the virtues, on which line, and in its proper column, I might mark, by a little black spot, every fault I found upon examination to have been committed respecting that virtue upon that day.

TEMPERANCE.							
EAT NOT TO DULNESS; DRINK NOT TO ELEVATION.							
	S.	M.	T.	W.	T.	F.	S.
T.							
S.	*	*		*		*	
O.	**	*	*			*	●
R.			*			*	
F.		*		*			
I.			*				
S.							
J.							
M.							
C.							
T.							
C.							
H							

I determined to give a week's strict attention to each of the virtues successively. Thus, in the first week, my great guard was to avoid every the least offence against Temperance, leaving the other virtues to their ordinary chance, only marking every evening the faults of the day. Thus, if in the first week I could keep my first line, marked T, clear of spots, I suppos'd the habit of that virtue so much strengthen'd and its opposite weaken'd, that I might venture extending my attention to include the next, and for the following week keep both lines clear of spots. Proceeding thus to the last, I could go thro' a course compleat in thirteen weeks, and four courses in a year. And like him who, having a garden to weed, does not attempt to eradicate all the bad herbs at once, which would exceed his reach and his strength, but works on one of the beds at a time, and, having accomplish'd the first, proceeds to a second, so I should have, I hoped, the encouraging pleasure of seeing on my pages the progress I made in virtue, by clearing successively my lines of their spots, till in the end, by a number of courses, I should he happy in viewing a clean book, after a thirteen weeks' daily examination.

This my little book had for its motto these lines from Addison's *Cato*:

> Here will I hold. If there's a power above us
> (And that there is all nature cries aloud
> Thro' all her works), He must delight in virtue;
> And that which he delights in must be happy.

Another from Cicero,

> O vitae Philosophia dux! O virtutum indagatrix expultrixque vitiorum! Unus dies, bene et ex praeceptis tuis actus, peccanti immortalitati est anteponendus.

Another from the Proverbs of Solomon, speaking of wisdom or virtue:

> Length of days is in her right hand, and in her left hand riches and honour. Her ways are ways of pleasantness, and all her paths are peace. iii. 16, 17.

And conceiving God to be the fountain of wisdom, I thought it right and necessary to solicit his assistance for obtaining it; to this end I formed the following little prayer, which was prefix'd to my tables of examination, for daily use.

> *O powerful Goodness! bountiful Father! merciful Guide! increase in me that wisdom which discovers my truest interest.*

✻
✻ ✻

strengthen my resolutions to perform what that wisdom dictates. Accept my kind offices to thy other children as the only return in my power for thy continual favors to me.

I used also sometimes a little prayer which I took from Thomson's *Poems*, viz.:

Father of light and life, thou Good Supreme!
O teach me what is good; teach me Thyself!
Save me from folly, vanity, and vice,
From every low pursuit; and fill my soul
With knowledge, conscious peace,
   and virtue pure;
Sacred, substantial, never-fading bliss!

The precept of Order requiring that *every part of my business should have its allotted time,* one page in my little book contain'd the following scheme of employment for the twenty-four hours of a natural day:

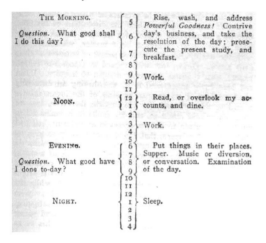

THE MORNING.	5	Rise, wash, and address *Powerful Goodness!* Contrive day's business, and take the resolution of the day; prosecute the present study, and breakfast.
Question. What good shall I do this day?	6	
	7	
	8	
	9	Work.
	10	
	11	
NOON.	12	Read, or overlook my accounts, and dine.
	1	
	2	
	3	Work.
	4	
	5	
EVENING.	6	Put things in their places. Supper. Music or diversion, or conversation. Examination of the day.
Question. What good have I done to-day?	7	
	8	
	9	
	10	
	11	
NIGHT.	12	Sleep.
	1	
	2	
	3	
	4	

I enter'd upon the execution of this plan for self-examination, and continu'd it with occasional intermissions for some time. I was surpris'd to find myself so much fuller of faults than I had imagined; but I had the satisfaction of seeing them diminish. To avoid the trouble of renewing now and then my little book, which, by scraping out the marks on the paper of old faults to make room for new ones in a new course, became full of holes, I transferr'd my tables and precepts to the ivory leaves of a memorandum book, on which the lines were drawn with red ink, that made a durable stain, and on those lines I mark'd my faults with a black-lead pencil, which marks could easily wipe out with a wet sponge. After a while I went thro' one course only in a year, and afterward only one in several years, till at length I omitted them entirely, being employ'd

in voyages and business abroad, with a multiplicity of affairs that interfered; but I always carried my little book with me.

My scheme of Order gave me the most trouble; and I found that, tho' it might be practicable where a man's business was such as to leave him the disposition of his time, that of a journeyman printer, for instance, it was not possible to be exactly observed by a master, who must mix with the world, and often receive people of business at their own hours. Order, too, with regard to places for things, papers, etc., I found extreamly difficult to acquire. I had not been early accustomed to it, and, having an exceeding good memory, I was not so sensible of the inconvenience attending want of method. This article, therefore, cost me so much painful attention, and my faults in it vexed me so much, and I made so little progress in amendment, and had such frequent relapses, that I was almost ready to give up the attempt, and content myself with a faulty character in that respect, like the man who, in buying an ax of a smith, my neighbour, desired to have the whole of its surface as bright as the edge. The smith consented to grind it bright for him if he would turn the wheel; he turn'd, while the smith press'd the broad face of the ax hard and heavily on the stone, which made the turning of it very fatiguing. The man came every now and then from the wheel to see how the work went on, and at length would take his ax as it was, without farther grinding. 'No,' said the smith, 'turn on, turn on; we shall have it bright by-and-by; as yet, it is only speckled.' 'Yes,' said the man, 'but I think I like a speckled ax best.' And I believe this may have been the case with many, who, having, for want of some such means as I employ'd, found the difficulty of obtaining good and breaking bad habits in other points of vice and virtue, have given up the struggle, and concluded that 'a speckled ax was best'; for something, that pretended to be reason, was every now and then suggesting to me that such extream nicety as I exacted of myself might be a kind of foppery in morals, which, if it were known, would make me ridiculous; that a perfect character might be attended with the inconvenience of being envied and hated; and that a benevolent man should allow a few faults in himself, to keep his friends in countenance.

In truth, I found myself incorrigible with respect to Order; and now I am grown old, and my memory bad, I feel very sensibly the want of it. But, on the whole, tho' I never arrived at the perfection I had been so ambitious of obtaining, but fell far short of it, yet I was, by the endeavour, a better and a happier man than I otherwise should have been if I had not attempted it; as those who aim at perfect writing by imitating the engraved copies, tho' they never reach the wish'd-for excellence of those copies, their hand is mended by the endeavor, and is tolerable while it continues fair and legible.

It may be well my posterity should be informed that to this little artifice, with the blessing of God, their ancestor ow'd the constant felicity of his life, down to his 79th year, in which this is written. What reverses may attend the remainder is in the hand of Providence; but, if they arrive, the reflection on past happiness enjoy'd ought to help his bearing them with more resignation. To Temperance he ascribes his long-continued health, and what is still left to him of a good constitution; to Industry and Frugality, the early easiness of his circumstances and acquisition of his fortune, with all that knowledge that enabled him to be a useful citizen, and obtained for him some degree of reputation among the learned; to Sincerity and Justice, the confidence of his country, and the honorable employs it conferred upon him; and to the joint influence of the whole mass of the virtues, even in the imperfect state he was able to acquire them, all that evenness of temper, and that cheerfulness in conversation, which makes his company still sought for, and agreeable even to his younger acquaintance. I hope, therefore, that some of my descendants may follow the example and reap the benefit.

[…]

Excerpted from *The Autobiography of Benjamin Franklin* (1793)

EDITORIAL (3)

by Lewis H. Lapham

They said, 'You have a blue guitar,
You do not play things as they are.'
The man replied, 'Things as they are
Are changed upon the blue guitar.'
Wallace Stevens

With this issue of *Harper's Magazine* I come to the end of my second term as its editor, and when I look at the bound volumes on the shelves of the magazine's library, I hear the voices of writers and readers with whom I've been acquainted for a very long time, still loud in their passion to get at the truth. I know of no task more difficult, but then neither can I think of one that makes for better conversation or brings with it as many changes on the poet's blue guitar. The tables of contents I regard as still current, and on reading down the lists of familiar names, I can imagine an orchestra tuning its instruments, restless with the promise of multiple themes and variations, which, heard separately or in concert, argue that the world of men and events eventually can be understood. Not yet, perhaps, not in time for tomorrow's deadline or next month's cover illustration, but sooner or later, when enough people with access to a new idea or a more accurate choice of word have had the chance to extend the reach of the human imagination and enlarge the realm of human possibility.

Writing some years ago in *Harper's Magazine* about the uses of the novel, the late Walker Percy put the proposition as follows: 'The point is that all fiction can be used as an instrument of exploration and discovery … to discover, or rediscover, how it is with man himself, who he is, and how it is between him and other men.'

Percy's observation pertains to all writing, whether discursive essay or investigative report, comic memoir or angry letter to the editor, that seeks to tell a true story. True in the sense that the authors root their discoveries in the ground of their own being—what they themselves think, know, have seen, can find language to express.

The telling of a true story usually puts the writer at odds with some sort of wisdom in office —a New York publisher's belief that literature died with Ernest Hemingway on a mountain in Idaho, the government's faith in its own propaganda, Hollywood's preference for fairy tales. I don't imagine that it was ever easy or profitable to conduct explorations unauthorised by a finance committee or unsupported by the judgment of a Mr Pecksniff or an Oprah Winfrey, but over the last few decades in the United States we've been learning the dead languages fitted out for television and better business management, and our newfound gifts for the art of saying nothing make it difficult to hear voices that haven't been swept clean of improvised literary devices, downsized into data points, reduced to an industrial waste product.

The achievement has been duly noted by numerous bystanders, most of whom applaud it as the wonder of the age. Never has so much information been so instantly at hand, not only on a cell phone and the Internet but also in department-store windows, on supermarket walls, behind home plate at Yankee Stadium. The promoters of the brave new world like to say that the 'key outputs' and 'innovative delivery strategies' broaden our horizons and brighten our lives with better-looking celebrities, more books available at Amazon.com, quicker access to 'valued customers', a finer class of politician capable of distinguishing between 'core' and 'noncore' promises.

Maybe I miss the 'key performance indicators' or misinterpret the 'risk assessments', but I don't know how a language that's meant to be disposable enriches anybody's life, whether that of an American citizen 'deriving synergies' from wellplaced 'knowledge entities' or that of an Iraqi national introduced to the joys of 'Operation Enduring Freedom'. I can understand why words emptied of meaning serve the interests of the corporation and the state, but they don't 'enhance' or 'empower' people who would find in their freedoms of thought and expression a voice, and therefore a life, that they can recognise as

their own. Although it's frequently said that the truth shall make men free, the commandment is almost as frequently misunderstood. What is meant by the truth as a synonym for liberty doesn't emerge from a collection of facts or an assimilation of doctrine, nor does it come with a declaration of war or the blessing of Christ; it's synonymous with the courage that individuals derive from not running a con game on the unique character and specific temper of their own minds, finding a story that settles the wilderness of their experience with the fence posts of a beginning, a middle, and an end.

Which is why as the magazine's editor for twenty-eight years (from 1976 into 1981, then again from 1983 to the present), I've been drawn to writers unafraid of the first-person singular, willing to think out loud, to experiment with narrative and cadence, bet the pot on a metaphor, take a chance with an argument or a line of inquiry that in other periodicals might be deemed ill-advised, unkempt, overly complex. Whether or not I agreed with what was being said didn't matter as much as the author's saying it in a way that couldn't be confused with the mission statement 'What We Stand for: Our Core Beliefs and Values' produced by the CIA—'Objectivity is the substance of intelligence, a deep commitment to the customer in its forms and timing.'

Often I have been asked, by Washington policy intellectuals and California environmental activists, why *Harper's Magazine* doesn't publish program notes for a brighter American future or blueprints for the building of a better tomorrow. All well and good, they say, to point to the flaws in the system, or to suggest that the leading cast members of the Bush Administration be sent to sea in open boats, but why so many jokes, and to what end the impractical criticism? Where are the helpful suggestions and the tools for forward-looking reform?

If I had ready answers to the questions, I'd stand for elective office; as an editor I've been more interested in the play of mind than in its harnessing to a political bandwagon. Some of the notions put forward by the magazine's contributors have been taken up by presidential candidates looking for something to say to the voters in Iowa or New Hampshire (single-payer health insurance, decriminalization of drugs); others have drifted into the backwaters of academic regret (an end to the two-party system); a few of them, much modified by circumstance and the available campaign money (less pollution in the oceans and the air) have made the passage into law. But no matter what the results, the impetus toward social or political change stems from language that also induces a change of heart. George Orwell made the point as long ago as 1946, in his essay 'Politics and the English Language'. The slovenly use of words, he said, 'makes it easier for us to have foolish thoughts … If one gets rid of these habits one can think more clearly, and to think clearly is a necessary first step toward political regeneration.' Or, more simply, how do we expect to find our way to the brighter future unless we can imagine it as something other than a Las Vegas resort hotel, or build a better tomorrow unless we have the words with which to construct it?

The decay of the public language in the mouths of the society's official sponsors (politicians, publicists, marketing directors, real estate salesmen) often has been remarked upon over the last few decades by people who know, as did Orwell, that a ceaseless burbling of lies, no matter how 'context-sensitive' or 'prioritised', cannot long sustain either the hope of individual liberty or the practice of democratic government. Don Watson, a once-upon-a-time speechwriter for a prime minister of Australia, makes the argument as well as it can be made in *Death Sentences*, a book published last spring in the United States by the Gotham Press and one to which I am indebted for the CIA's mission statement as well as for many of the phrases that I've borrowed as examples of the vocabulary administered as soporific.

Although Watson bears witness to our exodus into the neon deserts of audible silence, he doesn't mention the collateral damage— i.e., the increasingly hostile attitudes toward any use of language that fails to conform to the standard of television. Twenty years ago it was generally understood, not only by readers of *Harper's Magazine* but also by admirers of Johnny Carson, that the attempt to tell a true story sometimes entailed the writing of loose and periodic sentences, incorporated the tone of irony, employed words of more than one syllable, encompassed the turning of the occasionally artful phrase. To the degree that steadily larger numbers of people have been suckled at the machine-made breast of corporate entertainment —on the tone, substance, sense, and feel of the thing, the aesthetic of the beer commercials indistinguishable from that of the docudrama

news show and the authentic soap opera—so also they become irritated by anything that is not television. Subordinate clauses they view with suspicion, parentheses they regard as elitist and therefore condescending; messages must be delivered deodorised and free of ambiguity, which is disturbing and therefore wicked.

Similar attitudes of entitlement invaded the country's universities in the 1980s under the banners of political correctness, but again, as with the industrial language of business and government, the laziness of mind necessary to its acceptance has come to be seen as a consumer benefit. During the same week that I was reading Watson's book I came across Eric Larsen's equally fine *A Nation Gone Blind: America in an Age of Simplification and Deceit*, which approaches its topic from the perspective of a college English teacher alarmed by the progress that the last two generations of his students have made toward the notion of the classroom as petting zoo. The young inheritors of the world's supreme military and economic power apparently take it as an insult if anybody invites them to think. Why should they? Thinking isn't advertised on television. This is America, where everything good is easy, anything difficult is bad, and the customer is always right.

Read as tell-tales in the prevailing wind of our multitasking systems of global communication, the books by Watson and Larsen point toward a world in which, as Simone Weil once noticed, 'It is the thing that thinks, and the man who is reduced to the state of the thing.' It's conceivable that her premonition will prove well founded —as marker buoys in the data stream we have the rusting hulk of the Bush Administration, Harvard University floating on the rafts of grade inflation, the wreckage on the beach of prime-time television—but among the last people to lose consciousness I would expect to find the readers of *Harper's Magazine*. The writers whose investigations I've had the chance to aid and abet I admire not only for their talent but also for their courage and pride of mind; the readers I can count upon to know the difference between the hard coin of their own thought and the counterfeit currency of a White House press release.

Over the years I've exchanged letters with a great many correspondents whom I've never met nor do I expect to meet, most of their return addresses in cities and towns west of the Hudson River. The zip codes never matched a demographic profile that measured real estate

11

values or the consumption of golf balls and Sonoma County white wine, but if I couldn't guess at the size and weight of an individual's stock portfolio, I knew that I was talking to people bound together by their faith in the meaning of words. It occurred to none of them that they were being condescended to by a writer exploring the distant shores of sense and sensibility; instead of assuming that somehow they were being snubbed, they received the text as compliment, a sign of respect for their intelligence in line with J.M. Keynes's suggestion that 'Words ought to be a little wild for they are the assault of thoughts on the unthinking.'

When the readers found something amiss in one of my own essays (published under the rubric 'The Easy Chair' prior to 1981, and as 'Notebook' after the magazine's redesign in 1984), they took the trouble to correct a mistake, a wrong fact, a paragraph badly crippled with adjectives, my utter ignorance of the historical circumstances, etc.—instead of spewing forth a diatribe on my political, sexual, or religious orientation.

None of their voices could be mistaken for prerecorded announcements, and their remarks were free of the pretensions that tend to accompany the dramas of self played out in the Washington think tanks. No matter what the subject under discussion—the authorship of the Shakespearean plays, the moral bankruptcies of the Reagan and Clinton administrations, strange birds seen wading in the Platte River, the trouble with New York literary critics, a son's illness or a mother's new novel, the forgotten reasons for the fall of the Roman republic—the care taken with the composition of the letters (some of them printed out to a length of twelve typewritten pages) testified to the importance that their authors attached to the telling of a truer story. In other words, a long if desultory conversation with people whom I wouldn't recognise in a bookstore or a police lineup, but from whom I've learned that it is the joint venture entered into by writer and reader—the writer's labour turned to the wheel of the reader's imagination— that produces the energies of mind on which a society depends for its freedoms and from which it gathers the common store of its hope for a future that doesn't look like an early Mel Gibson movie.

I'll continue to write 'Notebook', six times a year instead of twelve, because I can rely on the readers of *Harper's Magazine* to further my continuing education. Otherwise unburdened

of the work on the editor's desk, I expect to undertake one or more of the ventures that over the last few years I've too often postponed. Together with notes for three books already long past their due dates with a New York publisher, I have in hand the preliminary design of a new journal, *Lapham's Quarterly*, intended to strengthen the knowledge and sense of history among people apt to forget that we have nothing else with which to build a future except the lumber of the past.

As the readers of this column know by now, I like to place the topic of the week or month in some sort of an historical frame, that absent at least a passing acquaintance with the prior record, I wouldn't know how to make sense of the newspapers, much less question the wisdom of what G.K. Chesterton once called 'the small and arrogant oligarchy of those who merely happen to be walking about.' Conjugate Walker Percy's dictum into the past tense, and the world in time becomes as good a place as any other, probably better than most, to discover or rediscover 'how it is with man himself, who he is, and how it is between him and other men.' I look forward to the exploration. If from the wreckage of modern-day Baghdad I can follow the lines of imperial conquest backward in time to Lord Kitchener and the Treaty of Versailles, through the centuries of somnolent despotism imposed on the Valley of the Euphrates by the Ottoman sultans of the Sublime Porte, to Caesar's legions governing what they knew as the province of Mesopotamia, at last to Hammurabi and the hanging gardens of Babylon, maybe I'll find reasons, better than the ones handed out at the Pentagon, that explain President George Bush's dream of Christian empire.

Originally published as 'Notebook: Blue Guitar' in *Harper's Magazine*, May 2006. Reproduced with kind permission.

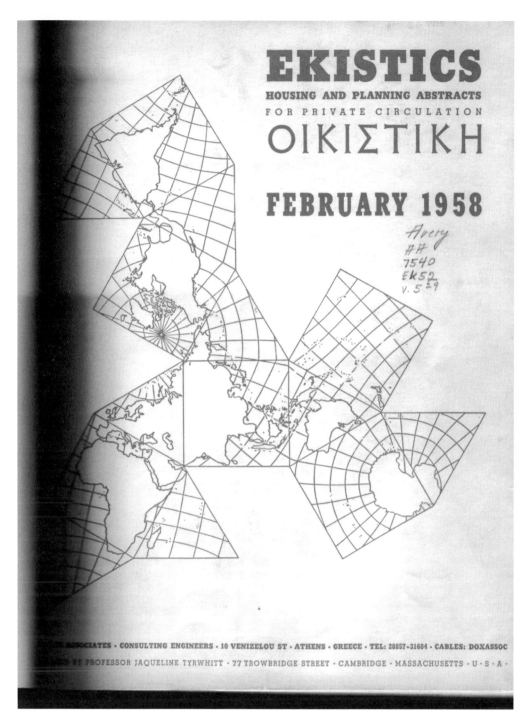

EKISTICS

HOUSING AND PLANNING ABSTRACTS

FOR PRIVATE CIRCULATION

ΟΙΚΙΣΤΙΚΗ

FEBRUARY 1958

...OCIATES · CONSULTING ENGINEERS · 10 VENIZELOU ST · ATHENS · GREECE · TEL: 28857-31604 · CABLES: DOXASSOC

... BY PROFESSOR JAQUELINE TYRWHITT · 77 TROWBRIDGE STREET · CAMBRIDGE · MASSACHUSETTS · U · S · A ·

SCANNED IN SITU

by David Reinfurt

Since 1955, *EKISTICS* has been published by Doxiadis Associates for dispersed employees of the global planning office, for U.N. technical assistance officers, and by subscription. Almost exclusively republishing, abstracting and re-framing existing articles, *EKISTICS* provided a distributed reader on global networks of communication, transportation, economics and human settlement. It was inextricably aligned with systems theory discourse growing out of Norbert Weiner's *Cybernetics: or Control and Communication in the Animal and the Machine* and developed by architects and planners including Buckminster Fuller and Christopher Alexander. Mark Wigley concisely sums up the role of *EKISTICS* in his article, 'Network Fever':

THE PUBLICATION of EKISTICS was started in the Autumn of 1955.

THE IDEA behind it was to supply members of Doxiadis Associates in remote field posts and U.N. Technical Assistance experts working overseas, with a timely selection of abstracts from international journals, papers and books upon the broader aspects of housing and planning.

THE TITLE EKISTICS, comes from the Greek verb OIKΩ, meaning settling down, and demonstrates the existence of a science of human settlements conditioned by man, influenced by economics, sociology, geography and technology.

THE CONTENTS are derived in large part from protected materials and may not be reprinted in whole or in part without the permission of the respective authors.

EKISTICS has become a means of developing interest in this more comprehensive approach to the problems of human settlements. It is addressed to all those interested in the planning and building of better settlements.

CIRCULATION is either:

> In exchange for other related publications issued by academic or professional organizations,
>
> or
>
> on a subscription basis; the annual subscription being $15, £5.6s.0d., or its equivalent.

Ekistics is itself a networking instrument. Indeed, it explicitly exaggerates the networking operations of all magazines. It only publishes abstracts of already published texts, repackaging and rebroadcasting existing data. The magazine is a scanning device, constantly monitoring information in other magazines … If all magazines are prosthetic extensions of their readers, far-reaching eyes monitoring a distant world for a particular community, Ekistics is a precise and efficient instrument.[1]

Appearing on the cover from the previous page is the Dymaxion World Map designed by Buckminster Fuller. Over its over 48-year run, the magazine continued to publish and republish a series of alternate network drawings—some kind of a never-ending search to articulate a post-modern web of interconnected networks. Bucky's Dymaxion map is tailored perfectly to the agenda of the journal—representing one continuous landmass, an amorphous form viewed at one time and drawn together with lines of connection

Ekistic grid index

The articles in this issue are coded by the scale of settlements and an aspect of an element indicated in the ekistic grid.

The content of each article is classified within an ekistic grid as follows:
- The scale of the settlement(s) with which the article deals is selected from among the 15 ekistic units:

Anthropos	1
Room	2
House	5
Housegroup	40
Small neighborhood	250
Neighborhood	1,500
Small polis	10,000
Polis	75,000
Small metropolis	500,000
Metropolis	4 million
Small megalopolis	25 million
Megalopolis	150 million
Small eperopolis	1,000 million
Eperopolis	7,500 million
Ecumenopolis	50,000 million

- The subjects dealt with in this article are selected from among the subheads of the five ekistic elements. The position of a dot in any square of the grid indicates which of the four subheads is being referred to. If the article arrives at a synthesis of these elements, either in a physical plan or in ekistic theory, the dot is at the top or bottom of the square.

key to placement
of subheads

①	②
④	③

The subheads of the elements are:

NATURE
1. Environmental analysis
2. Resource utilization
3. Land use, landscape
4. Recreation areas

ANTHROPOS
1. Physiological needs
2. Safety, security
3. Affection, belonging, esteem
4. Self-realization, knowledge, esthetics

SOCIETY
1. Public administration, participation and law
2. Social relations, population trends, cultural patterns
3. Urban systems and urban change
4. Economics

SHELLS
1. Housing
2. Service facilities: hospitals, fire stations, etc.
3. Shops, offices, factories
4. Cultural and educational units

NETWORKS
1. Public utility systems: water, power, sewerage
2. Transportation systems: road, rail, air
3. Personal and mass communication systems
4. Computer and information technology

SYNTHESIS: HUMAN SETTLEMENTS
1. Physical planning
2. Ekistic theory

Each article is described by key words, which are also used in the Ekistic Index, and by abbreviations referring to their illustrative content.

Key word letter code

D = diagrams
I = illustrations
M = maps
R = references
S = statistical tables and/or graphs
X = simulation and mathematical models, etc.

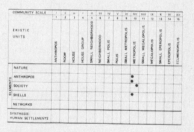

Up-to-date concepts
in traditional Cairo
*History 15th Century,
Housing, Building Design,
Egypt — D,I,R*

p. 96

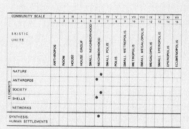

Al Jarudiyah, Saudi Arabia
*Housing, Building Design,
New Cities, Saudi Arabia — D,I,S*

p. 100

and continuation (latitude and longitude reimagined as pathways of communication, trade, and habitation.) The Dymaxion World Map would be used off and on in recurring appearences over the life of *EKISTICS*, becoming a kind of magazine mascot or default logo.

Classified material
EKISTICS provided an increasingly articulated frame for the articles that it republished. By 1965, the Ekistic Grid was instituted. Described and demonstrated on the inside front cover of the magazine, the Ekistic Grid attempted to sort each article that was republished in a strict categorization of subjects, subheads, and keywords. Further, the location of the dots within the box of the grid indicated the relative weight of topics addressed. The elaborate syntax of these intensely coded grids begins to form a specialist language for close readers. It is presented as if (!) a close reader might quickly scan the Ekistic Grid and identify relevance, degree and subject matter of the article.

Thinking about complex systems

C.H. Waddington

The ekistic outlook can be considered as part of the culture of our time. Therefore shouldn't everyone going to a university gain some idea of what the ekistics outlook is all about, and learn to see their dwelling places in the context of the whole city, or man in the context of the megalopolis? I personally think this is our minimum duty.

In its old elitist day, the university used to provide a general education for gentlemen. This was supposed to be an introduction to all the things that such a person should know something about if he wanted to understand society. We have swept that away entirely and concentrated on training specialists, either because there is no agreement on the nature of civilization, or because we have no time to consider it. But I believe that universities are failing in their responsibilities by not providing some sort of system for making the students acquainted with the developments of modern thought. Some universities are trying to do this. However, in my own university, "General Science Studies" (which is supposed to trace the impact of science on social affairs) has tended to become a series of very special case studies.

I would like to give some examples of the kind of thinking about complex systems that I think do not at present get across to students. They may perhaps pick some of them up for themselves, but I think it is worthwhile for us to present them more systematically.

1. We should for instance insist that we are almost always dealing with processes, and not things. Even theories have a life-time.

2. We are nearly always dealing with populations — universes — of things, and not single examples. That means you must know something about statistics and what are the valid conclusions you can draw, and what are not.

3. We are dealing with organized systems involving hierarchies of order — levels of order. Here I can refer to the analogy that has been drawn here between ekistics and medecine. This is a valid analogy, provided we remember that ekistics has got a much wider hierarchy of order: it has not only the complexity of clinical medecine and public health, but several other forms of complexity as well. Thus you need to have your mind fully attuned to the idea that anything you are going to deal with is going to be in hierarchies of order.

4. We must distinguish whether we are dealing with an open or a closed system. Are we dealing with a system which is an enclosed world, or are we dealing with a system in which things are coming in, being processed, and going out at the other end? Nearly always, in real life situations, we are dealing with open systems, but nearly all the classical thought you are likely to come across in ordinary, old fashioned based education was based on closed world premises. Therefore this is a new type of thinking that you have got to get into your mind.

5. Now, if you are confronted with a complex system, what you would like to do is to give a full analysis of it with identifiable elements and relations. That is what

Dr. Waddington is Professor of Animal Genetics at the University of Edinburgh and a frequent participant in the Delos Symposia.

410

Ekistics 193, Dec.

EKISTICS also introduced a host of neologisms to its committed readership. Most significantly, the word 'ekistics' was defined as the science of human settlements. 'Ekistics' derived from a Greek verb meaning (roughly) 'to settle' and with an application somewhere halfway between 'establishing a place' and 'rearranging your connections'. The adjective form, 'ekistical', the adverb 'ekistically', and the noun 'ekistician' have since been incorporated into a slightly wider lexicon.

Complexity and contradiction

EKISTICS developed from and within the discourse of systems theory as applied in the fields of architecture and planning. In *Cybernetics*, Norbert Weiner elegantly described a worldview that would hold sway at *EKISTICS* until the present. Weiner detailed the feedback mechanism in its many manifestations from James Clerk Maxwell's speed governor to the thermostat and the human body, along the way proposing a model for the thinking about the world

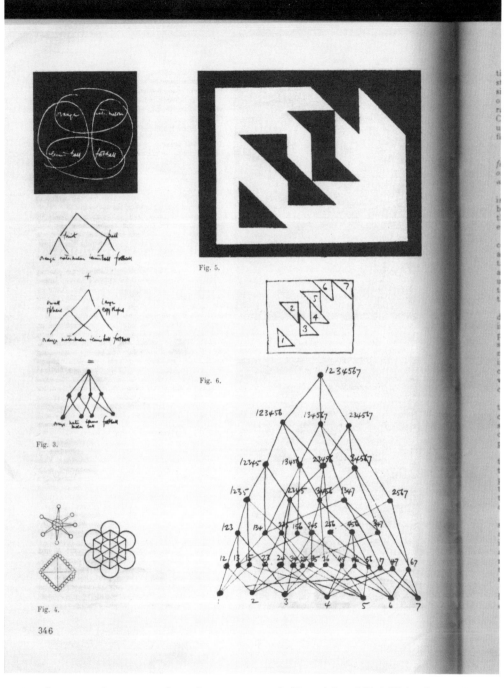

Fig. 5.

Fig. 6.

Fig. 3.

Fig. 4.

as a system of systems, an interconnected organism, feeding back constantly and regulating itself in realtime. This model of the world aligned precisely with the concerns of Doxiadis Associates in publishing the journal. *EKISTICS* travelled around the world in a tight, engaged and distributed audience of committed readers. Recurring topics dealt with networks of all sizes, shapes and configurations; whole systems, feedback and dynamic equalibriums, complexity in structure, kind, difference and degreee.

In 'Network Fever', Mark Wigley observes that the form and the content of *EKISTICS* are the same. As a republisher, scanner or even network device, the journal constantly trolled the flotsam and jetsam of various discourses and collected them in a small publication, distributing widely. For *EKISTICS*, the contents do not buttress the magazine, nor is the form of the magazine justified by its contents. Instead, it is a doubling, where *EKISTICS* actually becomes a model of the ideas that it is circulating—putting into practice

LYLE C. FITCH
U. S. A.

R. BUCKMINSTER FULLER
U. S. A.

Now President of the Institute of Public Administration of New York, he held successively from September 1957 to April 1961 the posts of Deputy Administrator and Administrator of the City of New York. Consultant on urban transportation, planning and finance, he has been director of a project to revise the accounting system of the Puerto Rico Commonwealth and member of the Shoup Mission to Venezuela (1958), which prepared a comprehensive report on Venezuela's finances; chief of staff and research director on Management Survey (1950-52); economic consultant and special assistant to Governor Chester Bowles of Connecticut (1948-50); and economist with the Treasury Department. He has also taught in the economics departments of Brooklyn College, Wesleyan University and Columbia University and is at present supervising projects concerned with urban government planning and administration in India, Venezuela, Peru, Nigeria, and the United States.

He is also author and co-author of several books and numerous articles on urban administration, economics, and public finance and has travelled extensively in Asia, Africa, Europe and South America.

«Planning, to be effective, must be closely identified with the political process; planners must work closely with the political leaders who are the community's decision-makers (in the governmental sector). Without a political base, planners are largely impotent. They have value only as community educators; while this value is not to be despised, the process of education alone, without the cooperation of the community's political leaders and other elements of its power structure, is long and slow».

Professor of Generalized Design Exploration, (S. Illinois University 19___; has been Charles Eliot Norton Pro_____ University (1961-1962); visiting p_____ turer at numerous universities in ___ abroad; honorary life member __ __ Institute of Architects and many ___

Inventor-discoverer of energe____ getic geometry and of geodesic ___ structures, including some 2,000 ___ in 41 countries, he was appointed __ __ mittee on Human Resources, cons_____ tists, to consider new educa_____ light of Russia's acceleration in s____ gical-educational field. Richard ___ ler was Editor of Convoy Ma_____ editor and publisher of Shelter ___ author of «Nine Chains to the ___ tion Automation» (1963); «No ___ Gods» (1963); «Ideas and Integ_____ Unfinished Epic of Industri_____ has been the subject of b_____ «Dymaxion World of Buck_____ and by John McHall, «Buck_____

«In discussing the popul_____ facing a total increment, ___ ___ The overall extension of li____ a major problem... The ___ brought about by automa_____ into whole months of pur___ an ecological sweep-out__ about it: the entire w___ fact be stacked under a ___ area of New York City__ of populations may l____ dynamic neighbourhoods ___ disappear in a period ___

224

the same dispersed and continually readjusting network that many of the articles attempt to describe.

On a boat, somewhere in the Aegean
EKISTICS also became a network of people. Extending the journal, Constantinos Doxiadis convened the Delos Meetings, a series of conferences on patterns of human settlement, by inviting a group of experts and engaged practioners in a wide variety of academic and professional disciplines to spend two weeks on a boat

travelling off of the coast of Greece. The first of twelve planned Delos meetings was covenened in 1963 (again, comprehensively described by Mark Wigley in 'Network Fever'). It consisted of a series of presentations, formal and informal discussions, meals, recreation and ceremony. The net result was a series of declarations, some mimeographed notes, and most productively, a set of fruitful relationships among the participants. When including accounts of the meetings,

SIR ROBERT MATTHEW
GREAT BRITAIN

MARSHALL MCLUHAN
CANADA

1953 Professor of Architecture at
...gh University, and senior partner of
...te practice with offices in Edinburgh
...don, he was knighted in January 1962.
... the Department of Health for Scotland
..., Sir Robert was appointed its Chief
... and Planning officer in 1945. He was
...puty Consultant to Sir Patrick Abercrom-
...the preparation of the post-war report on
...ning of the Clyde Valley region.
...e Architect to the London County Coun-
...-1953), he was responsible for the post-
...ools and from 1950 for all new housing
...mes.
...itect of the Royal Festival Hall, Sir
...has designed, among others, over the
...years, the Edinburgh Airport Terminal
...Edinburgh University Arts Faculty Build-
...Coordinating architect, at the moment,
...Administration Centre of the new Pa-
...capital of Islamabad, he is currently
...g a report on Building Costs for the
...n Nigeria Government and has prepar-
...recent Regional Plan of Northern Ireland.
...ident of the International Union of
...ects since 1961 he became President of the
...Institute of British Architects in 1962.
...ere are two kinds of problems: The ne-
...to bring together various intellectual
...nes bearing on physical development main-
...relation to the 'developed' ... and the
...y to link up the various professional and
...al know-how with the international or-
...capable of providing extensive technical
...the developing countries. At present, we,
...nting the isolated professional institutions,
...owerless without such coordination— yet
...esent a vast source of power».

Professor of English Literature, St. Michael's
College in the University of Toronto (1944).
He has also been Chairman of the Ford Foundation Seminar on Culture and Communication
(1953-55) and Director of Media project for the
National Association of Educational Broadcasters.
Recipient of Governor General's Award for
critical prose (1963), professor Herbert Marshall
McLuhan has published articles in many journals in the field of literature; has had frequent
appearances in TV and on the lecture platform;
and has published: «The Mechanical Bride; Folk-
lore of Industrial Man» (1951), «Explorations in
Communications» with E.S. Carpenter (1960),
«The Gutenberg Galaxy: The Making of Typo-
graphic Man» (1963) and «Understanding Media».

Professor McLuhan was appointed in 1963
by the President of Toronto University to create a
new Centre for the Study of the Extensions of Man.

«Electronic technology has extended the brain
itself to embrace the globe; previous technologies had only extended the bodily servants of
the brain. The result now is a speedup of information that reduces the planet to the scale of a
village — with this difference, that the volume
of information movement is on a planetary
rather than village scale. A global consciousness thus becomes the new human scale.

The electronic extension of our brain involves each of us totally in the family of man, an
involvement which constitutes a new kind of
continuous learning, as involuntary as seeing
when one's eyes are open. This global extension
of the human brain is an enormous upgrading
of man. We must not fail to exploit it. The most
important task of the planner is to prepare the
environment for the exploitation of this new
tremendous opportunity».

229

EKISTICS, as a republisher of existing articles, was
even forced to print an apology for including material
that hadn't appeared anywhere previously.

Invisible architectures
Through its adolescence and into middle-age,
EKISTICS continued to publish images of networks on
its cover. The restless search for a perfect networked
representation of the world as a cover image describes
concisely the mission and effect of the journal for its

readers. A slide show of forty-eight years of *EKISTICS*
covers would produce a perfect picture of an ekistical
network—one morphing image, drawing and redrawing
itself, rupturing, reconnecting and reconsidering.

On the following two covers produced eight years
apart, Fuller's Dymaxion World Map is again used.
But now, it is overlaid by a series of lines—a network
loosened from the boundaries of the map to describe
a series of relationships. Are they paths of flight, lines
of communication, areas of influence, new territorial

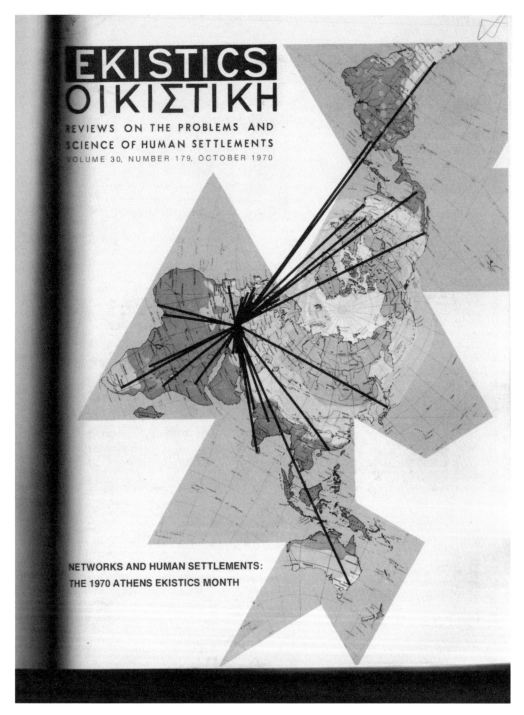

EKISTICS
ΟΙΚΙΣΤΙΚΗ

REVIEWS ON THE PROBLEMS AND
SCIENCE OF HUMAN SETTLEMENTS
VOLUME 30, NUMBER 179, OCTOBER 1970

NETWORKS AND HUMAN SETTLEMENTS:
THE 1970 ATHENS EKISTICS MONTH

boundaries or patterns of participation? Between the
180 degree rotation of the map and a reconsideration
of the network structure, the search continues for
a hidden architecture, organizing the world and
structuring the system of systems.

It is as if the journal set itself the task of solving
all the 'Problems and Science of Human Settlement'
(*EKISTICS*' subtitle), and as such, terminating the job
before satisfactory resolution is simply not an option.
Along the way, *EKISTICS* draws out lines of connection

between readers and writers, between places, between
things, between patterns of occupation, between a
journal and its audience, between complete discourses
and discrete ideas.

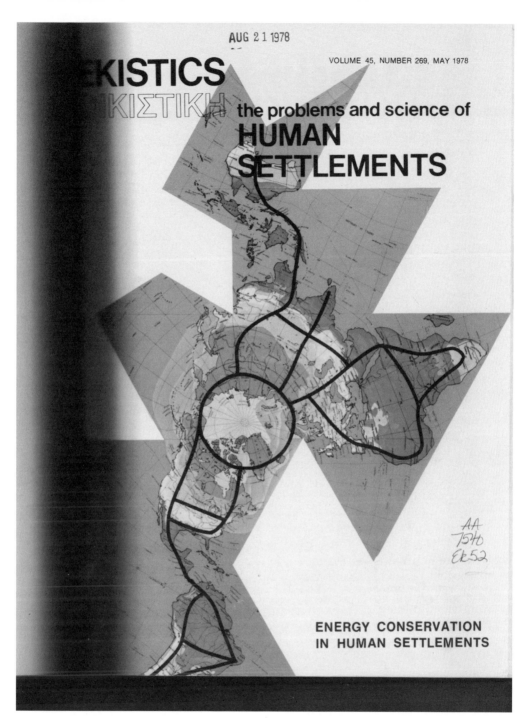

AUG 2 1 1978

VOLUME 45, NUMBER 269, MAY 1978

EKISTICS
ΟΙΚΙΣΤΙΚΗ

the problems and science of
HUMAN SETTLEMENTS

ENERGY CONSERVATION
IN HUMAN SETTLEMENTS

Although three shelves of carefully-archived volumes collect a network of articles, bound and ghettoised all under call number AA 7540 Ek52, *EKISTICS'* natural habitat was really in the field —a U.N. office in Kenya, a regional planning office outside of Delhi, maybe a Doxiadis Associates project office in Tehran. Maintaining a relatively small reader base, the magazine still enjoyed an exceptionally wide distribution pattern, both physically and socially. *EKISTICS'* small numbers found themselves

in the hands of a precise audience and, as a result, it was buoyed by a committed and supported readership.

By November 1970, *EKISTICS* had lost the disclaimer/proclamation on its front cover 'FOR PRIVATE CIRCULATION'. What began as a distributed reader for a limited number of a Doxiadis Associates employees developed into a self-sufficient, complex and self-regulating subscription-based information machine

EKISTICS
ΟΙΚΙΣΤΙΚΗ
REVIEWS ON THE PROBLEMS AND
SCIENCE OF HUMAN SETTLEMENTS
VOLUME 30, NUMBER 180, NOVEMBER 1970

BALANCED URBAN DEVELOPMENT VERSUS ECONOMIC DEVELOPMENT

(the final cover here offers a convincing self-portrait.)
EKISTICS, then, becomes a kind of *Whole Earth
Catalog* for the United Nations/NGO set, serving up
an inventory of links to previously published articles
and a constellation of ideas, writers and publications.
Sitting now on the library shelf and sewn up in
hardback folios, *EKISTICS* is for the moment settled.
The ideas continue to circulate.

NOTE
1. Mark Wigley, 'Network Fever', in *Grey Room*,
vol. 1, no. 4 (MIT Press).

ROYAL ITINERARIES

An interview with Sven Augustijnen
by Raimundas Malasauskas

Monday 20 March, 2006

Sven Augustijnen: Thanks for the invitation
of the interview, Raimundas. And what a coincidence: our King Albert II visited your country
today! I learned that Lithuania was a kingdom as
well a few hundred years ago and an extensive
one at that—it stretched from the Baltic to the
Black Sea! It's probably not helping my career,
but I am really getting into the history of the
Belgian royal family. To start with Leopold I,
for example, the founder of the dynasty, whose
funeral in particular is fascinating; or rather his
funerals. He requested to be buried with his first
wife, Princess Charlotte, in the Saint Windsor
Chapel, but this was denied because of his
protestant conviction and free-masonry relations.
When they finally decided to bury him in the old
church of Notre-Dame de Laeken, the Catholic
clergy refused that his mortal remains access the
church. And so he was without a final destination.
In the end a compromise was found: an opening
was made in the wall and the coffin was slid into
the royal crypt so that his corpse didn't have to
be carried through the church. Later, they created
an outside entrance to the royal crypt—one that
can still be accessed without having to enter the
church. Do you have any interesting stories to tell
about your king before I try to respond to some of
your questions?

Raimundas Malasauskas: Unfortunately our
only king, King Mindaugas, was assassinated
before your first king was born, and since he
was the one to Christianize Lithuania there were
no churches yet to accommodate his burial.
There is a national holiday on July 6 though.
But let me get to the first question: Have you
read Jack Burnham's book *Beyond Modern
Sculpture*? He argues that we are changing from
an object-oriented world to a system-oriented
world, and that art is involved in doing it
right now.[1]

SA: I didn't read the book. Maybe we are changing
from an object-oriented world to a system
oriented world and art is involved in it, but people
involved in the art market would rather stick to
the object. It gives them something to hold on
to. In the end we believe that a piece of wood or
a canvas is worth much more than its material
value. A world without the object might be too
confrontational—this might force people to
realise there's some enchantment or bewitchment
involved, and that realisation might break their
belief. For example, recently I made a newspaper
called *PANORAMA*[†] and one remark I got was
why didn't I print it on better paper, because now
it's used for peeling potatoes on.

RM: Is it normal to peel potatoes on newspapers
in Belgium? To me it's a very Broodthaers-type
image.

SA: Yes, it's a very common thing in Belgium.
Broodthaers did it as well, no doubt. After all,
he made use of common and popular Belgian
habits in his work. We can't escape our context
or nature, and why should we? There is nothing
wrong with peeling potatoes on newspapers, is
there? I live close to the European Parliament
and the Wiertz Museum which Broodthaers
wrote about. My newspaper tells the story of
how a handful of property developers created
a myth of an International Congress Centre
in Brussels, which, as if by coincidence, was to
be built very close to the branch of the European
Parliament. It was given the stature of a gigantic
parliamentary infrastructure, which perfectly
responded to the European Parliament's needs.

---

†

The newspaper *PANORAMA* was published on 12 October
2005 in the financial newspaper *De Tijd*, in the context of
the exhibition 'Information/Transformation' at Extra City,
Antwerp. In *PANORAMA*, an interview with Etienne Davignon
(a political and economic frontman in Belgian and European
history) provides the basis for the weaving of a meaningful
network: various texts which describe the genesis of the
European Union and the topographical implantation of its
institutions in Brussels are placed in relation to narratives
from Belgium's colonial past.

Contrary to all European treaties and the governmental agreements between Luxembourg, France and Belgium, three fourths of the activities of the European Parliament were established within this infrastructure, and Brussels subsequently became the capital of Europe. Why should I search for a great story when I can find it nearby?'

RM: Don't you think that the ethnic schizophrenia of Brussels perfectly reflects the state of Europe and that the profit-driven agenda of real estate developers only emphasises this (together with what Deleuze wrote about Capitalism and Schizophrenia)? By the way, have you ever done work under a different name? Can you imagine making the work of another artist?

SA: Brussels has served and serves still today as many metaphors for the state of Europe. One of them, Manneke Pis, has more than 700 costumes! Concerning doing work under a different name, I did once apply for a grant as another artist. Coincidence or not, in retrospect one could say that the artist was constructed within the realm of the ethnic schizophrenia of Brussels you are talking about—I gave the artist the identity of a *flamand franconisé*. His great grandfather was a Flemish labourer who moved to Brussels for economic reasons, as many did in the 19th century and the beginning of the 20th century. Speaking French was a matter of survival for them. And in the course of the century they unfortunately lost their mother tongue. On the basis of his Flemish roots and name he applied for a grant.

RM: And did he get the grant?

SA: No.

RM: Can your pieces be redone in another situation, somewhere else, by someone else?

SA: It was you, wasn't it, who asked how one could be sure whether a certain film of mine had not been stolen from the pocket of another artist? So why not the other way around?

RM: I was indeed wondering how anyone could be sure that, due to its content, *L'Ecole des Pickpockets*,[††] a film 'manual' of how to steal all kinds of valuables from pockets, had not been stolen from the pocket of another artist and simply presented by you, under your name?

By the way, what did the pickpockets—who appear as themselves in the film—say about your work?

SA: I invited them for the premiere, but they couldn't make it because they were busy. The audience was convinced they were watching professionals, so there was no need to demonstrate it in real time. When the screening was over, it was quite interesting to see people running out of the cinema. But the hilarity of the moment quickly turned as the screening took place in an auditorium in the most obscure metro station in Brussels.

RM: Have you ever worked for television? Would you? Or are you not at all interested in the formats and forms that the synopsis of a story created by you might ever take?

SA: Recently I read this little book *Surtout pas de journalistes!* [*Certainly no journalists!*] by Jacques Derrida. The sentence goes on '… et pas de nouvelles ! Pas de confesseur et de psychanalyse!' […and no news! No confession and psychoanalysis!] Considering the newspaper I mentioned earlier, you could say that I must have been very much involved with journalism, its formats and forms, despite Derrida's warnings.

RM: How did professional journalists react to your newspaper? If I am correct, 50,000 copies were printed by and inserted in *De Tijd*, the equivalent of the *Financial Times* in Belgium. The same amount was printed in French and

††

Charles Dickens framed petty theft (most famously in *Oliver Twist*) as a gesture of civil disobedience in a society that did little to care for the poor, yet today the sleight-handed art of the pickpocket is more often than not reduced to a side show element in the dizzy and contagious acts of prime-time TV magicians. In Brussels, like most major cities, however, pickpocketing is a day-to-day reality. Shot in a single working day, *L'Ecole des Pickpockets* (video, 48 mins, 2000) observes two master pickpockets initiating a fresh-faced young apprentice into the secret art of invisible theft. The film is shot in an underground room, a hidden place, where the viewer witnesses what the Surrealists described as the 'beauty of the perfect crime'.

Two fragments from Sven Augustijnen's *PANORAMA* newspaper (2005)

14th January 1992

On 14th January 1992, France and Luxembourg's Foreign Affairs Ministers of that time, respectively Roland Dumas and Jacques F. Poos, wrote a joint letter of protest to Mark Eyskens, the Belgian Foreign Affairs Minister. It was a vigorous protest against the signature of a purchase option rental contract for *L'Espace Léopold* on 8th January 1992 between the European Parliament and the *Société Espace Léopold*.

During a telephone conversation, we asked Mark Eyskens to situate this letter of protest and his 15th January response in the global context of tense diplomatic relations surrounding the "headquarters war" between Belgium, France and Luxembourg.

– Am I speaking to Mark Eyskens?
– Of course.
– If you don't mind, I would like to ask you a few questions about the "Caprice des Dieux", in my capacity as an independent journalist. If I'm not mistaken, you were Foreign Affairs Minister when the building was constructed...
– What building are you talking about? What does the "Caprice des Dieux" mean?
– I am talking about the building that now houses the European Parliament, the so-called International Congress Centre.
– I have never had anything to do with that building.
– I thought that you were Foreign Affairs Minister when the building was constructed and that you ensured that good diplomatic relations were maintained with France and Luxembourg. Can I ask you a few questions about that?
– When are you talking about

now?
– The end of the eighties. The construction of the building was announced in 1987 and shortly afterwards...
– I was Foreign Affairs Minister from 1989 to 1992. But the Foreign Affairs Department had nothing to do with that affair. You will have to speak to the Secretary of State in charge of the Belgian state-owned construction company at that time, Mr. Duprez. He was in charge of that affair and should probably be able to answer your questions better. I cannot help you. OK?
– It is true that you had nothing to do with the construction of the building. But in your capacity as Foreign Affairs Minister, you were confronted for years with what we called the "headquarters war" between Luxembourg, Strasbourg and Brussels. You played a major role in the success of that affair, didn't you?
– No, absolutely not! I cannot

```
1- Jan. '92 15:40       MIN. AFFAIRES ETRANGERES    FAX 0                    P. 2


                                        Luxembourg, le 14 janvier 1992



                              Monsieur Marc EYSKENS
                              Ministre des Affaires étrangères



    Monsieur le Ministre et cher collègue,
```

A brief history of Brusse
the capital of Europe

in
and
veral
have
and
er to
feel
h, in
run-
the
ple-
such
they
ease.
skin
are
The
althy
the
will
dogs
yet

rein-
lon't
vhite
hay
have
vul-
keys'
mely
most
door
res-
epri-
nals.
glec-
or is
ani-

s

ng in
sure.
dge-
the
does

(Panorama) – "Wiertz, a nineteenth century artist from Dinant, was famed for his paranoid delusions. To be greater than David, he painted on canvases of such extravagant dimensions that a studio had to be built to accommodate his desires which were taking on gargantuan proportions. Wiertz was a curious, original painter; to say the least.

His studio was to become the Wiertz Museum in the district of Brussels where an archaic Natural History Museum is still to be found, housing among other objects, enormous fossils of prehistoric creatures extracted from the memory of a coal mine… Such are the almost imaginary places that have survived the destructive exploits of property management companies. According to what I have just learnt, they are threatened with demolition to make room for more profitable constructions. There would even be a specific threat weighing on the Wiertz museum. Although I cannot say that I like Wiertz as much as I liked my great-grandfather, this is an opportunity for me to cry out: Save Wiertz and his memory; Wiertz, the (natural) unintentional caricaturist of a well-thinking society, now needs the solidarity of good architects. From a contemporary artistic viewpoint, let's consider this strange museum as a place where theoretical inflation is evident, that is certainly worth preserving and that can still be used as a critical model."

Description noted by a certain Marcel Broodthaers in the Belgian edition of *Studio International* in October 1974.

If you visit the Wiertz Museum situated only a stone's throw away from the European Parliament, you will find in the entrance hall the original drawing of Wiertz's virulent and visionary pamphlet, entitled *Bruxelles Capitale, Paris Province*. It was drawn up in 1840, in reaction to the incomprehension of his contemporaries and to the humiliation, by indifference or provocation, of the sarcasm of Parisian criticism. In a certain sense, he predicted the future: "(…) it's my plan, my new plan for Brussels Capital, the capital of Europe… Come on, Brussels! Rise up! Become the world capital and let Paris, to you, only be a provincial town to you! (…)"

The brief history of Brussels as the capital of Europe began in the post-war years, in 1951 when the Six (Germany, France, Italy, Luxembourg, the Netherlands and Belgium) formed the European Coal and Steel Community (ECSC). The *Le Soir*

From that moment on, temporary offices were used, mainly around rue de la Loi in the Leopold district. This situation lasted until the 3,200 employed civil servants became too spread out to work efficiently. And until 1960, when the grounds of the Berlaymont monastery, situated within one hundred metres of the European Economic Community headquarters in avenue de la Joyeuse Entrée, were chosen for the construction of a prestigious administrative complex large enough to accommodate all of the civil servants. The regular canonesses of the Order of Saint Augustine were subjected to increasingly insistent pressure from property developers attracted by a district whose administrative vocation was becoming increasingly stronger each day; they finally gave in and left rue de la Loi, where they had settled when they had been forced to leave rue de l'Etoile to make way for the Palace of Justice. The Berlaymont, finan-

34, MO 51, MO 59, MO 70, MO 75, N-9, N-85, N 105, ORBN, OVER, PALM, PHIL, RAV, REM, RMA, RP-3, RP-6, RP 12 RP 11, SC 14, SC 15, SC 27, SC 29, SC 41, SDME, SOUV, STAL, T 61, T120, TERV, TRMF, VDBR, VM-2, WILS, ZA. A total of 1,930,000 square metres of office buildings. It is difficult to keep check of all of the investments made over the years.

"(…)But for the completion of this great work… a law is required, a law which obliges the wealthy constructor to maintain the desired distances. Let us not cry out against such a law; it would be no more arbitrary, no more irritating than that which obliges me to renounce my garden, my field, or my house for the expansions of a road or railway, established in the public interest. We will leave to the governors, the knowledgeable economists, the major industrialists, the care of meditating on this matter."

Artist Antoine Wiertz's prophecy still remains intact even though the Wiertz Museum and its gardens were spared from demolition by bulldozers. Almost an entire residential district was sacrificed for Europe with, as the icing on the cake, the promise of an International Congress Centre that would soon accommodate European parliamentarians representing a vast territory reminiscent of the Roman Empire.

This is only an intermediate climax to a long "headquarters war", as demonstrated by the headline of a newspaper that has since gone bankrupt: "The first extraordinary session in the dark!" The chamber was plunged into darkness at 12:44 pm on 28th April 1983, on the first day of the extraordinary

English, and distributed in the European Parliament and Commission. What was the impact of the newspaper?

SA: What is certain is that the editors and journalists of *De Tijd* were in emergency meetings on the day of its publication. When they arrived at their desks that morning, they had unexpectedly found a totally new section in their beloved newspaper. Of course, as always in such cases, they tried to find a scapegoat—without success, since the person responsible was part of the editorial team. So they decided to sweep it under the carpet. Meanwhile, the newspaper was being promoted by the local television news, every hour. They were recommending the audience buy that day's newspaper due to its interesting contribution on 'Brussels, Capital of Europe'. The television journalist didn't differentiate between my insert and the rest of the newspaper —probably because of the similar layout. Since, some of the main characters of the newspaper have been contacted by professional journalists. One of the journalists was told that the story is under embargo for now.

RM: Does this mean that you've received good royalties to stay out of the picture?

SA: No comment.

RM: Whether the choreography of pick-pocketing or the invisible map of the Brussels Royal Gardens shared by cruisers, *Le Guide du Parc*,[†††] your work deals with a very specific type of knowledge; it is an unwritten and unofficial knowledge, and exists as a parallel universe within everyday life. Usually it is manifested by invisible structures and actions, and shared only by a small group of insiders. How did you first get initiated in it?

SA: One of the places where you experience pickpockets in Brussels is the Beursschouwburg, the central theatre of Brussels. So you get robbed on the street as well as in the wings of the theatre—I speak from experience. This is quite amazing if one thinks about the phrase the master pickpocket utters a few times in the video: '*C'est toute une comédie*' [It's all theatre]. It seems that parallel universes do experience crossovers, not only in terms of material objects, but also in terms of ideas. A similar reflection could be made about *Le Guide du Parc*.[2]

The *mise en scene* in the Royal Gardens, as we experience it in the video, occurs in the park between the Belgian Parliament and the Royal Palace. The prime minister simply crosses the garden when he goes to ask for his dismissal from the King. Living uptown, I also cross the garden when I go downtown or visit the Palais des Beaux-Arts, located at the border of the park. So it's a matter of daily observation and then of infiltration by camouflage, sympathy or other strategies to be invented.

RM: Are there any strategies you would like not to talk about?

SA: Another strategy could be straight out acting, without beating around the bush. Also, a deviation or a diversion could be sufficient. Sometimes it is just a matter of letting sleeping dogs lie or of being very patient and waiting for the right moment to act. In general, I can say that people are very willing to participate; creating is a wonderful thing to do and since the city is full of unexplored talents, it's a matter of tapping into these sources. Of course one has to consider that finding the right person in the right place is not that easy. Not everybody has the rhetorical talents like those of the guide in the park. And not every pickpocket is eager to share his philosophy and techniques in front of the camera. Some skills to find these 'talented people' are required, and of course you need a bit of luck. After that it's a matter of offering these people full scope to unfold their talents.

<hr />

†††
Le Guide du Parc (video, 44 mins, 2001) depicts an unusual visit to the Parc Royal in Brussels. The guide in this fake documentary introduces you to the habits of the park's gay scene, slowly relating details of the park's 'social life'. This is an educational film incorporating many historical facts of the park, as well as a 'sociological document', but most of all a humorous film revolving around the charismatic central character.

RM: So the role of the artist is to activate and connect creativity of other people? You work as intermediary rather than entrepreneur?

SA: It's quite enterprising to mediate and, don't forget, one still has to lead ideas in the right direction, within a form that will communicate.

RM: Would it work the other way round, where your creativity would be shaped and directed by other people and then introduced into their context, for example, introduced to a club of pickpockets?

SA: I have to admit I like to stay out of the picture. But what I mean is that for example in *L'Ecole des Pickpockets* my camera is following the hands of the pickpockets, and at the same time, they are attracted to the camera. It is not quite clear who is shaping whom or who is directing. Take for example the moment when the woman is picked up from the street to be the student's victim and becomes part of the psychology of the pickpockets very fast, at one point she even starts to teach the student. At that moment, she takes over control and sets the rules. So somehow the most interesting moments are those when somebody runs off with someone's ideas, when something unexpected happens.

RM: And did you ever consider leaving the art world and becoming a part of the people you film?

SA: One could define it more as a practice of stepping from one world into the other.

RM: So when did you most recently step out of one world and into the other, and what were those worlds?

SA: The newspaper project was one where I took some steps as a researcher and journalist into the history of the capital of the European Union, the history of Belgium and that of its former colony, Congo, and the relations between them. For this project, I walked through many doors of different parallel worlds. Those of the European Parliament and Commission, Suez-Tractebel, the Ministry of Foreign Affairs and the Cabinet of the Prime Minister, the Palace of Justice, the Wiertz Museum and the Museum of Central Africa, the private houses of the informants, those of the libraries and archives, the urbanists,

the newspaper and the printing house … and I've probably forgotten some.

RM: And where are you now?

SA: It seems to be that just like our King, I am tightening the bonds of friendship with Lithuania. But I have the feeling that you are suggesting that I am in many places and subsequently nowhere, that I have many costumes, many identities?

RM: Well, I don't think you have many identities, I think you have an opaque and fluid identity, which you prefer not to define (which is rather different from a multiple identity). Or maybe I should say you have an anamorphic identity. But let me get to another question. Lucy E. Smith, who is an editor of *Amgazine* from Brooklyn, writes about the notion of the invisibility of art and the artist in your work and claims that *L'Ecole des Pickpockets* teaches not a miraculous manual technique à la Houdini, but more complex concepts of the 'artist's dissolution and evaporation aimed towards revolution'. What do you think about this?

SA: I've often thought about this sentence and especially its ending. Particularly since I am doing research at the moment about Marx in Brussels. It was 1848, the February Revolution in Paris was taking place and King Leopold I almost abdicated under the pressure of a revolution threatening to take place in Belgium as well. The king won some time for his government by announcing that he would consider abdicating. The liberalists, who where in power meanwhile, quickly issued a law to reduce the voting tax to a minimum, which was a major demand of the opposition. And Marx was deported because he didn't keep his promise to renounce his activities as a journalist; so, no revolution in Belgium. They were afraid of another foreign occupation—after all, the revolution that took place in 1830 led to the foundation of the monarchy and of Belgium. It's clear about the artist's dissolution and evaporation, but what does the word 'revolution' mean and what does it imply within a Belgian context or more generally, in the art context? You also have to consider that in the 18th century our beloved valleys were the setting of the contra-reformation.

RM: Maybe everybody could be a king then? I think Lucy E. Smith speaks of evaporation and dissolution in relation to revolution in the same way Giorgio Agamben does when introducing the concept of 'anomie', i.e. atomised, lawless communal forms. You can dissolve there as an entity and re-emerge as another, or as part of 'an assemblage of forces', speaking through Manuel de Landa.

Francesco Manacorda, an Italian critic, interestingly transfers this view to the realm of art: 'Life dissolving into art is decadentism; art dissolving into life is utopian avant-gardism. But what would be an art that actively works to deprive you of the critical ability to distinguish between the two?' Don't you think that the concept of anamorphosis[3] which, according to Dan Collins, 'is a technique for bringing what still remains outside the field of the gaze into the line of sight and into consciousness' could be a productive formula to articulate the type of art Manacorda is talking about—removing our critical faculty to distinguish between art and life. Would you agree that in this respect your art is essentially anamorphic? And what do you think Sven Augustijnen, the journalist, has in common with Karl Marx, the journalist?

SA: At first glance the representations that I make look very normal. For example in *L'Ecole des Pickpockets*, the technique and the format are very familiar and what we see is real, at least that's what we believe. Before we realise, we are charmed and captured by the pickpocket and taken into his illicit ideology. By sympathizing, we comply. Something similar is going on in *Le Guide du Parc*. In a very realistic way 'the guide' takes us along his 'promenade' full of historical and philosophical, poetic and romantic details. With a touch of humour he totally convinces us of the 'truth' of his presentation. The reality might be slightly different. We might be misguided (or we could use the terms 'dérives' or 'détourne-ment' as proposed by the situationists). It might make us wonder what is going on. And that's interesting because then the spectator creates the 'picture'; he becomes self-aware of the process of seeing. He stands at a distance, he is an ex-centric observer. Here we have a parallel with the observer of anamorphosis. So there is a connection to be made, although the technique is different. The strange thing is that the revelation of the technique or the mechanism doesn't change its effectiveness. One is enchanted by the power of the voice of the protagonist and the magic of the kinetic image. The pickpocket

says: 'We'll do it even though you know it.' He is talking about stealing of course. So there is a lot of circulation and exchange going on. Which brings us to Marx. Reading *Das Kapital* is very interesting in order to discover its mixture of philosophy, history, economics and journalism. Alongside its all-encompassing, monumental unity, it retains a hybrid nature.

My interest in different fields and my attempt to unite them in a film or a newspaper gives them something in common. Of course, the reality of the context of journalism has drastically altered since Marx wrote *Das Kapital*. Then there was no television or radio, not to mention the Internet. The newspaper had a different impact in its time than it has now. So the 50,000 copies of *PANORAMA* in *De Tijd* and the 50,000 in the European Parliament and Commission in fact might all have been used for peeling potatoes on while watching television … I should get my films on television!

Next month *L'Ecole des Pickpockets* will be presented once more in a public place. We'll see what happens. When it was first shown it was forbidden after only one day of screening. It must have caused too many short circuits in the brains of the passengers in the underground station where it was shown; consequently, measures in social and security control were started. Despite the disarming charm of our pickpockets, something was triggered.

RM: Who is your favourite detective: Sherlock Holmes or Hercules Poirot?

SA: I should do some more investigation into the detective genre. But to pick up our royal itinerary again, the death of King Albert I in 1934 is still a mystery! Being an alpinist, the official version holds that he died falling off the rocks in Marche-les-Dames. But since there hasn't been an autopsy and as his climbing outfit together with his glasses—without which he couldn't climb—were discovered intact later on, the assumption is that he was murdered in his castle in Laeken and afterwards transported to Marches-les-Dames. Of course the question then arises, who murdered him? Some suggest he was murdered by the French secret service because of his refusal to integrate the Belgian army into the French forces during World War I. Another option is that he was shot by the husband of a mistress *in flagrante delicto*. Others suppose that he was murdered by Queen Elisabeth, who was tired of his extramarital escapades. And concerning art, there is of course the ongoing detective story of the stolen panel of *The Adoration of the Mystic Lamb*, 'The Just Judges' by the Van Eyck brothers. Until now it has never been found. One hypothesis is that the panel —stolen in 1934!—was buried together with King Albert I. A post mortem autopsy of the latter could kill two birds with one stone.

RM: I don't know about killing the birds, Sven, but do you know who killed the King?

SA: The point is that there has never been any serious investigation done on the case and this is because—as some presume—there is the possibility that more skeletons could come out of the closet.

RM: The detective genre is driven by the pursuit of truth. What role does truth play in your thinking?

SA: It is quite interesting how the way this mechanism of the pursuit of truth, once one is contaminated by it, doesn't allow one to escape it. But I believe—in contradiction to its construct —that truth is always subjective and multiple. Think about *Rashomon*[4] from Kurosawa—where is the truth?'

RM: Or maybe 'when is the truth'? I guess it's a temporal phenomenon.

SA: Yes, of course, we need only to think of the four different versions of 'truth' on the murder constructed in 'time' in *Rashomon*. It becomes very concrete indeed to speak about it in terms of film. We can probably also speak about revolution as a temporal phenomenon. The turning of the page is by definition a temporal phenomenon.

RM: Is it true that you don't differentiate between fact and fiction?

SA: Is there a difference? Should we believe there is a difference? The question probably goes back to the distinction between nature and culture. Can we distinguish ourselves from nature? Isn't every construct of the human mind imaginary? If you make it happen, it's real? What is the origin or nature of this interview? Fact or fiction? In the beginning was the word? Is that a fact or a fiction?'

RM: So you claim that word starts with the letter F? Fake for F?

SA: A question of belief or disbelief, no?

RM: Is it true that you often experience picno-leptic[5] moments, where the difference between the production of memory and imagination becomes increasingly blurred?

SA: A special moment in Belgium's royal history worth mentioning in this context is when King Baudouin informed the Prime minister on 30 March, 1990 that in accordance with his conscience he could not assent to the law on the legalisation of abortion. But as a third section of the Legislature according to the Belgium constitution, the King has to sign the bill for it to become a law. King Baudouin's refusal to sign jeopardised the very basis of the Belgian Kingdom and the country's constitution. After a few nights of secret consultations, the Council of Ministers stated that on the basis of article 82 the King was deemed unfit to govern and the Council would take over his constitutive power. The King abdicated—for a day—and the bill was assented to and the law proclaimed. So it seems that in Belgium we even have articles in the law that enable picnoleptic moments. By the way, Carsten Höller was inspired by this historical event and followed in the footsteps of King Baudouin to lock himself up in the Atomium in Brussels for 24 hours, together with a few dozen selected people, in order to see how it feels to step outside society for a day. According to one testimony, the experience was like being pawns in an abandoned chess game. After all, to come back to our first king, what was Leopold I thinking when he was carried from one church to the other, unable to find a place to be buried? Maybe he thought he was somewhere in limbo? I wonder if he considered it a sublime moment?

RM: To be buried in several places at the same time is quite a sublime (or, I would claim, 'royal') moment indeed. Jozef Pilsudski, the Marshal of Poland, was so much in love with Vilnius that he requested his heart be buried in Rasu cemetery in Vilnius, while his body was buried in St. Leonard's Crypt in Wawel Cathedral in Krakow, the other city he favoured. What are your favourite cities?

SA: It seems that I am a bit stuck in the Brussels swamp at the moment. But recently my eye caught a very strange building in Cairo, some kind of Hindu Palace that happened to be constructed by the Belgian Baron Eduard Empain at the beginning of the 20th century. The Baron was a great industrialist who built railroads all the way from the Congo to China, as far as Russia and Egypt. As an amateur Egyptologist, he conceived the city of Heliopolis at the time. From his Palace and garden full of busts, statues, elephants, snakes, Buddhas, Shivas and Krishnas he could oversee his city rising out of the desert.

Today his palace is integrated in Greater Cairo, but unfortunately severely derelict and subject to countless fables, legends and rumours.

It's supposed to be haunted by bats, stray dogs, and others believe by ghosts. Some say even some devil worshipping takes place there. Maybe it would be interesting to find out what is the 'truth' about all this. So I might consider visiting the palace, as well as the Baron's graveyard—since the Baron was buried in the Basilica of Heliopolis, which he constructed as well.

RM: Would you like to be buried there?

SA: I'll let you know when the end is nigh.

A version of this interview appeared in *Metropolis M* magazine, 2006/3. Reproduced with thanks.

NOTES
1. The interview was done with a help of questions from *Answer is Never the Same*, the title of a series of interviews with a growing number of artists made by Raimundas Malasauskas. They are based on the same questions coming from older interviews with Lawrence Weiner, Robert Barry and others from the 1960s and 1970s, as well as more recent conversations with Jonathan Monk, Carsten Höller, plus some newly-fabricated inquiries such as those from the questionnaire *Are You Dora Garcia?*.
2. *Le Guide du Parc* (2001, 36 minutes) was realised and first shown in the context of the Prix de la Jeune Peinture Belge, Palais des Beaux-Arts, Brussels. The video didn't win the prize. Michael Tarantino, who was a member of the jury, wrote: 'I don't understand what this has to do with cinema. Is it a documentary or is it fake? It can't be a documentary. I don't believe that these things could happen like that, in the middle of the city. If it's a fake, it's a disgrace. People shouldn't be led to believe that things like this happen. And those camera movements. What's the purpose of that?' (Michael Tarantino, *Wiels!*, catalogue, Contemporary Art Centre, Brussels, 2003).
3. The most famous example of anamorphosis is the painting *The Ambassadors* by Hans Holbein the Younger (1497/8–1543). The figure floating in the foreground of the main painting is an anamorphic projection of a skull.
4. *Rashomon* (1950) is a film by Akira Kurosawa: 'In 12th century Japan, a samurai and his wife are attacked by the notorious bandit Tajomaru, and the samurai ends up dead. Tajomaru is captured shortly afterward and is put on trial, but his story and the wife's are so completely different that a psychic is brought in to allow the murdered man to give his own testimony. He tells yet another completely different story. Finally, a woodcutter who found the body reveals that he saw the whole thing, and his version is again completely different from the others.' (www.imdb.com)
5. 'Picnolepsy' (noun. from the Greek, Picnos: frequent): 'Even the most perfect reproduction of a work of art is lacking in one element: its presence in time and space, its unique existence at the place where it happens to be.' (from Walter Benjamin, *Illuminations*); 'The return being just as sudden as the departure, the arrested word and action are picked up again where they have been interrupted. Conscious time comes together again automatically, forming a continuous time without apparent breaks ... However, for the picnoleptic, nothing really has happened, the missing time never existed. At each crisis, without realizing it, a little of his or her life simply escaped.' (from Paul Virilio, *Aesthetics of Disappearance*).

Prospectus for the Invisible University correct at 07.00, 19th June 2006, 35 Clerkenwell Road London EC1

Imagine yourself with a lap-top on a lawn by a shed, the screen is your tutor, the lawn is your classroom and the web your university.

So what is the shed for?

EXP Research into the architecture of the culture of smaller and faster.

Pastoral: relating to, or associated with shepherds or flocks and herds. Portraying country life, usually in a romantic or idealised form.

Arcadia: a mountainous district in the Peleponnese of Southern Greece. In poetic fantasy it represents a poetic paradise, the home of song loving shepherds.

Arcadian: an idealized peasant or country dweller. Especially in poetry. Simple and poetically rural.

Arcady: an ideal rustic paradise.

33

THE BLOODY LATTE

Vampirism as a Mass Movement

The penchant for a culture to imbibe drinks and drugs en masse, in a collective ritual-orgy, is a phenomenon which transcends mere fashion.

This, in itself, is unworthy of remark; the quest for transcendence through intoxication is as old as history itself. The cultural particularity of the proclivity is what is striking: the strange uniformity of every epoch's beverage cult.

Personal taste amounts to little; instead, for each era, there's a distinctive mass hysteria for the imbibing of a particular beverage or substance.

The drinks at this juncture in American history are indisputably coffee from Starbucks and the vodka of Absolut. The popularity of these drinks stems from their value as symbolic war booty from recent conquests. A culture's adopted beverage represents the blood of their vanquished foe.

Coke Adds Life

Drink is transubstantiation à la the Catholic cannibalism of Christ's blood and body. The smell of coffee is the odor of the Sandinista hospital, maimed by Contra bombs. Ice-cold vodka is the blood of the Russians, raped and murdered by capitalism.

And so it has been through history. Each imperial culture imports a liquid memento from their vanquished foe to serve as a totem of their power and glory. Tea, the Englishman's beverage, is falling out of favour as their neo-colonial hold on the Sub-continent wavers. For two centuries the English supped on their well-steeped leaves and tasted the sweat of the slaves in the Empire. Now, tea is for old mums, while beer swilling "lads" form the visible majority. The British love their beer; a cold pint brings fond memories of dead Germans, falling out of the sky in the battle of Britain.

Beer first attained great popularity in America immediately after the First World War, when the US had tipped the scale against the Kaiser in the last days of the conflict. That war had been highly unpopular to a then-isolationist nation, with American involvement cynically contrived by Anglophiles in government. The war transformed

the country profoundly, much to the consternation of its activists.

The women who had raged for abolition and suffrage now turned their eyes to alcohol, successfully banishing it in 1920. Prohibition, then, was unconsciously a moral crusade against imperialism and the blood sucking and chest beating that followed the Treaty of Versailles. Of course, beer made a comeback, especially after the depression hit and veterans needed to boost self-esteem by slurping the entrails of the wretched Kraut. A cold beer in a bar with one's buddies brought one's thoughts to the bread lines in Berlin, with all its one-legged soldiers.

Beer was big in Germany 1000 years earlier, when King Otto had pushed back the Slavic Wend and Magyar interlopers from the East. For the German, it is essentially the blood of the Slav. Its popularity was reinforced when Frederick the Great struck into the bread basket of Poland, expanding Prussia, a conquest that led to German domination of the continent under Bismarck.

Years later, to invoke the German's bloodlust, an Austrian man named Hitler held meetings in Munich beer halls, and cited the loss of those wheat fields, now occupied by Slavs.

This name was changed to "Java" in the '60s, when the US helped install the dictator Suharto in Indonesia, who murdered so many of his subjects at the behest of insecure multinationals. Although this was a proxy war, not directly fought by the US, coffee's taste still reflects the power imparted by the struggle. Its flavour was enriched and it grew in popularity. Whether Indian or Indonesian, coffee was the blood of the vanquished and it tasted good.

Now, in the global economy, coffee is grown across the entire subjugated Third World. When Starbucks sells a bag of beans, it's always marked with the region from whence it sprang, making the consumer an imperial cannibal connoisseur.

Coca-Cola is another toast of imperial conquest; it initially drew its flavor from the coca plant from Central America, but switched to another regional flavor (Tamarind root) when this was outlawed. Coca-Cola's ascendancy coincided with the Spanish-American War and the annexation of Puerto Rico, Cuba, etc. It was often mixed with rum, the sugar-based flavor of those very islands.

Coke was provided to all American soldiers during the Second World War as a way to "blood" the army. Coke plants in Germany changed their

When Hitler rose to power, after the "Beer hall Putsch," he allied himself with the Italian dictator Mussolini, who dreamed of imperial glory in Africa. The Italian conquest of Ethiopia, the birthplace of coffee, resulted in the espresso craze in Italy. During the Second World War, each Italian soldier carried an espresso maker in his mess kit. The Starbucks aesthetic — garish, Fascistic murals combined with Futurist mechanization of the work force and absurdist shouting — can be traced to Mussolini.

America's love of coffee has always been tied to the affection for conquest. Coffee fuelled the "winning of the west" and the usurpation of the former colonies of Spain at the turn of the century. Guatemala, Salvador, Nicaragua, Colombia, etc., have all been virtual colonies since then, with frequent US-armed interventions to ensure servitude.

These nations constitute the mainstay of our coffee supply, and much blood has been spilled to maintain it. Coffee was the blood of the Indian, and gave one the adrenal rush needed to achieve "manifest destiny." Coffee was "joe," as in Joe Nobody or John Doe, as the racist dehumanization of the native peoples refuted any necessity for their identification.

trade-name to FANTA, so as to deflect charges of corporate two-timing in the war effort. FANTA was orange, a flavor homage to the smashed Republican army in Spain, where the German army had first honed their killing skills. When a German drank an orange pop, he was gnawing the jugular of an Anarcho-syndicalist in Valencia.

Vodka is the refined fruit of the peasant's potato. Under the Tsars, Russia's border relentlessly expanded, from the Baltic to the Black Sea, and then on to the Pacific. Conquered people, impressed into serfdom, were manifest in the vodka drink favored by the Russian ruling class, both before the execution of the Tsar and then later with Stalin.

Vodka can actually be made from a variety of grains and fruits, appropriate to the vast and varied lands of Muscovite conquest. For the Russians, this drink, the blood of Swedes, Finns, Lithuanians, Ukrainians, Uzbeks and Khazars, became suddenly, under the creed of Communist internationalism, the celebration of fratricide. This accounts for the existential mania and depression that famously accompanies modern Russian drunkenness.

With the conclusion of the Cold War, and Russia under the yoke of exploitive capitalism, vodka

is more and more beloved by Americans, who gulp it smugly as proof positive of their power to sculpt the earth. Sweden, the traditional nemesis of Tsarist Russia, is the producer par excellence of the trophy drink.

As we can see, the cultural specificity of the blood represented by a drink is contingent on the race or nationality of the person drinking. So, while a German drinking a beer would be enjoying the life-force of the Slav, an American popping a "Bud" would be eating the guts of that same German man. Similarly, a toast of expatriate brand "Bacardi" rum is a celebration of the assassination of Che in Bolivia, while a splash of "Habana Club," the Cuban national brand, is the bloody froth from the surf at the Bay of Pigs.

And so it goes: tequila's worm is the dead Yankee at the Alamo, as "gusano" or "worm" is the Latin revolutionaries' name for the *Yanqui* imperialist. Even the introduction of Perrier to America coincided with the death of the nationalist de Gaulle and the subsequent compliance of France with NATO (the boycott of an intransigent and undefeated foe's imported foodstuffs follows a similar repressed logic, as with Cuban rum or French wine during the Iraq War). Wine was championed by the Gauls upon the disintegration of its drinkers, the imperial Roman occupiers. The Romans had snatched it from their Greek competitor, whose empire they had eclipsed, while the Greek slave states begat their wine from the stamping feet of their war-captives, and so on, ad infinitum to the prehistoric dawn of life on the planet.

Food rituals have always been centred on hierarchy and power. The cow is ingested because he is essentially defenseless against us. We assert our primacy over nature by ingesting it in a gory ceremony of flesh chewing. The animals we admire are felines and canines, bears, and eagles: predators like us. This is an ancient warrior's ethic, echoed in the American craze for Nazi memorabilia. The milk of the breast is the first liquid imbibed by the newborn child. The baby learns that his mewing automatically summons the mother, whereupon she administers the juice of subjugation from her teat. Therefore the taste of liquid is psychically paralleled with subjugation and enslavement even in the semiconscious baby state.

Once again, while Stoker's *Dracula* story per se addresses the genetic concerns of the European upper classes, vampirism — an ancient legend

shared by many different cultures — is also a mass movement, enjoyed by every conquering race.

Excerpted from *The Psychic Soviet and other works* by Ian F. Svenonius (Drag City, Chicago, 2006)

1

GREETINGS FROM BHUTAN

by Alex Klein

The year was 1951, and it began with a message sent via telegram: 'Please come now to Bhutan. Jigmie leaves May 21st for Ha Dzong. We have received permission for you to join him.' As recounted in Burt Kerr Todd's 1952 essay for *National Geographic* magazine, upon receiving this invitation Todd packed his bags and was soon the first American to visit Bhutan, a country also known as 'The Land of the Thunder Dragon' or 'Druk Yul'. Prior to Todd's well-documented trip to the small land-locked nation in the heart of the Himalayas, only a handful of Western visitors had preceded him, such as James Hill, who dubbed it 'Shangri-la' in his 1937 novel *Lost Horizon*. And surely the shift to monarchial rule that had occurred at the turn of the century due to the influence of the British meant that Bhutan was a vastly different place than that documented in the survey *Political Missions to Bootan: Comprising the Reports of The Hon'ble Ashley Eden.*[1] Published in Calcutta by the Bengal Secretariat Office in 1865, the same year as the signing of the Treaty of Sinchula, the Honorable Ashley Eden's account described Bhutan as a 'country in which there is no ruling class, no literature, no national pride in the past or aspirations for the future, ... no reliable history and very little tradition.'[2] In short, prior to Mr Todd's visit the country was largely a terra incognita in the eyes of the Western world, shrouded by colonial ignorance and insulated by its strict ban on foreigners.

In 1949, two years after India's independence, Bhutan declared its sovereignty. It was from this moment on that the country began what could be considered an emphatic leap from feudalism directly into Western modernity. It would be incorrect to say that any of this was a transition as much as it was a series of calculated intro-ductions and innovations by a monarchy deter-mined to preserve the rich culture and traditions of Bhutan even as it was becoming increasingly curious about its relationship to the world at large. Returning to the year 1952, King Jigme

Dorji Wangchuck, the recently-appointed King of Bhutan, eliminated the system of feudal rule and introduced wheeled vehicles into the lives of farmers who had previously relied upon their own manpower to plow the fields and transport their crops. In the meantime, his friend, Burt Kerr Todd, had returned to the United States and was beginning to reflect upon his recent journey (he would later spend a year-long honeymoon there in 1954). Although it was but one in a series of exciting adventures, the first trip to Bhutan had left a lasting impression on Mr Todd, who maintained a lifelong fondness for the country until his death in April 2006. And thus, today we might remember him not only as the first American visitor to Bhutan, but also as its first modern tourist.

Born in Pittsburgh on May 15, 1924 to a wealthy family whose fortunes were built on steel, glass and banking, Burt Todd was never one to stay still or to let a deal pass unnoticed. A man from the imagination of another era, tales abound of Todd's insatiable hunger for travel and adventure. An oft-told story posits the industrious Mr Todd just back from World War II, where he had been enlisted in the Air Force as a radar instructor, attempting to enroll in a graduate program at Oxford. Undeterred by the fact that he only had one year of college at Williams under his belt, Todd managed to track down the one person with the authority to accept him. The official in question happened to be on his honeymoon at the time in a remote part of Norway and one can only begin to imagine the circumstances under which Todd, who had traveled there in person, was able to persuade him. Graduating with a masters degree in law in 1949, Todd left England with a broader appreciation of the world and a new, elite, international friendship circuit that included among them the future queen of Bhutan, Ashi Kesang-La Dorji—the first person from Bhutan to study in the West and to cross an ocean.

A lover of flying, hunting and antique cars; friend to the ruler of Fiji, the sultan of Brunei, and the premier of the island of Mauritius, Mr Todd made a living out of enthusiastic ventures and fortuitous opportunity. As recounted in his obituary in *The New York Times*, Todd's 'exact job defied description, though it entailed both the businessman's art of the deal and the confidence man's gift of gab ... Officially, Mr Todd was president of the Kerr-Hays Co., an importing and manufacturing concern, now based in Ligonier [Pennsylvania], that he founded in 1963. But even before that, and for many years afterward, his portfolio included advising heads of state—mostly of small countries in Asia and the Pacific—on attracting U.S. investment.'[3] Of Todd's accomplishments and business schemes it is worth mentioning his role in facilitating the re-sale of luxury vehicles formerly belonging to maharajas and in helping Fiji to produce rum and Singapore to market seaweed—a product with which his family is still involved to this day. One of his more outlandish projects was trying to 'found a small kingdom himself, on a deserted coral reef in the South Pacific'.[4]

Ten years after his first visit to Bhutan King Jigme Dorji Wangchuck called upon Todd for advice regarding the expansion of the country's economy. Todd, who had been retained as an official advisor to the Kingdom, was only too happy to assist. He suggested that a postal system be installed and with it a series of unique stamps. On October 10, 1962, four years prior to the publication of Thomas Pynchon's prescient postal network novel *The Crying of Lot 49*, Bhutan issued its first series of stamps for use outside of Bhutan.[5] Numbered A1_1−A1_7, the stamps depict scenes of Bhutanese life and national symbols such as the yak, a map of Bhutan, the royal palace, and the national sport of archery in a reduced two-tone palette designed by Todd himself. Quickly, however, the designs of the stamps became increasingly unique. Oddities to true philatelists yet highly collectible, there were Bhutanese stamps made out of silk and steel; hologram stamps, and triangular-shaped stamps that depicted the local abominable snowman.[6] Most of the stamps included text printed in both Dzongkha and English so as to encourage their distribution beyond the region. There were also stamps that depicted indigenous plants and animals and commemorated significant world events ranging from space travel, the postal system itself, the Olympic Games, and Bhutan's 1971 entry into the United Nations. However, some of the most fascinating stamps were issued in the series SC 152−152F, released on April 15, 1973.

Created in the same year that the Bhutanese National Broadcast Service installed its first national short wave transmission and one year after King Jigme Dorji Wangchuck's unfortunate death, the 'talking stamps' entered circulation. Issued as a set of seven in red, yellow, green, blue, purple, white, and black and in various sizes, the talking stamps were in fact miniature phonograph records. Constructed of a normal adhesive back and a flexidisc-like front, the stamps featured audio recordings of folk songs, the Royal Bhutan Anthem, the history of Bhutan in Bhutanese and the history of Bhutan as told in English by Mr Burt Kerr Todd himself. In a voice straight out of a 1940s newsreel Todd reported on the geography, government and economics of the nation, describing the Bhutanese as 'a strong and well-built race whose religion is Buddhism.' He duly reported that 'over 1,000 kilometers of roads criss-cross the country, there are one hundred schools and sixty post offices.' Each stamp, which could be used both for national and international mail, came in a small envelope with the statement,

> This envelope contains your BHUTAN postage stamp. In order to develop a national economy, these unusual beautiful stamps are now the principal industry. Bhutan is a tiny 90 mi. kingdom high in the Himalayan mountains. This stamp, one of a series, is a collector's item.

Today, as when Todd first visited, Bhutan remains primarily agrarian. However, instead of an economic system sustained by stamps, close to 75% of the current economy is dependent upon the sale of hydro-electric power to India and, increasingly, a reliance on tourism. In 1974, the year that the present currency of Bhutan, the ngultrum, was introduced, King Jigme Singye Wangchuk (son of the former king) was coronated. In celebration of the occasion several foreign guests were officially invited to attend the ceremony. For the first time in Bhutan's history, tourists slowly began to trickle in and a small tourism industry was allowed to ferment. Although visitors were and still are severely limited, it was becoming clear that the slow program of modernization overseen by the government could not entirely be controlled. Acutely aware of the onslaught of globalization, Bhutan has subsequently enacted a series of measures in an attempt to protect itself. For example, specific laws require that all Bhutanese wear traditional dress in public and be schooled in the native customs of the country. Most notably the kingdom has received wide attention for its efforts to curtail what it sees as a negative or neglectful dominant international economic model. The growing pressures for a broader,

2

4

3

1. 'Talking Stamp', Bhutan History (English). Photograph by Alex Klein.
2. Bhutanese listening to a radio brought to Bhutan by Burt Kerr Todd. First published in *National Geographic* magazine, December 1952. Photograph by Burt Kerr Todd.
3. 'Travel to Bhutan', Lindblad Travel, Inc. print advertisement, 1975.
4. Burt Kerr Todd and his wife Susie on their honeymoon in Bhutan in 1955. Photograph published in Burt Kerr Todd's obituary in *The New York Times*, May 7, 2006.
5. Radio stamp, Bhutan, issued March 2, 1966.
6. King Jigmie Wangchuk and Queen Ashi Kesang-La Dorji displaying wedding silks and brocades, First published in *National Geographic* magazine, December 1952, Photograph by Burt Kerr Todd.
7. Cover of the Voyager Golden Record, 1977. Photograph courtesy of NASA.

5

6

globalised development strategy raised concerns that the unique culture of Bhutan was being threatened and that the individual well-being of its citizens was being ignored. In response, the Dragon King proclaimed that the happiness of his people should be considered first and foremost and that a new economic model be set in motion. Thus, on the eve of the 21st century, Gross National Happiness was set to supercede Gross National Product.

Gross National Happiness (GNH) is an economic model rooted in the tenets of Buddhism that encourages the development of a 'self' that is community oriented rather than self-involved. Although the Bhutanese have conducted scientific studies abroad regarding the base level income for contentment, in a country where the median annual income is reported to be US$1,321, it became necessary to try and measure success by other means. Described as a way of fostering both 'inner spiritual and external material development' GNH is meant to encourage a 'harmonious psychological, social and economic environment.[7] As happiness cannot be measured through traditional data, it was surmised that in order to promote happiness the population required not only that its basic material needs be met but also environmental, spiritual, cultural and socio-political concerns.

As part of the effort to increase Gross National Happiness, Bhutan spends close to 18% of its national budget on healthcare and education and continues to maintain one of the most diverse climates of any nation in the world, comprising an estimated 64% forest land. Furthermore, in 1998, concluding that a people who have a say in their destiny will be happier, King Jigme Singye Wangchuk ceded his absolute power and began to rule with the advice of the government. Circulating a draft of the new Constitution to every household, he gave the Council of Ministers the power to remove him from office with a two-thirds majority vote. In an effort to move the country closer to democracy the king also announced plans to relinquish office in 2008, a move that placed him in *Time* magazine's 2006 hundred most important people of the year. In his speech on GNH, His Excellency Lyonpo Jigmi Y. Thinley, Chairman of the Council of Ministers, summed up the King's intentions by stating, 'A growing income does not always lead proportionately to an increase in happiness. Consumption patterns everywhere seem increasingly to be based on emulation of the consumption patterns of our admired peers elsewhere. Our need is increased when we find that others in our reference group have more. As psychologists and economists say, happiness depends on relative income not on absolute income. In a world where everyone who has less is trying to catch up with everyone who has more, we may become richer but happiness becomes elusive.'[8] These sentiments are not only affecting the lives of the Bhutanese, but are gaining an audience with policymakers around the world.

Prior to 1999, Bhutan had strictly monitored the process of modernization by outlawing satellite dishes, carefully introducing modern vehicles, prohibiting rampant advertising, Coca-Cola and, most recently, smoking in public. However, despite its national ban on television, by 1998 Bhutan was no stranger to World Cup fever. The King arranged for the Olympic Committee of Bhutan to broadcast the final matches of the World Cup in the capital of Thimpu on a large screen in Changlimithang stadium. In June 1999, hoping that the population would be able to judge good television from bad, the ban was officially lifted, making Bhutan the last nation to officially enter the age of the small screen (soon followed thereafter by Internet and cell phones). With television, however, all of the aspects of modern existence that the Kingdom had attempted to keep at bay were beamed directly into its citizens' lives with the widest selection of programming available. Some studies have speculated whether this late and extremely sudden introduction of television has the potential to undermine the very fabric of Bhutan's society. Confronted with a world which until then had been relatively invisible, the younger generations now find themselves caught between the principles of Buddhism and the pleasures of capitalist consumption.

Unlike the predominant approaches to economic development, it would seem that Gross National Happiness is not necessarily dependent upon technological advances or conventional measures of material wealth. In H.E. Thinley's aforementioned speech, the year of Bhutan's modernization is dated to 1961, the year before the first Bhutanese stamp was circulated. Although Burt Kerr Todd surely continued his relationship with the country, there is little readily available documentation of his involvement after the release of the talking stamps. If the advent of Bhutan's postal system marked a turning point in the country's modernization, we might add that the talking stamps epitomise its shift from utter reticence to a tentative, yet optimistic desire to communicate. Occupying a moment between two kings and on the cusp of a period of international relations, a new currency, a burgeoning tourist industry, and an era of information exchange, the talking stamps offer a material trace of a moment of unprecedented possibility.

In 1977, the year of Steven Spielberg's *Close Encounters of the Third Kind*, NASA launched the Voyager I spacecraft, which had been preceded by Pioneer 10 in 1972 and Pioneer 11 in 1973, just when the talking stamps were first circulated. These missions were meant to collect data and, for the first time, inform alien life about the inhabitants and history of planet Earth. Chief among the objects included for this purpose on Voyager I was the Golden Record. Created by a committee chaired by Dr Carl Sagan, its contents include hundreds of images of flora, fauna, animals, landscapes and different cultures from around the world in analog format, greetings in fifty-five languages, various natural atmospheric sounds found on earth, addresses given by President Jimmy Carter and U.N. Secretary General Kurt Waldheim, and ninety minutes of music. Engraved on the face of the record are instructions written in a symbolic pictorial language explaining how it should be played and the history of the Voyager I space-craft. Although no one has responded to these recordings as yet, the vessel continues to transmit data back to Earth as it searches the outer reaches of the galaxies. Currently, Voyager I is the farthest man-made object in the cosmos, having reached one hundred astronomical units from the sun as of August 15, 2006.[9]

Coming in the first decades of the post-modern era, the Bhutanese talking stamps were not only contemporaneous with these initiatives, but actually anticipated the Golden Record by a number of years. In this respect, we might think of the earliest stamps issued in Bhutan not simply as a tool for economic advancement, but also as the first attempt by an isolated, essentially pre-capitalist nation to communicate with the rest of the world. Like the Golden Record, the stamps represented an opportunity for the people of Bhutan to tell the story of their culture and preoccupations in their own voice and pictorial language, culminating with the actual recorded

voices of the Bhutanese and their enthusiastic translator, Burt Kerr Todd, on the talking stamps. Hearing these voices today, one can't help but begin to think of one's contemporary capitalist self as a type of alien life form. And in our present moment of geopolitical and ecological urgency, one can only hope that the message of Gross National Happiness has arrived just in time.

NOTES
1. Although it has been reported that the centennial of the monarchy is technically this coming year—Gongsar Ugyen Wangchuck unified the fragmented nation in 1907—the official celebration will take place in 2008 as the Bhutanese calendar deems 2007 'inauspicious'.
2. The full title of the survey reads *Political Missions to Bootan: Comprising the reports of The Hon'ble Ashley Eden. 1864; Capt. R.B. Pemberton, 1837, 1838 with Dr W. Griffith's Journal and the account by Baboo Kishen Kant Bose* (Munishram Manoharlal Publishers Pvt. Ltd, New Delhi, 2000), p. 108.
3. Margalit Fox, 'Burt Todd, 81, Entrepreneur Who Dreamed Big, Is Dead', in the *New York Times*, May 7, 2006, A31.
4. It is worth noting that the economy of this new nation was to be based entirely on stamps. Fox, 'Burt Todd', A31.
5. Although Bhutan has had internal courier services for centuries and issued a domestic stamp in 1955, it was not until the 1962 series of stamps that mail could be sent to international destinations directly from Bhutan. It is reported by the CIA World Factbook that Bhutan's primary foreign exchange earner was from the sale of stamps until the influx of tourism replaced it in 1974.
6. The stamps are so collectible that mail in transit is often delayed due to the removal of stamps mid-route.
7. Lyonpo Jigmi Thinley. 'Values and Development: Gross National Happiness', in *Gross National Happiness* (The Centre for Bhutan Studies, Thimpu), p. 17.
8. Thinley, *Gross National Happiness*, p.20.
9. NASA JPL, 'Voyager 1: "The Spacecraft That Could" Hits New Milestone', http://www.jpl.nasa.gov/news/features.cfm?feature=1150.

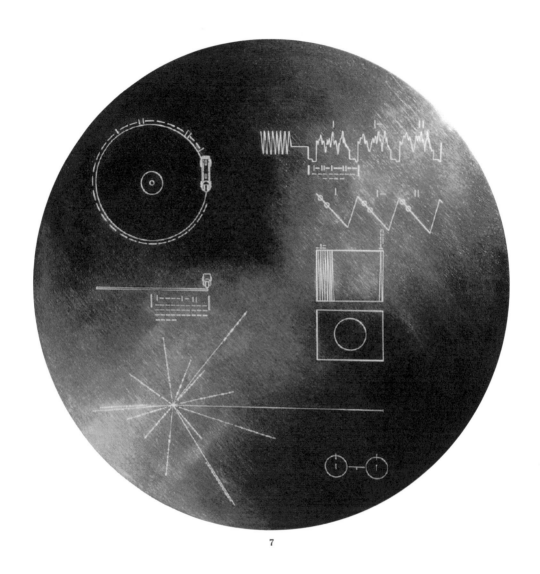

7

46

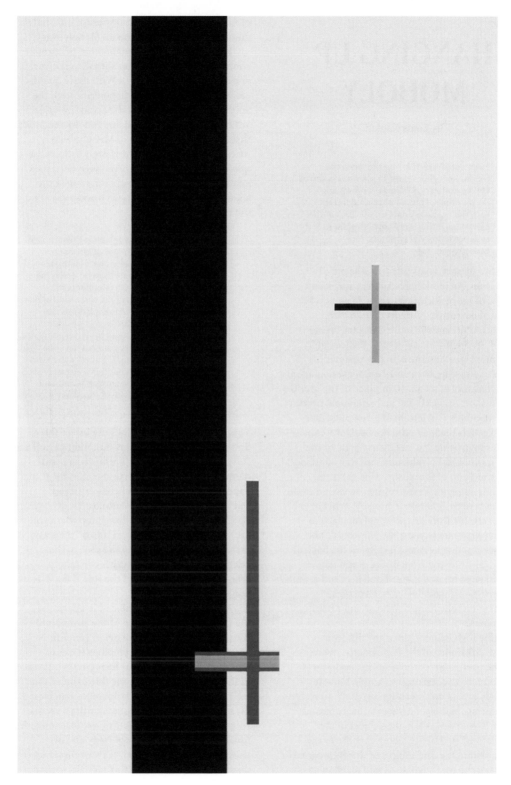

László Moholy-Nagy, *Telephone Painting* or *Em 3*, enamel on steel, 24 × 15 cm, 1922
(Reproduction, Bauhaus-Archiv, Berlin. Copyright Hattula Moholy-Nagy)

47

HANGING UP MOHOLY

by Louis Kaplan

I was not afraid of losing the 'personal
touch,' so highly valued in previous painting.
On the contrary, I even gave up signing
my paintings. I put numbers and letters
with the necessary data on the back of the
canvas, as if they were cars, airplanes,
or other industrial products.
László Moholy-Nagy

A number of paradoxes tie up this scene of
resignation. An identifiable subject speaks of
his loss, of becoming anonymous. In an autobiographical narrative, *Abstract of an Artist*,
he writes of his artistic techniques for losing
himself, for losing his signature, the loss of
assignment to a signature. In this manner,
the text written as *Abstract of an Artist* documents
the abstracting of an artist. In place of the identity
of the maker, one will read an impersonal product
label—numbers and letters of a computer bar-
coded system stamped onto the back of a canvas
in order to provide the 'necessary data' in the
age of mechanical production and reproduction.
But at the point of this abstracting gesture,
one reads about an 'I' who returns to assign each
of the acts of resignation to himself. What of the
'I' who refrains from the personal touch, who
will have given up signing 'my paintings', who
will have put numbers and letters on the back of
the canvas or on the front of the graph paper,
who will have treated himself and his productions
like impersonal models—cars, airplanes,
guns or even telephones? Who, if and when,
anonymous?

While it should not make any difference
—in the difference of the anonymous—who says
this, the particular 'I' who gives up, and who is
given up for dead, belongs to László Moholy-
Nagy.[1] By giving up and resigning the 'I' that signs
the painting, Moholy, or whoever, has crossed
out the 'I' who writes (i.e. the subject of the
enunciation) so that the material shifts to the 'I'
who is written (i.e. the subject of the enunciated).
These are the basic dynamics and mechanics of
the unsigning 'I'. Its inscription converts all of
the 'necessary data' into an unhooked generation,

of numbers and letters, anonymous, unlisted or
unnameable which hang up on Moholy-Nagy.

It is the impossibility of making the proper
connections, of hooking up with the receiver
at all (or once and for all?). With these qualifi-
cations, disclaimers and dispensations of the
anonymous hand that get the speaking subject
'off the hook', so to speak, one follows the process
through another passage of Moholy-Nagy's
writing, which almost immediately follows the
quote above. The following passage describes
another specific instance of resigning of the
signing of works of art. These works are called
the telephone paintings.

In 1922, I ordered by telephone from a sign
factory 5 paintings in porcelain enamel.
I had the factory's color chart before me
and I sketched my paintings on graph paper.
At the other end of the telephone, the
factory supervisor had the same kind of paper,
divided into squares. He took down the
dictated shapes in the correct position.
(It was like playing chess by correspondence.)
… Thus, these pictures did not have the virtue
of the 'individual touch,' but my action was
directed exactly against this overemphasis.
I often hear the criticism that because of
this want of the individual touch, my pictures
are 'intellectual.'[2]

This paragraph also employs the use of the
first person pronoun to play out other paradoxes.
It is a four-fold authorial 'I' who orders and
dictates from a sign factory, sketches on graph
paper, studies, plays, and hears criticism.
But if this is the same 'I'—another 'I'—who gave
up signing, who prefers anonymity, who eschews
the virtues of the 'individual touch', then who
is there to talk about, or in the case of the
telephone pictures, who is there to talk to?
Who is on the other end of the line if the 'I' is
put on the line?

These pictures have placed in operation
the telephonic solicitation of the author and
the production of works of art in general.
He (the authorial 'I') still employs terms of
mastery and authority, but he is caught unaware
in the work carried on by the fine print of the
telephone directory which detaches him from
his signature. The telephone paintings are the
connecting, and consequently, the disconnecting
link between László Moholy-Nagy and his
passing away into anonymity. From dictating to
dispatching and transmitting signals, with the
dispensing of the author, the Romantic conception
of the artist has been put at risk. Smoothly,

48

László Moholy-Nagy, *Painter's Works in Switzerland*, photograph, 39 × 30 cm, 1925
(Reproduction, Bauhaus-Archiv, Berlin. Copyright Hattula Moholy-Nagy)

facilely, with the greatest of ease, the telephone has turned Moholy into an operator for feeds and feedback. He has also brought into question the concepts of the creative genius and the original artist. In the book *Kunstismen/Isms of Art*, these art exchanges, telephone exchanges, make the ex-Bauhaus master seem quite common—a common house painter, a common name, a bedroom farce, a simpleton or even a nobody. Moholy overheard the following advice: 'Now the production of works of art is … so facilitated and simplified that nobody can do better than order his works by telephone from his bed, from a common painter'.[3] Oddly enough, a Moholy photograph from the same period illustrates the same basic elements, as a house painter is set off against a backdrop of telephone lines.

This mode of production, utilizing a sign factory and a design charted on graph paper, has sketched a network that interrogates the structure of the sign. The telephone paintings set up static in the lines, on the graph paper, in the sign factory, in the final product—a buzzing for telecommunications and for communication in any form. With the gesture of the dialing or the push-button hand that generates art by telephone, it is the impersonality and anonymity of the language machine or of the telephone machine which has gone into a remote-control reproduction.

But even as we listen to Moholy's words, the effaced 'I' of the telephone paintings does not like the sound of a certain criticism raised against him. From where did this personal affront come and to where is it going? 'I often hear the criticism that because of this want of the individual touch, my pictures are "intellectual".' He claims the pictures as his own through the most possessive of all the pronouns ('my pictures'). But, in giving his reason, he says a personal touch is missing. Meanwhile, the terms 'intellectual' and 'individual touch' are indicated with quotation marks. They are marked off from the communication that surrounds the telephone paintings and are overemphasised in the presentation. These acts of quotation also remove the communication from the authorial origin and place them in an anonymous hand, in that this quoted material invades the space from an unknown origin. Perhaps these terms, or the criticism itself, have been effaced (like the 'I' that resigns from signing the paintings) through their quotation and through the anonymous gesture of the telephone paintings.

One wonders what the pedagogical value of this production could have been or even where its teacher might be found. Lucia Moholy decides this question by going back to the source, but she overlooks the consequences of the telephonic action upon this source. She argues that since Moholy *himself* did not talk about the telephone paintings in his posthumously published text *Vision in Motion*[4], or deal with their educational implications in *Abstract of an Artist*, they are not intended to teach anything. 'These are significant symptoms; for Moholy-Nagy's wisdom and circumspection as a teacher being of a high order, any gaps left in the didactic system must be understood as intention.'[5] I agree that the telephone paintings do not serve to instruct, but not for reasons that Lucia Moholy cites, nor for the sake of reason. The pictures do not circumscribe a didactic system of the highest order of any kind. If these paintings do instruct, it is through the gaps, the holes, the patterns of interference they leave between the author and the work, between both of these and their significance, and between the 'I' who writes and the 'I' who is written—through the insertion of an anonymous hand dialing or a coin placed in the slot of a machine. It places a long-distancing device, a telephone or a sign system, between the author and the production of the art work. Therefore this anonymous hand writing distances every intent from the teacher and from the records.

Lucia Moholy's *Marginal Notes* also offers strong opinions on the role of the telephone in the paintings. Lucia disputes the paintings' removed origins. According to this Moholy, that Moholy did not really order the paintings on the phone. This is a telephone prank, minus the telephone, and Moholy is a *tele-phonie*. Later on, Lucia transforms the story in this game of telephone talk in a version that goes in one ear and out the other. She says he did the job in person. Lucia turns the crank and recalls: 'I distinctly remember the timbre of his voice on that occasion—"I might even have done it over the telephone."'[6] Lucia Moholy invokes the format of a personal memoir in order to speak with an authoritative voice. This memoir is similar to the photo portraits of her partner in which Lucia seeks to capture László as visual image rather than as voice. But, in the act of quotation, an indistinct overtone slips in through the wavering of the words 'I might have done it over'. Between this future conditional tense and the certainty of the version in the

Lucia Moholy, *Portrait of László Moholy-Nagy, Dessau*, photograph, 23 × 15.9 cm, 1926
(Courtesy Bauhaus-Archiv Berlin / Lucia Moholy-Nagy / VG Bild-Kunst Bonn)

Abstract of the Artist (i.e. 'I ordered by telephone'), this remounting of remembering has afforded another detached and detaching possibility that blurs the borders of fact and fiction.

Furthermore, Lucia Moholy states that the name 'The Telephone Paintings' is a misnomer. She insists that these works, which border on the namelessness of anonymity, were originally named 'The Enamel Paintings', 'Email' for one, 'Emaille' for plural, or simply 'Em' in Moholy's abbreviated style of naming and numbered from 1 to 5. She insists that the enamels were intended only for experimentation with the effects of colour in relation to the size of their reproduction. But with the logic of the dispatch in the production and reproduction of the paintings, something has been lost in the mails and later recalled—that is, the telephone paintings.

Through a later call, the telephone paintings receive another calling. This is emblematic of the secondary role of a biographic writing practice that assumes a reality of its own and that estranges an artwork or its author from an original entitlement. Speaking against herself, Lucia Moholy senses how the margins creep into her notes via her telephonic reconsideration of Moholy. 'The role played by industry, a secondary consideration for him to start with, gradually assumed in his mind a reality of its own, the metaphor of the telephone becoming the emblem of the day.'[7]

Telephone becoming, taken as metaphor, rewires the signals from message unit to message unit. The 'assumed' character of the graphics that later rewrote the history of art carry over to the point where, according to some critics, Moholy becomes the primary source for conceptual or telephone art—ideas that were not on his mind at all. Again—this regrafting operation of telephone becoming surpasses intentions, hand executions, ideas—even what László Moholy-Nagy, in person, dubbed the 'mental process of the genesis of the work'[8] Lucia Moholy argues that Moholy could have had nothing to do with the origins of Conceptual Art or its thinking. ('It is erroneous to think of Moholy as the ancestor of those tendencies'[9]) But at another point, certainly unintentionally, she acknowledges the unintended consequences of telephone becoming, of a production in reproduction, outside of the power of intentions of the author of the work of art. It pulls the present argument apart. In *Marginal Notes*: 'The present argument apart: the notion of

Telephone Art might, in the computer age, take on a new meaning with connotations of a very different nature hardly foreseeable today.'[10] In the slip of a disk or on the tape of a telephone answering machine, this talk doubles back on Lucia Moholy and produces doubletalk—that is, statements that 'take on a new meaning with connotations of a very different nature hardly foreseeable today.'

For *telephone becoming*—very different from nature—the redialings of the telephone game, take and transform. Present and future arguments aside, it can give new meaning to anything Moholy might have said about it—especially when he who executes the anonymous telephone pictures has given up his signature, that which attaches something to himself. But this difficulty in tracing the call will not have been made in service of meaning. *Telephone becoming*, to cite a phrase, takes away from authorial intentions—puts meaning on hold—only through an anonymous handwriting, the 'I' that is written and rewritten. It produces every autobiographical statement in an anonymous hand, un-naming it with an anonymous hand.

All of these telephonic switches raise a chorus. It is an affirmation that rises to ever new heights, again and again. It is the party line of the dispatching signature taken upon by different voices and by different timbres. Amid the din, his voice becomes distinct: 'So they came to a new device of the literary expression—to a crisscrossing, zigzagging thought-pulsation of as many currents and messages as could be transmitted at the same time. We have an analogy in the synchronous multiplex telegraphy and in the coaxial cable system.'[11]

With these reflections, Moholy returns yet again to the metaphor of the telephone—to the super-syncretistic science of 'synchronous multiplex telegraphy'—as the meanings to describe contemporary literary and artistic production, to describe the telegraphic writings and practices that sent him and his voice through the wires. At that juncture and with that device, in the space of 'literary expression', where the history of ideas gets tangled up in the materials and materiality of writing, this crisscrossing and zigzagging of thought—its currents and messages that put the term 'intellectual' in a marked form, in the intertwining of the lines, the patterns of interference, the static of that dispatch network, the systematic overloads of the coaxial cable system, this long drawn-out death sentence, the telephone rings, sounding the death knell of the author.

This scenario posits a world where an anonymous phone call, a telephone painting or a biographical experiment in defamiliarization —and the risks that these pose to authority— would not automatically be called a practical joke nor considered obscene.

It resembles the H-U-M of a dial tone, of an anonymous phone call—Hanging Up Moholy.

An earlier version of this piece appeared in Louis Kaplan, *László Moholy-Nagy: Biographical Writings* (Duke University Press, Durham, 1995).

NOTES
1. László Moholy-Nagy, *The New Vision* (Wittenborn, New York, 1947), p. 79; László Moholy-Nagy, *Abstract of an Artist* (Wittenborn, New York, 1947).
2. See Moholy-Nagy [1], pp. 79–80.
3. Anonymous, 'Constructivism', in Hans Arp and El Lissitzky, *Kunstismen/Isms of Art* (Eugen Rentsch Verlag, Munich, 1925), pp. x–xi.
4. László Moholy-Nagy, *Vision in Motion* (George Wittenborn, Chicago, 1947), p. 314.
5. Lucia Moholy, *Marginal Notes* (Scherpe Verlag, London / Krefeld, 1972), p. 79.
6. Moholy [5], p. 76.
7. Moholy [5], p. 77.
8. László Moholy-Nagy, 'Domestic Pinacotheca', in *Painting, Photography, Film*, Janet Seligmann, trans. (MIT Press, Cambridge, MA, 1969), p. 26.
9. Moholy [5], p. 77.
10. Moholy [5], p. 79. Lucia Moholy refers to the 1969 exhibition 'Art by Telephone' at the Museum of Contemporary Art in Chicago.
11. Moholy-Nagy [4], p. 314.

1984
AND BEYOND

Screenplay by Gerard Byrne

CAST:
Jur van der Lecq
Jos van Hulst
Ruud van Andel
Rob van Gestel
Rien Stegman
Pieter Verhees
Leon de Waal
Dion Vincken
Wim Bouwens
Reinout Bussemaker
Michiel Nooter
Herman Boerman

1963, A LARGE GENERIC OFFICE BUILDING,
THE HEADQUARTERS OF AN ANONYMOUS
LARGE ORGANIZATION. OTHER SCENES
ARE SET IN A CONTEMPORARY SCULPTURE
GARDEN OF THE TIME, AND IN THE STREET.

Sc. 1: PROVINCIEHUIS (2:05 mins)

BUDRYS: I think the Russians will reach the
Moon ahead of us and soon. And once there, they
will claim the entire orb, and declare any landing
by any other nation's hardware, manned or not,
an invasion of territorial rights.

ANDERSON: Well, I think it's a toss-up whether
we or the Russians will get there first. But whoever
it is, I don't believe it will be possible for any
country to claim the Moon, or an entire planet,
merely because one of its ships gets there
first.

STURGEON: It looks to me as if we'll have to go
along with the famous remark Wernher von Braun
made years ago when asked what we'll find when
we get to the Moon. 'Russians', he said.

ASIMOV: At the time the Americas were being
colonised, the main squabble in Europe was
not between the English or French or Dutch or
Spanish; it was Catholicism versus Protestantism.
Today this great battle of ideologies, which cost
many millions of lives, is forgotten. To see the
future solely in terms of a capitalist-communist
fight to the death is being parochial in outlook.
We will be taking frontiers into space, but who,
at this point, can predict which frontiers?

POHL: It doesn't much matter who gets there
first any more than it mattered what whaling
ship first saw Antarctica. Consider the United
States: America was discovered and explored
independently by the French, the Spanish,
the Italians, the Norse, the Dutch, perhaps even
the Chinese. The English were quite late on
the scene, but they were the ones to establish
successful colonies. However, the English
held America only briefly, and it was held finally
by a new nationality who called themselves
Americans. I don't know what nation will first
colonise the Moon, but I know what nationality
will hold it: It will be the Lunarians.

BRADBURY: I agree. If you'll forgive a reference
to one of my own stories, I act out this point at
the end of my 'Million-Year Picnic' in *The Martian
Chronicles*. Two Earth boys, stranded on Mars,
keep pestering their father to show them
the Martians. Finally the father takes them down
to a canal and points down, saying, 'There are
the Martians.' The boys look and see their own
reflections in the shimmering waters.

Sc. 2: PROVINCIEHUIS (4:45 mins)

PLAYBOY: How soon do you estimate that manned
bases, Russian or American will be established
on the Moon? And how long afterward on Mars
and Venus?

CLARKE: The generally accepted time scale is:
Moon, 1970; Mars and Venus by 1980. I'll be very
much surprised if these figures are more than
five years off. We'll be establishing temporary
scientific bases on the Moon around 1975 for
astronomical, geophysical and all sorts of other
observations. I think we can visualise permanent
bases around 1980. These will lead to permanent
colonies as soon as we've perfected techniques
for extracting air and water and possibly other
essentials from the lunar rocks. I suggested in my
book, *Prelude to Space*, that the low lunar gravity

may be invaluable for many forms of therapy. It may even be that men will live much longer under low gravity. If so, one can foresee quite a rush to the Moon.

PLAYBOY: How much will it cost to finance a lunar or interplanetary voyage?

CLARKE: Billions at first, while we continue to rely on liquid-propellant rockets using chemical fuels. It will drop to millions when nuclear propulsion systems and ion or plasma jets are perfected.

HEINLEIN: The time will come when we can put a pound into orbit for ten cents by using cheap fuels like kerosene. We are going to be able to put people on the Moon so cheaply that it will cost less to rocket to the Moon than it is now to fly to Australia. It's a simpler engineering problem.

BUDRYS: Our children will doubtless be able to buy a ticket to the Moon on a civilian ship, and it's quite likely the process will be as simple as buying an airline seat today. The per-mile cost will likely be a fraction of present airline fares. Right now we're all very impressed with the hardware and the investment involved in extending our concept of what belongs to man, as if the Moon were the Seven Cities of Cibola rather than just another chunk of real estate. This awe will pass at about the same time the lunar communities acquire tax assessors.

POHL: Whatever it will cost to get there, only one thing will be found on the Moon or anywhere else in space that is truly valuable in an exploitive sense. That commodity is knowledge, and this is valuable forever.

HEINLEIN: I don't disagree with you on finding knowledge there, but we are going to find something else that is more immediately important to the human race: We're going to find a lot of real estate. And we're going to find an awful lot of raw materials. The human animal can live and create a high standard of living anyplace where he's got power and mass.

TENN: Well, with all that real estate and all that knowledge, another factor will come into human affairs which has been out of it for some time: Any outlawed sect or political minority, any discontented group which doesn't like the way

things are done; will be able to pick itself up and go elsewhere in the Universe like the Mormons did in our West.

HEINLEIN: I would like to amplify that. The human race is going to split off into a minority who travel into space. People who are smart, able, healthy and fast on their feet. The ordinary run of Joes will just stay where they are. And the human race is going to spread out through space with this Darwinian elite, a type of human being who probably won't even interbreed with those back on Earth.

BUDRYS: As has always been the case in the past, those who feel restricted and repressed within their cultures, those who find no peace at home will be those who go faring outward. And so they go out. Yesterday they became seafarers; today they become space-farers; tomorrow, star-farers. What will stay behind, as always, is the happy remnant, those content to put their life cards in a slot and have their homes, jobs, mates and off-spring delivered to them in a polystyrene package. In their little colonies of contentment, those back on Earth will cultivate the static arts. They will bring a great many crafts and entertainments to a high point of refinement. Those who leave, meanwhile, will have no victory except the contemplation of their next defeat but they will be the winners. The contented ones, those who stay behind will be the losers. We Earth-bound men have had it. The next century belongs to the space-farers.

Sc. 3: SONSBEEK PAVILION (7:20 mins)

PLAYBOY: Though the possibility of encountering intelligent life within our Solar System is considered slim, most scientists concede the probability, if not the inevitability, of its existence elsewhere throughout the Universe. As mankind moves deeper and deeper into space, do you foresee the likelihood of contact with such alien races?

CLARKE: We may not need to venture beyond our own Solar System. Although with the exception of Earth it would seem to be inhospitable to all the forms of life that we can imagine, we shouldn't be too ready to write off even cold, giant planets like Jupiter and Saturn. Are they really cold, as a matter of fact?

SLAM

It's much more probable that, owing to strong gravitational pressure, there is some level in their atmospheres where it is hot enough for water to exist, and for the complex chemical reactions which animate life. Sheer pressure itself is no obstacle to life, as our own oceans demonstrate prolifically. The facts of astronomy have always turned out to be more surprising than anyone could have dreamed.

TENN: Well, suppose, while cruising out toward Mercury or Pluto, we actually do bump into some alien civilization or other. Suddenly we'll find out for certain what we've been dreading and hoping and suspecting and speculating about for thousands of years: that we're not alone in the universe. Only then will governments begin to wonder frantically, 'How are we going to handle this? What are they like? Get the sociologists, psychologists, anthropologists; now they're almost as important as nuclear physicists.' So all these social scientists will be brought down to Washington with TOP SECRET stamped on their foreheads. And then, possibly, since they won't know too much about these aliens either, the Government may dig up a couple of grubby science-fiction writers and ask them, 'How strange can these characters be?' At that point, we will run through the multitudinous permutations which science fiction has presented. We will suggest, well, whether they are collectivists or individualists may not be nearly as important as whether they are asexual, bisexual, transsexual or products of precision manufacture.

HEINLEIN: Any condition in chemistry, whether it's within our present scope or not, which allows the building of large molecules, provides a situation where life can exist and inevitably will, I think.

STURGEON: Well, I operate on two adages. One of them is Sturgeon's Law, which says: Nothing is always absolutely so. The other adage states: Nature tries everything. I go further: Nature tries everything everywhere. And modify that to: Nature tries everything everywhere where it is possible.

ANDERSON: Yes, but let's modify that just a little further down to: Nature tries everything that the laws of physics permit which in turn includes just about everything we can imagine.

POHL: I think perhaps the laws of physics may subsume things we can't imagine.

STURGEON: That's a chilling thought when you think of some of the things we have been able to imagine. Bob Heinlein's Titans for example, in *The Puppet Masters*—intelligent slugs which could fasten on your back and thereafter control your thoughts and actions; or the creature in Hal Clement's *Needle*, which could ooze into and through your tissues and live there. And Stanley Weinbaum's silicon beast in *Martian Odyssey*. A creature which absorbed sand, grain by grain, very slowly extracting what it needed, and every year or so, laid a brick and then moved on a few inches. But I wouldn't doubt for a moment that nature can out-imagine these trifles.

HEINLEIN: Writers like Jack Williamson, Fred Hoyle and Olaf Stapledon have suggested that stars and nebulae might themselves be forms of life.

BUDRYS: We are certainly going to run into life as we don't know it but we may even have run into it 8000 or 30,000 years ago and as Dr Asimov suggests not recognised it as alive. We may be living with it at this moment and not know it. The obvious point being, you can't know what you don't know. Maybe it's totally neutral toward us, and so doesn't have to be accounted for. How can we know? Maybe the Rocky Mountains are alive on some extremely long time scale. Maybe the Earth is inhabited by some life form so unlike ourselves that we don't recognise it as anything but a rock, a tree or a cloud; and so we formulate 'Laws of Physics' to account for physical properties which may actually be behavior patterns.

TENN: Well, for the sake of such creatures as yet undiscovered, I find myself hoping that they will be so unlike life as we know it that we will ignore them completely. If they are life as we know it, Heaven help them.

VAN VOGT: I'm inclined to agree. In science fiction we have dabbled harmlessly with countless alien characterizations, but when you consider that a standard novel about a Gentile marrying a Jew or a Negro sleeping with a white is still considered an inflammatory subject, you can gauge how far we've come in our social development.

BRADBURY: The study of aesthetics, I think, will be essential to the task of comprehending the bizarre life forms we are going to be encountering just as aesthetics has a lot to do with the problem of assimilating the various colored races here on Earth. We don't want to accommodate ourselves to new art forms. Hence the violent reactions of critics to new techniques, new uses of color. Every artist with any individuality has done things with color and shape that we can learn from. These are the lessons we can teach those who will be going into space. We must say to them: Because a living thing looks horrid, because it has an unfamiliar color, because you do not like its odor or its texture, do not be afraid of it, do not lash out instinctively to destroy that thing; quite possibly it will find us no less repellent to behold.

BLISH: When you consider the vast variation in human behavior that we already know about, I think that any alien we might imagine would be far less likely to horrify humanity or even surprise an anthropologist than my confreres seem to assume. Bob Heinlein wrote *Stranger in a Strange Land*, in which the Martians practice ritual cannibalism, since they live in a desert climate and want to keep the organic compounds in circulation as much as possible. Now this is a rash and rather startling notion for a story, but that kind of practice actually prevails in many parts of Africa today, and I can think of rites even more startling. Among some of the Andean Indians, for example, when a child dies, the mothers of the tribe ritually cook and eat it as their form of mourning. It's not a question of their being short of protein it's a religious ceremony. What I'm trying to say is that few aliens are apt to be more startling than man himself.

Sc. 1: PROVINCIEHUIS (3:32 mins)

PLAYBOY: The Russians have served notice that they intend to continue their non-violent ideological and economic competition with the West until they 'bury' us. Do you think they will?

HEINLEIN: Well, the mystique of collectivism has seized upon the world. Whether its nearly universal magnetism will endure and prevail, we just can't estimate now.

BUDRYS: What is far more important and immediate is the bloodless, or proportionately bloodless, struggle for power between the Asian communists and the European communists. It seems to me that we ought to consider the possibility of our being caught in the middle of a war between Russia and China.

STURGEON: Do you mean Russia in particular or communism in general? I agree with you in either case, of course; but I think we may be in danger of equating one with the other in our conversation as if they were ideological synonyms. If you will, go along with me in a fantasy about ourselves and the Soviet Union in the hypothetical future. Once upon a time, Nikita Khrushchev wakes up and says to himself, 'You know, this collective stuff makes good propaganda; the only thing is that people don't seem to be getting fed. So I'll tell you what we're going to do. The Americans seem to feed their people pretty well; let's try giving private ownership back to the farmers.' Well, the rest of the population doesn't hold still for that and they all start petitioning right away for their own shoe shops, hardware stores, factories, etc. until Khrushchev has to give in completely. He says, 'I guess you Americans have something there after all. At least you're living better than we've been living; we'll try it your way whole hog.' Now the Soviet Union is a monstrous country with enormous resources, many of them untapped. So with all these resources it suddenly blossoms out into a full capitalist society and collectivization disappears. Do you think for one moment that we would be any safer in terms of world peace? Do you think that there would be any less of a space race or economic race than we have now? Do you think along with our arch-conservative brethren that Russia is our number-one enemy only because it's communistic?

CLARKE: I agree with the moral of your fantasy, Ted; but I can't see U.S. democratic capitalism lasting any longer than U.S.S.R. state socialism. They'll pass each other about 1980, heading in opposite directions.

BUDRYS: If I understand you correctly, you see us getting more socialistic while the U.S.S.R. becomes less so, to the point where we become redder than they are. Well, I don't think we will. It seems to be a fact of human nature that 'planning' cannot win in the face

63

of accumulated resistance by individual human beings. I think we may well pass each other around 1980, but I rather think we'll be going in the same direction. And when we do, we'll be talking about winning or losing the Individual Freedom Race.

Sc. 5: PROVINCIEHUIS (3:50 mins)

PLAYBOY: Even if the threat of nuclear war were to be alleviated the world will still be confronted by a peril which many economists regard as no less ominous: the population explosion. Will our planet be capable of accommodating let alone feeding, the global population of 6,000,000,000 recently prophesied for the year 2000 by the National Academy of Sciences?

HEINLEIN: Most of the curves call for doubling the population every 50 years, wars or not. The most conservative projection I have seen for this planet calls for 4,000,000,000 people by the end of this century, which is only 37 years away. Today, as Ray Bradbury said, we're living in a golden age: We've got nothing to worry about but Cuba, hydrogen bombs, Billie Sol Estes, and things like that. But 50 years from now, 100 years from now, 200 years from now, we're going to be starving to death standing on each other's shoulders.

POHL: I recently did the arithmetic on what a population gain per annum similar to the present rate in Brazil or one of the new African countries might mean if protracted over a period of time. I found that if the population had begun to double at the time of the birth of Christ, by this year we would have a planet composed exclusively of human flesh. I don't mean just the surface; I mean every atom of the Earth, including the core, transformed into human bodies. So at some point there has got to be a stop.

ANDERSON: I am not particularly optimistic, but I think we may be in some danger of taking this one further than it's actually going to go. There will be new economic and biological factors coming in as history moves on. A number of studies, for example, on the breeding habits of rats under highly crowded conditions indicate that there are natural forces which provide a certain check, that some kind of balance will be struck by nature. I don't think it necessarily

has to be a balance of starvation; it might, but it doesn't have to be.

POHL: You're right, Poul. Population doesn't multiply itself indefinitely, because natural checks do come into play eventually. But meanwhile we may find our grandchildren all going as loopy as the undoubtedly claustrophobic rats in that experiment you mentioned. The point is that these natural checks are decidedly unpleasant. But all may not be lost: John Campbell, the editor of *Analog*, once proposed a delightful alternative to all these problems: a contraceptive drug which would be both euphoric and mildly habit-forming.

BLISH: Oral contraceptives have been widely hailed as an all-but-ideal solution to the birth-control problem. But I'm afraid I have my doubts. If bacteria can find a way to neutralise a cell-wall-dissolving antibiotic like penicillin, it won't be too many generations before the human organism can immunise itself against any fertility-suppressant drug. I hope, therefore, that Arthur is right about our adopting sterilization as a social custom, because I don't see any prospect of a less drastic solution.

ASIMOV: As a matter of fact, there are a number of erotic practices which cannot possibly lead to conception. Under the pressures of geometric population growth, it may well be that such modes of sexual expression will actually be encouraged and come to be considered moral in a society which finds them useful, if not inescapable, as a solution. The so-called 'unnatural' sex practices, both hetero and homosexual, may become legal, ethical and who knows, even patriotic in years to come.

Sc. 6: SONSBEEK PAVILION (3:20 mins)

PLAYBOY: Do you foresee any new frontiers in the realm of enhancing sexual pleasure chemically?

BUDRYS: A society which has completely dissociated sexual pleasure from procreation will inevitably devise and use with gusto countless drugs and devices of every description for intensifying and prolonging one's sex life.

ANDERSON: I don't see any reason, for example, why we couldn't develop a safe contraceptive-potency pill for men and women which would

For good or for worse, we would cultivate the belief that we could transcend our earthy, physical shortcomings by means of prosthetics and projections. We would continue planting technological seeds of concepts in the future of this belief, as our grandparents did, in the hope that somewhere we would arrive at an agreeable level of human existence. Generations pass, children become grandparents: the type of human being that is internally more confident, and less bothered and preoccupied with the ever hopeful projection of oneself onto things that bring us places.

Our friend walked through the airport, absorbed by the commerce that had stuck to the snowball of powered flight, since 1903 when the Wrights first fitted out their assembly of sticks and canvas with an early combustion engine. He wandered through the makeshift department store, as bored and tempted to browse as any other traveller, his mind submitting, as usual, to the state of light-headedness he normally associated with these moments in transit. He acknowledged the forthcoming distorted perspectives that usually accompanied travelling, especially flight, thinking back to Buckminster Fuller's explanation of modern philosophy, as told by John at the table the night before:

"'I remember the year when I met him (B.F.) at Black Mountain." John told us. "One day he told us that the wind around the earth always went from west to east. There were people who went with the wind, others against the wind. Those who went with the wind went to the East and developed an Eastern type of thought; those who went against the wind went to Europe and developed European philosophy. And he suggested that the two tendencies met in the United States, and that their meeting produced an upward movement, into the air."

"What is the movement into the air? Spiritual ascension?" Daniel had asked.

"No," said John. "It was the invention of the airplane."

Our friend had become used to this frequent
state of mind, but that was not to say that
he felt completely comfortable with it. In
fact, he sensed a heightened awareness of a
physical mistrust towards the side effects of
technological advance, in play with his consciousness. Only the fact *that* he sensed it,
but could not pin it down, confused him,
and the confusion in turn made him even
more wary of the effect on his observations,
and of what seemed to be relevant outside
of his daily schedule. He put it down to
either an altered state of mental control or
the numbing of said sense, as a side effect of
the technology of travel. Was there benefits
in the awareness, or would fault be found in
it's intangible nature? Only too often had he
pursued the same circling questions whilst
travelling, and the more frequent he flew,
the greater the conviction of the presence
of this altered state. After all, airports were
abound with visible proof of the manipulation and control of human urges.

What he had been noticing was that the
packaging, the agent of mutual exchange,

19

and its projected beneficiality was already on the decline. Travel was not the spiritual luxury it had been in the very recent past, and the qualities of the production of flight were caving in to the simple economics of higher demand and everyday use. What was once subject to religious awe, and considered a means to an alternative view of the world, was now becoming yet another attainable component of our mundane existence.

These thoughts had pushed aside any sense of time, and he arrived late at the departure lounge, where the plane's freight had lined up while he was elsewhere with his thoughts. Taking a seat in a battery of moulded plastic chairs, he sat patiently, waiting for the queue to disappear before he would join it. After all, chairs functioned to relieve our legs of the body's weight, as opposed to standing in line, waiting...

Aware of the restless nature of this situation, he sat and observed it. A young girl in a grey polyester uniform of unisex waistcoat and trousers (the latter, being washed more often than the former, denied any concept of uniformity), was tearing off boarding passes and controlled their printed names with the name on the passports, validating her function by stamping each boarding pass stub with a ready-to-order, self inking rubber stamp as each passenger went past. She stood at a console, which was moveable, like most other items of furniture in the airport. Not including the small wheels that were screwed to its base, it was a one metre tall box, 50cm square at the base. On the side that the girl stood at, a small door was affixed, with a drawer above it. Both drawer and door were fitted with chrome locks and dark grey handles. A small compartment had been made on top, which was another 20cm taller, with sloping walls on either side, 10cm at the top, and 25cm at the bottom. Passengers laid their passport and boarding pass on the top of this compartment, and the girl took both down into it, on top of the box. Her functions there were secluded from view by the compartment's sloping walls.

A Morning Bath

The whole construction was made of chip-board, laminated with a thin layer of plastic, coloured to match one of the greys of the two-tone patterned carpet it stood on. The other tone of the carpet was identical to the grey of the draylon shirt, as worn by the girl and her colleagues. The whole scene was grey with black highlights, found in her hair and the leather of her shoes, and the rubber protective edges added to all corners of the console, attached for the benefit of all involved parties: to soften the sharp nature of the chipboard's veneered corners, and protect it (the airline's property and the girl's uniform as part of said property) from any damage, and protect any third party's clothes, skin or property from being harmed by the nature of said material.

One edge of the console, however, was damaged. Perpendicular to our friend's line of sight, a strip of laminate edging had come loose, and a thin rectangle of chipboard was exposed on the all-grey side of the box. This light brown detail stood in such contrast with the darkened colours of it's surroundings, that it screamed for as much attention as if it were painted in day-glo. He was in such a mind that this sign grabbed his attention in a way that no advertising for whisky, cigarettes, electronics or perfume had done that day. The thin edge of chipboard was asking to be repaired and its exposed weakness covered up again, under the terms of its existence. The exposure of the underlying low-cost structure of recycled waste, was a sore thumb. It was an icon of disrepair, a blatant logo of the ultra thin, almost invisible yet opaque veneer of the projected surface of these grey objects of exchange, standing between the airline and their customers.

When the line had diminished, and he could be sure that the tunnel just around the corner was not full of queuing people, our friend stood up and walked towards the girl, gave her his documents and walked to his seat in the plane. His fellow passengers stared at him with expectant yet glazed eyes as he passed between them towards the back of the hull. Having attempted to find some form of comfort against the inhuman amount of legroom in this and all airplanes, he had requested an aisle seat weeks ago whilst booking the flight. As he approached his seat, he saw that that tickbox had had no relevance at all to his current situation: two young obese teenage boys with crewcuts sat on either side of an empty seat which he assumed was his designated place for the next nine hours. He looked at them again, and judging on their haircuts, clothing, age and build, assumed they were together.

"Are you together?" He asked in a friendly voice, wanting to be seen as having purely altruistic motives. They replied that they were, so he asked whether or not they would rather sit next to each other. They assumed grateful expressions of mutual, adult relationships, and began to rearrange the complementary components of the flight in return for his kindness: magazines, headphones, emergency cards and blankets, which had already been inspected by the boys, were all re-arranged so he could start his flight in an undisturbed setting. The less obese of the two boys moved to the middle seat, and he sat down, holding back the urge to stretch his legs into the aisle with a sigh of satisfaction.

His awakening thousands of metres in the air, combined with the fact that he always fell asleep before take-off, set off more alarms of suspicion towards this unnatural state of being. Looking around for distraction, he saw that the in-flight film was already playing. He ignored it and stood up to take his computer out of his hand luggage. There was a New Yorker article called on the Mass-Observation movement that a friend had passed on to him recently, and which he had saved for the flight. As he sat down again and unpacked the silver laptop from its black case, the young boy next to him gasped.

"Wow! that's a nice computer."

"Thankyou," he replied, appreciating the object that he took for granted, as familiar and unnoticed as his right hand. He opened it up and the layout of two columns of text on a double-page spread filled the screen.

The boy looked over, and asked "Are you writing a book?"

"Yes, I'm trying to." He went on to explain the nature of the book to his neighbour, and the boy spoke of a book that he had read that sounded similar to him. All the while our friend had the strange feeling that he was being thoroughly cross-examined. The boy only asked a stream of short questions, allowing our friend to generate the greater part of the content of this interview, that certainly wasn't a conversation. The boy was simply over-eager to gain information. Yet our friend was not of a forthcoming nature. Intermittent silences fell, and after a while he turned his head back to the screen, and started typing. The boy reached under his seat and pulled out a large, ringbound book. It had a stiff card cover, on which there was a photograph of the gable of a house that flew two American flags. The boy turned the cover over, and thumbed through the pages, looking for a particular page. Each page had a light grey reproduction of the same photograph, which was covered with black ruled lines. As the pages passed, our friend saw that much of the book had been filled with black, teenage handwriting. Endless pages of handwritten paragraphs, all headed with single large numbers. The boy was saturated, and seemed eager to clear his head by writing his observations, and it slowly became clear that could well be writing the account of his neighbour in these pages.

"You keeping a journal?"

"Mm-hmm."

Our friend couldn't help but try to read how the boy edited his life into this series of entries, and whether he himself would figure in them. He would have to wait, as the boy seemed to be going through a ritual of numbering the pages, or numbering the paragraphs before they were even written. He left fifteen or twenty lines, then wrote another large number, up till 20. When this was done, he went back to 1, and started writing:

U woke up this morning. U had to get up very early. U did not shower, but only brushed your teeth. U took your suitcase downstairs and waited 12 minutes till the others came down. It was still dark. U got in the car and U fell asleep again...

The boy could sense his progress was being monitored, and he leant over his journal, using his left hand to screen his records from sight. Our friend could not sit and watch and wait to see if the words concerned him, whether he was deemed important enough for an entry into the boy's life. On paper, the boy had not even arrived at the airport yet, so he turned his gaze back to his own screen, and continued writing. The boy quickly glanced over and it became clear that there was less privacy in the pixellated words on the screen. Leaning over the computer to hide what was being written, would make writing impossible. How could he observe the boy, without the boy observing him doing so and writing it in his own journal? If so, would he write

U were sitting next to a man with a cool laptop who was writing about U writing about you writing about him.   ?

28

He thought not. Yet, taking caution to avoid any kind of feedback from this slightly embarrassing intimate situation, made the size of the text much smaller and hoped the boy would not read along for the present. Luckily, it seemed as though he was more engrossed in catching up with his own past. Glancing over, he saw the word "airport" being written down. He also noticed a 'T' which made him look further across the page at the formal qualities of the handwriting, noticing how elaborate the boy's capitals were in comparison to the childish nature of the rest of the writing. He caught himself spying again, and looked to his own observations, but soon realised the futility of the situation he had got himself into, and switched to other matters. He opened another document that needed his attention, and worked on it for a while, when his concentration was halted by the passage:

This audience is made up of the spectator who [...] are, as Yvonne Rainer herself perhaps ironically describes as the "spectator of my dreams", someone who "gives the same attention to the fiction and to the production of these fictions".

His thoughts were dragged away by this passage. All his observations seemed to acknowledge and feed into the text, tying his whole environment together into its self-constructed proof. He looked away and took in his surroundings, in the still heightened understanding that up here, any observation could be of relevance. However, the static object he was in seemed to offer very little material for the fictions of a potential spectator, and he realised that observing life or the role of exchanges that objects represent between lives had more promise than even more thin, grey compressed waste, this time in the form of the cabin's plastic construction. Then again, the plane was a huge distributor, with people becoming the objects of exchange. Perhaps it is no longer necessary for objects to represent us, or us to have objects represent us, when the distribution of self was becoming so facilitated.

He was reminded of a newspaper article he had read earlier that day. In what has been described as both a virtuous and a vicious circle, one of Britain's biggest exports to China is waste plastic—which is turned back into the soft toys and decorations that the largest freight ship ever constructed, the Emma Maersk, brings back to Britain in time for Christmas. The costs of transport were obviously a negligible part of the total costs involved in this cycle of exchange. Transport was highly demanded and therefore low cost. How does the mass transport of humans compare with the ease of transport of raw materials? How does the quality and comfort of that transport compare to mass consumption and demand for fast food or Christmas presents, for example?

The discomfort of his surroundings was underlined by the high pitched noise of the air conditioning and the lack of insulation from the sounds of the engine, and once again, he had little to do but fall asleep, only to be woken again by the attendant pushing her trolley of microwaved food past him.

The silence that had fallen on the plane star-
tled him. The altered pressure and inter-
nalised hum and rush of air inside the cabin
gave him the sensation of having headphones on. All audible signs of life had been
blocked out by the anti-social surroundings.
For the remaining nine hours, having little to
observe besides the inanimate plastic object
around him, he slept off and on through the
300 passengers' silence in the noisy plastic
tube, only punctuated every so often by crying babies, whose urge to communicate is
not yet inhibited by their surroundings.

CHAPTER 3

THE GUESTHOUSE
AND BREAKFAST

The plane finally touched down and he was
released back into more comfort and the
accompanying peace of mind. This would
not last long, however, and by the time he
reached home he realised he couldn't be

absolutely protect us from impregnation while making us all as athletically and inexhaustibly potent as we like to think we are. Paradoxically, this might lead to a de-emphasis of sex in our thinking. In a liberated society, sex might begin to lose both its mystery and its obsessive importance.

PLAYBOY: Experiments with LSD, peyote and the other hallucinatory drugs would seem to have opened the door to many new horizons. Do you foresee the use of these psychochemicals as a means of intensifying the sexual experience?

POHL: It's a damned good guess that if in 1984 you feel depressed it will be because you want to feel depressed; if you don't, you'll need only open your medicine cabinet to feel just about any way you want, including erotic to the nth power. Compress that down into a single pill and you'll be able to experience a transcendental orgasm that any Reichian would sell his orgone box to attain. Of course, we've had a pretty good primitive drug for releasing sexual inhibitions on the market for some time; we call it liquor. But that's kid stuff. Why should we limit our ways of getting bombed to those provided by the happenstance products of fermented plant life? Let the chemists cook up some new alcoholic libations: smoother, more palatable, odour- and hangover-free. Or let's not bother with alcohol at all. I remember writing a story in which the characters got on a jag by incubating smallpox viruses: nice flush, nice delirium, nice sense of spatial and temporal disorientation; while at the same time they dosed themselves with antibiotics so that they wouldn't get too sick to enjoy themselves.

BLISH: This would eventually lead, of course, to the extinction of all the 'talk' psycho-therapies; and a society devoid of Freudians, Jungians and Adlerians strikes me as Utopian almost by definition.

STURGEON: I think it would be relevant, at this point, to suggest another line of pioneering research in this uncharted area. For some years now, using a technique called stereotaxia, medical scientists have been mapping brains. They clamp the head of a cat, a monkey or a human rigidly in a frame and by manipulating three thumbscrews, one for each dimension, they can position an electrode precisely where they want it deep in the tissues of the brain. This way they can

stimulate tiny areas and chart the reactions. Not only have they found out what part of the brain controls the hand; they can discriminate among the individual fingers. Experiments like these, in the past two years, have explored more deeply into the labyrinth of the mind, than humanity has probed in the past two millennia. You just don't make breakthroughs like that and expect life and society to amble on as before.

Sc. 7: PROVINCIEHUIS (2:35 mins)

PLAYBOY: The elimination of disease would seem to bode well for the prospects of lengthening the human lifespan dramatically in years to come. What do you predict will be the longevity of the average American by the year 2000?

BUDRYS: I think that the first man to live forever, or for two centuries, at the very least may already have been born. But before we can attain true immortality, we'll have to hurdle a few remaining obstacles. Once we eliminate disease as a causative factor in fatality, we'll have to apply ourselves to the task of expunging irrationality from the species. It's not such an impossible dream; conceivably we could instill everyone hypnotically, chemically, or electronically with the same general view of life, so that people will be deprived of their moral, racial, and ideological, pretexts for destroying each other. That leaves us with the simple deterioration of old age. This you won't solve by transplanting the brain into a fresh body because the brain, too, is not immune to aging. But I think the day is not far off when we can decelerate or even suspend the aging of all the individual cells of the body. Their control is the next logical step.

POHL: Recently I bought for *Galaxy* a manu-script by R.C.W. Ettinger, called 'Prospects of Immortality', in which he explores the possibilities of eternal life through 'frozen sleep'—a process in which a human body is frozen in liquid helium for years, centuries, millennia, or even eons if you wish. It is already a fact, Ettinger says, that we can freeze a man's body to that temperature without irreparable damage. All it will take is money, about $8,500 per person; we already have the know-how. It's a pretty good gamble that no matter what you might die of today, heart attack, stroke, cancer, TB, a bullet in the

POW!

belly, this damage will be surgically, medically or prosthetically reparable. Thus immortality of a kind may very well be attainable for you and me, right now.

BUDRYS: It seems to me that actual emancipation from death may not become a reality within the next generation or two, but some of our children will live actively and usefully for perhaps 200 years. And after that generation, the figure will go up exponentially, so that our grandchildren may live to a ripe old 1000, and our great-grandchildren essentially forever.

Sc. 8: PROVINCIEHUIS (1:45 mins)

PLAYBOY: Reducing or eliminating the need for sleep. What do you gentlemen feel are the prospects of fulfilling that wish?

POHL: I'm afraid the Russians may have beaten us to it. The other day I heard the first glimmerings of a most unusual technique of sleep abbreviation which they have developed and claim to have perfected. By taping the brain waves of a sleeping subject and playing them back to another man, they are reported to have materially shortened the amount of rest required by the second subject. If my information is accurate, they've come uncannily close to duplicating one of the hoariest and heretofore most improbable gimmicks in science fiction's overflowing bag of tricks: Instant Sleep. You put this shiny helmet on your head, press a button, get up, stretch, yawn and go back to work—completely refreshed.

ANDERSON: I have my doubts that either we or the Russians will ever be able to capsulise sleep quite so neatly, but I will venture to predict that it should be possible inside of 20 years, with the help of nontoxic drugs, to work or socialise for several days at a stretch without getting tired.

POHL: I don't really see why it couldn't be possible to eliminate the need for sleep entirely and permanently—conceivably by surgical removal of the sleep center from the brain; the dangers of disturbing the body's metabolic balance would seem to be negligible, for people whose sleep centers have been accidentally damaged or destroyed lead what seem to be essentially normal lives in every way except that they never sleep.

Sc. 9: PROVINCIEHUIS (7:40 mins)

PLAYBOY: So far we've been discussing future life rather generally and impersonally. And now, your conception of an average day in the life of an affluent city-dwelling bachelor at the turn of the coming century?

ANDERSON: Well, assuming that he bothers to sleep at all, our bachelor will be awakened more gently than by a yammering alarm clock. He'll get soft music off a tape piped into his pillow. His bed, which rocked him to sleep and fell quiet when his regular breathing told it he'd dropped off, now gives him a mild shaking till he orders it to stop, and then rises at the head to become a chaise lounge.

POHL: Then a timed mechanical servitor offers him freshly brewed coffee, maybe with a touch of amphetamine.

ANDERSON: And while he sips it, he dials for his breakfast, choosing from a menu that flashes onto a panel.

POHL: Next a recorded voice reminds him: 'Today is August 4th. You have an appointment with Esterhazy at 11am, a dinner date with Rosemary at 7, and your vacation begins the day after tomorrow.' When he steps out of bed the floor is warmed with radiant heat. His shower cubicle is preset to sluice him with gentle floods of water just warm enough to be relaxing.

ANDERSON: He uses an electric massager on his gums, not a toothbrush; cavities are a thing of the past. And he won't have to shave this morning, because his last depilation, which included a beard-inhibiting hormone, is good for another week.

ANDERSON: All of his suits, incidentally, will be entirely synthetic, designed more sensibly and comfortably than the contemporary business suit, and tailor-made by an automaton which takes his measurements and follows his specifications about cut, color, pattern and material, all at very little cost.

POHL: So little cost, in fact, that they will be as disposable as Kleenex.

ANDERSON: At any rate, when he finishes dressing, our man presses a button to inform the robot chef that he's ready for breakfast. In the minute or two he has to wait, he checks his television phone to see if it visitaped any messages for him during the night. The machine-made meal that comes up the delivery shaft and rolls on its tray to his table is typically delicious. Afterward he smokes his first cigarette of the day; the tobacco contains a mild euphoric to put him in a cheerful mood. He lives in a gigantic urban complex of interwoven buildings that forms a city within the city. Almost all of his material needs can be fulfilled without leaving the premises, and from his wall windows, when they aren't opaqued for privacy or sleeping, he commands a spectacular view of the city: a forest of glass-sheathed skyscrapers extending in all directions as far as the eye can see. But his job is elsewhere, so he catches the high-speed elevator down from the 100th floor to street level.

POHL: On his way down he orders transportation over his wrist communicator, and by the time he is at the curb the robot doorman has electronically flagged a robot cab, the door is open and the destination already set. The only thing missing en route is the hackie's conversation, though Cyril Kornbluth and I once wrote a story in which auto-cabs were programmed to discuss baseball, politics, weather and women by means of a library of selected tapes.

BUDRYS: Or our man might spend the time in transit getting a start on the day's work, dictating memoranda into his pocket recorder, and phoning ahead to his office on his wrist communicator to get the day's mail and messages.

PLAYBOY: He's on his way to work, but you haven't told us yet what kind of job he has.

POHL: Let's say he's a young white-collar executive; whatever his field, he'll have to possess a commodity in great demand on the labor market of the 21st Century: originality and freshness of thought. There won't be many dull, routine jobs available anymore; machines will be doing most of them.

ANDERSON: But today is a workday, so on to the office for five or six hours. He works four days a week, and has three months' paid vacation;

unlimited paid sick leave, too—of which he uses very little, thanks to modern medicine.

POHL: He's greeted at his desk by a mound of messages and mail, which he deals with by means of an automatic stenographer. He'll still have a live secretary, of course, but he won't waste her on mechanical chores like typing or running out for coffee.

ANDERSON: If one of his letters is going to a foreign country, it's automatically translated, then dispatched immediately by wire or radio directly to the address given. He'll also have face-to-face communication via visual telephone with associates around the world. Of course with correspondence so easy, there'll be an unholy lot of unnecessary calls and memos, but at least people will finally have acquired enough regard for health and sanity to take an hour off at lunch and not spend it talking business. He dines in an excellent restaurant near his office.

POHL: Big Brother picks up the check, because such things are still on the almighty expense account.

ANDERSON: At the end of the workday, our man hops a robot cab and relaxes with a drink while it threads him through traffic to the apartment of the young lady with whom he's planning to spend the evening. Of course she isn't ready yet; some things will never change. Over the intercom she invites him to pour himself a drink while he's waiting. He presses the autobar button for a vodka martini, very dry, with a twist of lemon. While he sips it he lights up another euphoric cigarette and watches live three-dimensional scenic color projection which covers one wall of the living room with a live television view of the Swiss Alps; it's a bit overcast tonight. When she's finally ready, they take the elevator up to the roof heliport and shuttle out to the city's vast aerospace port. In an hour or so they're in Hawaii. They have a swim in the surf, lounge around on the beach awhile. Finally they catch a submarine to a seafood restaurant famous for spectacular view of coral reefs, from within the giant plastic hemisphere which encloses it on the ocean floor. Afterward they go back topside for an evening of island hopping. First stop is a new club which has been built cantilevered directly over Manna Loa crater, where they can watch the lava bubble beneath the transparent dance floor.

M

POHL: Anyway, before the evening is over,
our man will suggest that they get together again
the following weekend, perhaps for a cham-
pagne-service rocket flight to Pago Pago, or a
hydroplane-liner cruise to Cap d'Antibes.

ANDERSON: Or if things are really going well,
he may even invite her to join him on a summer
vacation in space. It's as expensive as hell,
but well worth the cost. Let's hope she's duly
impressed, and that he doesn't have to return to
his apartment alone.

POHL: He can always invite her up to see his
etchings in this case, perhaps, a collection of
rare trading stamps from the 1960s. His door
key turning in the lock, of course, dims the lights
inside and flips on a continuous tape of the latest
electronic mood music. The divertissements
which ensue, unfortunately, can't be programmed
so predictably; nor are they likely to be conducted
any differently than they are today. There
are some things, after all, that simply can't be
improved by automation.

Sc. 10: PROVINCIEHUIS (3:00 mins)

TENN: That was a virtuoso vision of things to
come, complete with happy ending and fade-
out clinch. I agree that we're coming to an
age of unexampled social emancipation and
scientific revolution, an age abristle with all the
blandishments you've described. But I believe
that it's going to be repetitious in many ways both
of our present and our past, though in exactly
what ways we can't yet imagine. Thoreau wrote
over a hundred years ago that 'the mass of
men lead lives of quiet desperation'. Well, the
world has changed fantastically since then,
but the mass of men still do.

STURGEON: I can't help getting a bit impatient
with all this prognostication about how we must
continue to be as stupid as we are. Bill Tenn
insists that we are going to continue to behave
the way we do and remain what we are in the midst
of an immense pushbutton society, but it's just not
going to be so because we're not going to be the
same kind of people after it happens.

TENN: Ted, you have faith, and it's something I
respect. But when it comes to the human race,
I firmly believe that faith is what keeps mountains

firmly in place. We will have to understand one
basic fact about progress: that every advance
that we might make is an advance that can be
prostituted to vicious and vulgar ends. This will
continue to be true as long as man remains what
he is. And I don't see man changing.

HEINLEIN: I agree that mankind is still
barbarous and ignorant. But I disagree with you,
Bill, that we're destined to remain this ignorant.
I expect our descendants to exceed our grandest
achievements at least as much as we exceed
the cavemen.

BUDRYS: You make our destiny sound almost
too golden to be true, Bob. But I don't doubt it
will all come to pass more or less as you predict.
This age, in which 60 years have carried us
from Kitty Hawk to Venus, will someday seem
a stagnant time to most men of the future.
But the future, is constantly arriving, whether
we like it or not.

BRADBURY: I think that what we have been
leading up to is the fact that we are part of a
miraculous explosion of the senses. The important
thing is that the race is on the move, and that
we, selfishly, as writers, have long dreamt of this
movement and cannot help but be exhilarated
at our own involvement in this voyage of self-
discovery. We know so very little. But this we
know irrevocably: We love life and living, we hate
death and darkness. Love of day and motion,
fear of dark and immotion is all we need know
now. The rest will come. We will find it along
the way.

THE SEARCH FOR THE FOUNTAIN OF PROSPERITY

by Michael Stevenson

The theme of the quest is ancient. In many versions, it is the search for a precious object with magical properties: the Golden Fleece, the Holy Grail, the Elixir of Life. The precious object in most of the stories either remains elusive or is a disappointment when found …

Fifty years ago, in the aftermath of World War II, we economists began our own audacious quest: to discover the means by which poor countries in the tropics could become rich like the rich countries in Europe and North America. Observing the sufferings of the poor and the comforts of the rich motivated us on our quest. If our ambitious quest were successful, it would be one of humankind's great intellectual triumphs.

Like the ancient questors, we economists have tried to find the precious object, the key that would enable the poor tropics to become rich. We thought we had found the elixir many different times. The precious objects we offered ranged from foreign aid to investment in machines, from fostering education to controlling population growth, from giving loans conditional on reforms to giving debt relief conditional on reforms. None has delivered as promised.

William Easterly, *The Elusive Quest for Growth: Economists' Adventures and Misadventures in the Tropics* (MIT Press, Cambridge, 2001)

This is the story of a search for a quest—not the quest itself, but the search for what purports to be the only tangible object of the quest, the 'fountain of prosperity'. The story is as much mystery and fantasy as it is economics or history, or even sculpture for that matter. Like the quest itself, the search is steeped in superstition and magic. Forecasting economic growth is, after all, a form of divination or scientific fortune-telling and, like all predictions, remains permeable to the irrational. While the quest involves looking into the future, my search involves divining the past. Over a number of years, in diverse locations, I pieced together the following story.

Some years ago, while I was researching the automobile industry in New Zealand, I heard rumours of the existence of a physical model of the country's national economy. Intrigued, though unsure at first exactly what I was searching for, I found the Phillips Machine hidden in plain view at the Institute for Economic Research in Wellington. The machine stood there, on display yet still somehow undiscovered, concealed by its own obscure history and, perhaps, by its improbable form. I found myself standing before a large, upright Plexiglas and metal device, built partly into the ceiling. Almost biological in appearance, like some kind of cyborg vascular system rather than an instrument of use to economic science, it was crammed awkwardly into the tiny foyer beside the communal drinking fountain. This juxtaposition began to seem more than accidental when it was explained to me that the Phillips Machine itself runs on water. More precisely, it is a hydromechanical analogue for total national income—a hydraulic computer.

I learned that the economist Alban W. ('Bill') Phillips had built the machine in 1949 while a student at the London School of Economics, apparently to fathom the complexities of Keynesian economics. Confused by the various macroeconomic theories, Phillips fell back on his skills in both engineering and dairy farming and set to work in his landlord's garage. Using mostly war-surplus materials, including parts salvaged from a Lancaster bomber, he began to experiment with a system that represented capital reserves as tanks of water and monetary flows as that same water circulating around interconnected plastic tubes.

What is most striking about the machine is that it gives 'the national economy'—that invisible yet omnipresent being—a physical body. The hitherto unseeable multitude of social processes and restless circulatory activity that we call the economy and recognise only via its abstractions can, with this model, be viewed in its entirety, in the round. With its various tanks accumulating water/money via emissions from the central circulatory flow, a number of economic variables can be determined; thus the machine presents an illustrative simulation of economic processes. The machine is apparently quite accurate in its calculations, but beyond these

WHACK

economic capabilities it is also an undeniable sculptural presence. Economics is full of fluid metaphors, and Phillips's insistence on a cascading flow of water brought to life something beyond the functional. Quite inadvertently, Phillips created a fountain from whence, it can be said, a plentiful flow of magical, biological, and alchemical allegories spring forth. These allusions are not entirely unfamiliar, reminding us of metaphors employed by Karl Marx when describing the processes of the economy: 'crystals forming out of liquids, liquids passing back to crystals, metamorphoses, social metabolism, the dramatic encounter of life and death.'[1]

I was told that Phillips had also attempted to use electronic technology to realise his macroeconomics model, but it seems he was dissatisfied with the results. Apparently, this was not due to a lack of processing power but to a concern with the way the results could be displayed. At the time, the industry standard was to input information using punched paper tape, with numerical results tabulated off-line. This method was not only visually uninspiring, but it also failed to show the computations in progress. Phillips constructed his machine with the classroom in mind, and it seems he chose the hydromechanical solution because he felt it was more likely to capture the imagination of his students. In doing so, he brought about a strange convergence, fusing the objectives of the economist with those of the sculptor. He liked to dye the circulating water blood red, purely for dramatic effect, unleashing the full sculptural possibilities that lay dormant in the machine. This act of economic transubstantiation was not new: Thomas Hobbes had compared monetary circulation with that of blood 300 years earlier in his most influential book, *Leviathan*. Now the Phillips Machine called forth not only the power of the living but also that of the dead.

The Phillips Machine was first presented at a seminar held by a Professor Robbins at the London School of Economics in 1949, where it stunned both students and faculty. Some had simply shown up to scoff, but interest spread rapidly in the academic world. Phillips soon put the prototype into limited production, and in total perhaps fifteen machines were built.

Most Phillips Machines were destined for academic institutions in England. Scholarship on the subject has concerned itself primarily with these applications, but in the March 1952 issue of *Fortune* magazine I found indications that the machines also had a life in America. At the London School of Economics archives, which are the only real repository of information pertaining to the Phillips Machine, I began a more intensive search. I discovered that Abba P. Lerner, the economist credited with popularizing Keynes's ideas in America, had become an enthusiast for the machine after seeing it in London in 1950 and had secured the rights to sell the device in the United States. Lerner, always the populist, applied good old American business know-how to his new enterprise and christened the machine the 'Moniac', a corruption of 'money' and 'mania', and also perhaps a reference to a well-known early computer called the 'Eniac'. The name change was bemoaned by Lerner's colleagues, who thought it a devaluation of Phillips's work. A letter I later read at the archives of the University of California, Berkeley indicates that at one time Lerner proposed calling the machine the 'nymph' (or 'NIMF', for National Income Monetary Flow), thinking perhaps that the frolicking, semi-naked maidens of the fountain would bring him buyers. He acknowledged, however, that this new name would probably have engendered further bad jokes, in this case about nymphomaniacs. After spending several days at the Berkeley archives, I became aware of Lerner's fondness for this kind of salesmanship.

The name change was not the only modification that was made to the Phillips Machine when it entered the United States. Structural differences in the U.S. economy meant that further engineering work had to be carried out before it was fit for U.S. consumption. The American Moniacs were calibrated in dollars, and additional development work was done by the research division of General Motors in Detroit. It was there, in Motor City, that a so-called accelerator was developed. A brake, apparently, was not thought necessary.

Although the machines rapidly fell out of use in Great Britain (by the late 1950s they had been all but banished to the basements of their respective institutions), Lerner peddled his machine way beyond its obsolescence date. Seeing in it, perhaps opportunistically, a way to spread his own message, he brought this cumbersome machine along with him wherever his itinerant academic career led. (There is an account of Lerner with a leaky machine at an American Economic Association meeting in a New York hotel lobby in the 1970s.) He passed up no chance to publicise himself, or the machine.

86

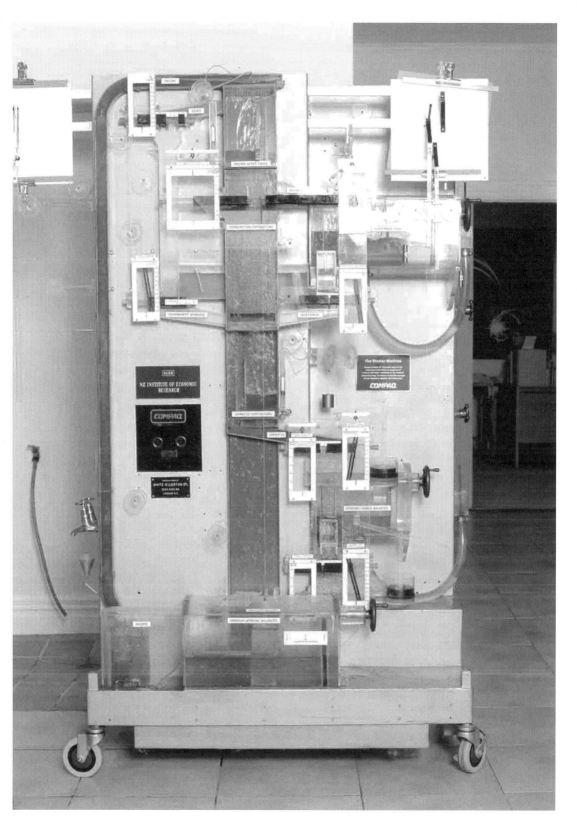

A Moniac at the New Zealand Institute for Economic Research, Wellington, New Zealand.

In correspondence with *Life* magazine, he urged the editor to include a piece on the machine and followed that with, of all things, material on his recent wire sculptures. (It is interesting to note that at this time economics still existed in a sphere that included the arts—indeed, even wire sculpture). Of all the accounts and letters I uncovered at Berkeley, however, one detail was enticing beyond anything else: a passing reference to the fact that, sometime in the early 1950s, a machine had been ordered by, and dispatched to, the Central Bank of Guatemala.

The search therefore brought me to Guatemala City. On busy 7a. Avenida, downtown in Zona 1, I came upon the Central Bank, situated in a complex beside the other fabled institutions of the modern nation-state. It was an extremely optimistic building—mid-century Latin modernist—and, like the other structures, it was concealed behind a deep, carved concrete façade replete with Mayan flourishes. A series of fountains were arranged to welcome the visitor, but it had been some time since the water had actually flowed in them. I had to take care, as I attempted to cross the dry plaza, not to walk into the empty, tile-lined pools that ringed the complex. It seemed that, metaphorically at least, the bank had lost its power over the forces of circulation. As I passed the grand façade, rusted steel reinforcing rods could be seen through the concrete rendering.

Inside, I was met by an elderly, bespectacled gentleman named Elvidio Aldana. He was the longest-serving employee of the bank and was known to all in the building simply as Elvis. It was not just his name that distinguished Elvis from the buttoned-down bankers; he wore a large tweed cap and his shoes shone with an unusual radiance. He would have been more at home in a Latin jazz club than at the Central Bank, and he had the tempo to match. He seemed very excitable and immediately launched into conversation. One of the first things he said to me was 'Phillips was brilliant!'

Elvis signed me in at the front desk and escorted me around the building. We paused in front of a red-lit glass case containing a rather badly stuffed bird with peculiar tail feathers. The bird was a quetzal, the country's national symbol, which shares its name with the official unit of Guatemalan currency. Given that the Central Bank issues quetzals, and the bird has, over the years, been brought to near extinction,

the symbolism was hard to miss. Next I was escorted to the office of our host, Lic. Sergio Armando Hernández Rodas, on whose various desks was arranged a curious collection of model sports cars—Lamborghinis, Ferraris—none of which were to be seen on the streets outside.

Elvis, who is the bank's chief librarian, an economist, and—some say—a historian, handed me a document. It seemed that rather than show me the archival material pertaining to the Moniac; he had instead prepared his own three-page account of its history at the bank. Not reading Spanish, I could only pick out obvious words from the text and wonder what Elvis had uncovered. Everyone who had read the Spanish agreed that it was not only accurate but also brilliantly observed. I noted that there was no bibliography and that nothing was footnoted. Our host took it upon himself to read it aloud for me in translation, and it was at this point that I realised the original sources would probably remain elusive. The account itself was written from so deeply within its subject that, even with my knowledge of the machine, it sounded like science fiction.

There was a fourth man in the room, who sat quietly; he spoke only Spanish. This was Señor Alberto Muñoz. After a chance meeting in the streets of Guatemala City, Elvis had invited this former bank employee to meet us. It seemed that most of the new information about the Moniac had been passed on in the street. On a number of occasions, Elvis turned to me, his index finger directed toward his large bifocals, and exclaimed, 'This man saw it … with his eye!'

Later, in the library, I mentioned to Elvis that in my birth country, New Zealand, the national symbol is also a bird—the kiwi. The colloquial name for the New Zealand currency also comes from the country's national symbol—the 'kiwi dollar', or even simply the 'kiwi'. Upon hearing this, Elvis took me to his chaotic desk at the back of the room and opened a drawer that appeared to contain freshly printed banknotes. The notes were in bundles, each with a paper band around it, as if straight from the mint. It was unclear if this was actual legal tender; since the bundle he removed was made up of one-quetzal notes and I had seen only one-quetzal coins since I had arrived. Nonetheless, he sat down at his desk, signed the notes as if he were the president of the bank, and formally presented one to me.

It was clear that a Moniac had been sent to the Central Bank, though the details about its time in Guatemala remained shrouded in mystery

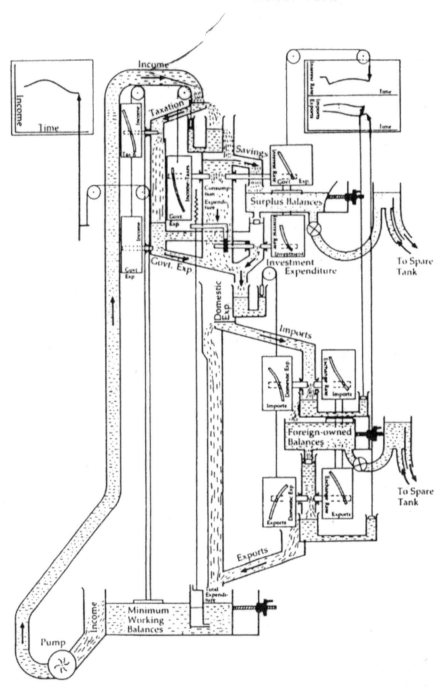

and its actual function at the bank may never adequately be understood. Also, it seems that it arrived damaged, and it is unclear exactly how or indeed if it was repaired. I later discovered that Lerner had visited to instruct the bank in its use, the knowledge of which seemed to have vanished soon after he left town. At the Library of Congress, turning the pages of one of Lerner's sweat-ridden pocket diaries, I finally came upon the relevant entry. It simply stated: 'Arrived Guatemala, set-up Moniac.' The date was March 23, 1953.

Beyond the hearsay and theater of my visit to the bank, the symbolism of the Moniac animated each and every conversation I had there. It had arrived at the bank at a crucial time, right at the climax of a period known as the Ten Years of Spring. This time of liberal reform was dramatically curtailed by a CIA-led coup in 1954, which in turn ushered in a forty-odd-year period of largely uninterrupted military rule and then civil war. The coup was—unofficially at least—launched in response to the land-reform program enacted by the government of Jacobo Arbenz Guzmán after it gained power in the 1950 election. The program returned land to the indigenous population by shifting ownership from the large landholders—the upper classes and foreign corporations. The foreign interest that stood to lose the most in these reforms was the Boston-based consortium United Fruit Company, the largest banana producers in the world.

The Moniac entered service at the Central Bank in 1953, just as the land-reform process began, and became an accidental witness to the tumultuous events of the next fifteen months. In desperate times such as these, there is no reliable counsel; no one knows what is being plotted, what pressures are being applied, or who will turn where. In such times, confidence can spring from the most unlikely places, and perhaps this is a clue in understanding the Moniac's true function at the Central Bank. It is often the case with complex machines that we attribute mysterious powers to them, powers they simply cannot possess. It may turn out to be that the Moniac—whose economic capacities were impaired—functioned more as a talismanic advisor on the economy and perhaps even the state. With the enforced regime change in 1954, the machine—and everything it stood for— was cast out.

From Elvis, I learnt that the machine had been given to the University of San Carlos, and so I resumed my search. The cab driver finally located building S8, the Economic Sciences Faculty, on the university's sprawling, run-down campus in Zona 12. It is the only public university in Guatemala, and though it is publicly funded, it maintains a certain autonomy from the government by invoking its founding decree —the pursuit of pure academic thought. Like the Central Bank, such independence has not always found favor with the government of the day, and the long-term result seems to be that the funding tap has been turned off, or at least reduced to a trickle. I walked over dry, bare terrain to approach the school, while in the distance I could see that the weather was changing.

I had an appointment with Lic. Eduardo Antonio Velásquez Carrera, dean of the Economic Sciences Faculty. He brought me into his spartan conference room, where a large desk stood beneath a frieze of framed black-and-white photographs of men in academic dress—this was the history of the deanship of the school. We sat down, and I showed him pictures of the Moniac. He was completely unfamiliar with the machine, though he had no trouble in describing to me the exact functions it could facilitate. From my cursory view of the building, and indeed the university as a whole, I guessed that the campus dated to the 1960s. Assuming that the school had relocated here a good ten years after the Moniac had been donated, it seemed unlikely that the Guatemalan machine was still in existence. It certainly was not here at the school, although the dean would not let that hope die. His secretary brought in large bound records dating from 1954 and 1955, and the dean scrutinised the handwritten inventory, but nothing of interest was found. He then began making telephone calls, and eventually an elderly gentleman appeared. We were introduced, and he sat down to read Elvis's account. Later I was informed that he too had seen the machine at the Central Bank. No further information was divulged.

Señor Velásquez Carrera had initially brought me into the conference room to introduce me to Dr Manuel Noriega Morales, a former dean of the school, by way of the framed portraits hung high on the walls. The dean pointed to the picture of Morales stationed in the middle of the frieze; the dates under his picture read '1948–1952'. The dean was convinced that Dr Morales had, along with President Guzmán, been responsible for bringing the Moniac into the country. If this was the case, the machine had certainly been in contact with extraordinary personalities. The title 'Dr' was important, it turned out, as Morales was the first Guatemalan to receive a PhD. He was also the only Central American present at the United Nations' Bretton Woods Conference in 1944, where the U.S. dollar's supremacy in the international monetary system was institutionalised—against the advice of John Maynard Keynes, the British advisor. But more importantly, Dr Morales was the founding president of the Central Bank, a role he maintained into the 1950s. When I asked why he was so sure Dr Morales was involved in the Moniac's history, the dean simply said that it was very much Morales's kind of machine. Again I was reminded of the mythology of the times and how neatly the Moniac story fitted this unfulfilled desire for economic autonomy. History in Guatemala, it seemed, was not a topic open to debate, and many aspects remain off-limits to this day. Unknowingly, I had introduced a new personality into these events—in the form of the Moniac—which had yielded at least some new grounds for discussion. Perhaps this is why so much of what I heard in the city circulated only in the form of allegory.

The real history, however, was not allegorical; it was brutal. Researching the history of the school on my return to San Francisco, I discovered another aspect of the story. The school had for many years taught a brand of economics with a distinctly leftist bent; it was described by some as Marxist. During the worst years of the civil war, in the 1980s, the military government added the dean of the school to a long list of assassinations. A faculty member attending his funeral was gunned down on his way home, and a third member of staff was also killed. All this took place in the period of about a month. The portraits above the table where I sat and talked with Señor Velásquez Carrera were hung with a regularity that revealed nothing of these events. As with a number of other subjects, these stories remain unutterable in Guatemala.

My return from the university was a disorganised affair. No taxi driver would pick me up in Zona 12 that late in the afternoon, and so eventually I was driven by the secretary in the dean's own vehicle. The threatening rain had now arrived and was turning the dry, dusty ground to mud. With the car doors locked, I passed through the squalid, desperately poor neighborhoods of Zona 8.

We drove in tandem with a decrepit diesel loco as it attempted to haul three wagons of scrap metal down a ramshackle railway line. I had wondered for some time about this railroad system, which in the 1950s was still the only transport link from the Atlantic. If the Moniac had been sent from London by sea, it eventually would have been hauled along these wet tracks. They were at the time part of a system entirely owned by the United Fruit Company. From the ripening bananas on their vast plantations in the Motagua Valley to fruit stands across America, United Fruit had developed what you could call a vertically integrated business system that guaranteed them money from every transaction. By the 1950s, their operations in Guatemala included electricity generation, mail delivery, a telephone network, and, of course, the railroad system. In short, it was difficult to do business in Guatemala without involving 'The Company', which became known as *El Pulpo* [The Octopus].

While the Moniac bore the hopes of economic independence, the hypothetical path it took to arrive at its destination suggests just what it was up against. If it came to Guatemala by sea, it would have been paid cargo on the United Fruit shipping line, the Great White Fleet. It would then have been off-loaded at their facility at Puerto Barrios, the only port on the Atlantic, where it would have incurred further fees. It would then have been hauled—for a price—along the United Fruit railroad network to Guatemala City. Hemorrhaging from these costs, the 'fountain of prosperity' would have arrived at the Central Bank damaged (also perhaps courtesy of United Fruit), drained of funds, and already in debt.

Ultimately, perhaps, the Moniac functioned neither as a Keynesian economic calculator nor as a tropical talisman for safe passage through the mysteries of global finance. Rather, it might be seen as a symbolic victim of the accelerated obsolescence of Keynesian thought in an international financial system dominated by the United States—a system committed to the relegation of all competing ideologies, with military force to back it up. It is this reality that led to the disappearance of the Guatemalan Moniac—and so also to its contemporary re-creation as the symbol of an alternative to the very real political, economic, and social miscalculations that defined Guatemala and other countries that strayed from the path. The Moniac, in this incarnation, stands not for the quest for a fountain of prosperity, but for the abandonment of that quest. The search for the Moniac turns out to be the key not to understanding the economic vision of a lost revolution, but to understanding the ways in which that vision was liquidated.

NOTE
1. Michael Taussig, *The Magic of the State* (Routledge, New York, 1997), p. 138.

Below: Reverse of the one-quetzal bill showing the Central Bank of Guatemala.

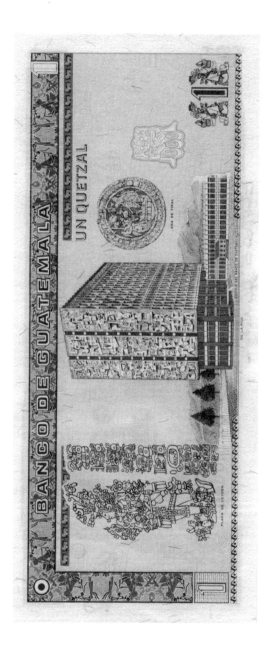

LIFE AFTER LIFE AND AFTER

An interview with George Maciunas
by Raimundas Malasauskas
featuring psychic medium David Magnus
and a specially-collected database
of questions

Tuesday 28 May, 2002

A small reproduction of Van Gogh's night was hanging above a sofa in a small room in New York's Gershwin Hotel. Yet this was late Tuesday morning, and David and I were sitting at a table in positions more reminiscent of Cézanne's card players. After offering me a glass of water, David switched off the air conditioner and placed his hands on a small woven object which reminded me of an old-fashioned telephone pad. Apart from the tape recorder, there were no other electric or electronic devices on the table. Just four arms, the pad, David's spiritual guides and 60 questions for Fluxus founder George Maciunas collected from a variety of people.

'So, what's the name of the person you want to talk with?' David looked at me.

'George Maciunas,' I said, grabbing a few photos of the Fluxus founder for the psychic to look at.

'No,' David shook his head, 'the name is enough.' He repeated the name again and pressed the REC button.

The channeling session had begun, although I am sure that it was always going on.

In the course of the conversation, George Maciunas described in great detail what it is like to be dead. In some respects his description was not too different from most techno-utopian cyberdelic visions of reality where communication and creation happen in realtime and with absolute speed. Telecommunication technologies—and particularly the Internet as a certain model of reality—encourage us to perceive the world as a database and to delve into subjective fragments of it, blurring distinctions between professional and amateur, high, low

and lower, global and local, dead and alive. By adapting the idea of Open Source to reality we enter an endless process of remixing and translation. Here the notion of the 'dead artist' is abandoned, the concept of artistic ego is rendered futile, and we are gripped by our own afterlives (in terms of delayed feedback or unmediated experiences) while drinking coffee with friends. If you'd like to experience it more vividly, just add some ketamine to your coffee instead of sugar.

There was no ketamine in the tea I drank with Jon Hendricks, curator of the G.L. Silverman Fluxus collection, who contributed greatly to our interview by suggesting people who would be interested in getting in touch with the late Mr Fluxus.[1] A peculiar mix of dead and living characters entered my notebook, opening up a virtual space where, for example, Joseph Beuys was supposed to get in touch with Gertrude Stein via Maciunas.

In the end, George talked for almost two hours, though I'm not sure whether it was exactly him or not. In fact, the whole notion of identity was called into question by his elusive behavior during earthly life (or in this context, his pre-afterlife), and perhaps it is even fundamentally reactionary to speak of isolated souls and egos when considering a transpersonal afterlife. To add to the confusion, on one hand the entire concept of the afterlife was effectively dismissed by the Fluxus preoccupation with everyday life liberated from the grand narratives, such as religion. On the other, Fluxus was equally concerned with contradiction and the illogical. Methodologically speaking, creative misreading is the key here, and as such, the main adventure of the interview involved the re-animation and development of some ideas inherited from Fluxus.

Nam Jun Paik remembers that Maciunas once confided that he would like to be reincarnated as a frog. While collecting questions for David Magnus' psychic interview with Maciunas, I realised that I was *just another medium* myself, or what Seth Siegelaub calls a 'point of infor-mation'. If we combine the idea of reincarnation with the idea of parallel existences, then all of our reincarnations are here and now, and all our interpretative practice is a form of channeling —in other words, an experiment in transpersonal reality.

...

David Magnus: So, what's the name of the person you want to talk with?

Raimundas Malasauskas: George Maciunas.

DM: OK, George Maciunas. Maciunas, Maciunas …

Well, his intellect, or his mind, his intelligence, served to set him apart from, say, the norm. He wasn't as a young person the most academically recognised individual. I think, in a way, he felt he was a sham. There is a real hunger of this energy to reestablish, reconnect, and reorganise what he feels is an injustice done to him. My sense of this guy, this energy, is that he wants just, almost to let go of the past.

As I said to you, you may have wishes towards the dead, or what you call the 'dead', but that doesn't necessarily mean that they are going to answer them the way we want them to, funny enough. And what he is doing, basically, is showing me a few things and I will then tell you what they are. It's like he is showing me inside his world.

Okay. Now, let's move on from there. Let me just say, he is in a much happier place then he was when he was here. I think, one other thing that I am feeling is that it's not an easy read. It's as if you enter into the mind or into world of people who were involved in, you know, the 'dirty side of life', let's just say … the more criminal and all that goes with it. He was responsible for either … what is this 'manacuso'? Oh, 'Maciunas' is his name, okay, okay.

He interfered with the system. He took advantage or, was taken advantage of … he took advantage of that life span to explore the deadly, the dark, the underside of life and of living, and of really not even of living … it was surviving. He had something to do, or he was connected with, people in, what I would say, something to do with productions.

The jail term, or yes, the jail term. I don't know why … would the mob have anything? The mob, the jail term, the mob, really, is connected to this.

A younger male, a young boy, left to his own accord isn't who he pretends to be, leaves his country and sets off on a journey, or embarks on a journey that will reveal or uncover history. And will make history.

You are attributing your work, your life it seems like, to the pursuit of what appears to me, to be almost justice, as if justice was not done. I would say that this work that you are doing,

I think will result in much more than you bargained for. It might take a little maneuvering, however.

It sounds like a bit, in a certain way, you want to be left alone, but you want to be involved. Or you don't want to be involved, but you want to be involved. It sounds like an oxymoron, this is almost as if you are exploring yourself while, perhaps, you are exploring and investigating somebody else. There is almost a strange relationship between the project or this work that you are doing and the work, the person that you are investigating. It probably doesn't come as a surprise to you. It shouldn't. It doesn't, does it?

RM: No, it doesn't.

DM: No it doesn't! Because, there is far more than, say, what meets eye. You are, let's say, revealed. Has the military been of any interest to you? The military? That might not be the word.

RM: I would like to ask some questions submitted by people curious about George Maciunas' afterlife. What is it like being dead?[2]

DM: What is it like being dead? Oh, alright, alright. You want to ask this guy? You know, the emphasis is being placed on not being alone. He emphasises also that it is much easier. I think, he is also emphasizing that … A card player? Royal flush? Royally screwed! Royally flushed! Yes, the card reference is being used.

RM: Definitely, he designed cards.

DM: And, the royal flush … His father was a young entrepreneur of some kind? Or he was a young entrepreneur, as well, OK, I am getting onto other things.

This also being emphasised with relation to the question that you asked is that, people in a physical form think less of themselves, and he doubts the reasoning connected to that.

When you are older you'd like to be young again. When you are young you'd like to be old, older. When you are in a body, you want to be out of a body. When you are out of a body, you think it's better being in a body, sometimes (laughter). The focus is entirely on love, primarily. Entirely on relationships, entirely on whatever you particularly are focusing on, whatever you focus on, that's it.

94

It manifests. It is created. Thought is very fast. You are not conditioned by time. You don't have a liver, or heart, or all of these organs. Instead, you have a force. And if you want to be a part of this force, while you are in the living, so to speak, then acknowledge it, yes, acknowledge its presence. For, if it weren't for that force, these organs would mean absolutely nothing.

RM: Can art cure the world?[3]

DM: Can art cure the world? Okay, cure it. They want to emphasise that, 'cure it'. That's an interesting question. Let's just say that art is responsible for explaining … one possible way of looking at it is explaining your history, past lives. You recognise yourself in it, whether that particularly intellectually makes sense to you or not. Also if art were emphasised in the world, recognised by the authorities as being a valuable tool for knowing the human condition.

Art permits us to recognise our mortality, our immortality. Art allows us, allows someone to see the bigger picture. They can't win the wars that they are fighting without greater awareness of themselves and who they really are. And in biblical times, when the men disconnected from the force, as Jesus was a channel, a prophet, and a whole bunch of other things.

And they are saying something about 'it is all in the scriptures'. It's talked about by many philosophers, many teachers over there, you know, Buddha, Sartre, all of them. The artists know and recognise this … the value, and validate it, and continue to put it in front of the masses in hopes to quietly awaken them. 'Alone' is what he doesn't feel anymore, being out of the body. He doesn't feel separate.

RM: What shall we put on the back cover of this publication?

DM: The back of the publication … the less is more. Take, not necessarily the usual approach, apparently, the more eclectic. Present what it is that you have to offer. Divulge or reveal what it is that gives the reader, perhaps, insight into … like a tease, almost, but not a tease. That way you provide them with something more than just what might captivate them into wanting to know, of course, more.

He's talking about the publication being a selling tool. There in words, they will take leave

of their intellectual mind and enter into their imagination. And that's the world that he would like them to be able to go in, to go into more of a looser, less rigid, focused, you know, this is not a workshop. This is an exploration, of oneself, not just this man, but of oneself, through this character, much like a play, or the theater. That's what I was talking about, the theater!

He becomes the main character, the central character, through which, vicariously, the reader lives through. That position ought to interest the appropriate reader, because as I've been told, in a sense, not to try to answer all of the questions in one small thing. They all can't be. And in a way that, even with all this book being written, publication, that there are answers, so to speak, to questions that … there are answers to the questions that have yet to even be asked out there. You are approaching this … you are happy to do this, are you not?

RM: Sure.

DM: Yeah! There is an enthusiasm that will be expressed to the reader. The reader will pick up on that energy. It may be symbols. Little, tiny little letters, you know, but inside, that is energy.

Don't be limited. Not to limit it, again, in short, not to limit it to any one particular thing right here, right now. Your doubts, your concerns, your fears, whatever. Leave a little bit more to the imagination. They'll thank you for it. You don't have to explain everything. It doesn't have to be verbatim. Because you want the reader to be a part of the process, you don't want to just inform them. You want them to be a participant, much like the audience is the participant of the theatrical experience. You just don't tell them. You share with them. Kind of what is going on right now.

RM: George, are you still aware of what is going on in the world, and, if so, what do you think about it?[4]

DM: You can't get past it without first going through it. Every individual comes with a sort of plan of action, or a destiny, a course of action. You're as limited or as expansive as you allow yourself to be.

As much as everybody would like to think peace on earth, there will never entirely be peace everywhere. The nature of the universe is to destroy and create. And that relationship will always be binding. The way in which people

?

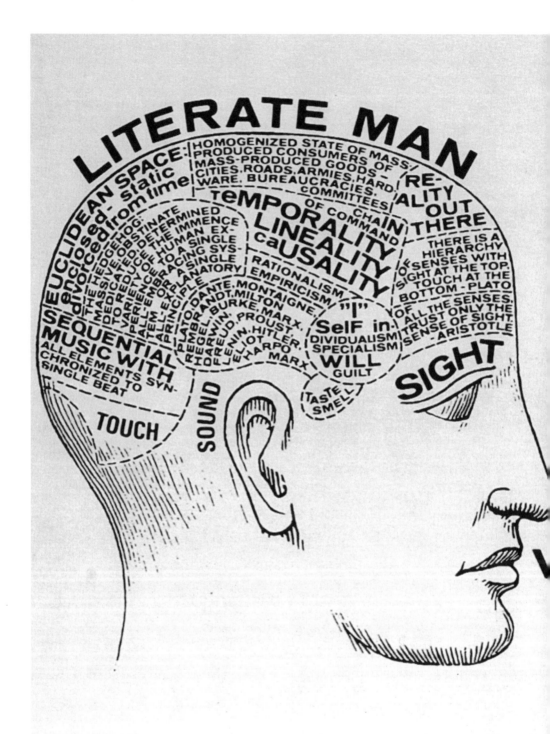

LITERATE MAN

EUCLIDEAN SPACE: enclosed - static divorced from time

HOMOGENIZED STATE OF MASS-PRODUCED CONSUMERS OF MASS-PRODUCED GOODS - CITIES, ROADS, ARMIES, HARDWARE, BUREAUCRACIES, COMMITTEES

REALITY OUT THERE

CHAIN OF COMMAND

TEMPORALITY
LINEALITY
caUSALITY

HOG: OBSTINATE DETERMINED THE IMMENCE HUMAN EXPERIENCE REDUCE TO A SINGLE RACING SYSTEM ALL-EMBRACING A SINGLE ALL-EXPLANATORY PRINCIPLE

THE HEDGEHOG: MASSIVE, DEDICATED, VARIETY

RATIONALISM
EMPIRICISM

PLATO, DANTE, MONTAIGNE, REMBRANDT, MILTON, HEGEL, BURKE, MARX, DARWIN, PROUST, FREUD, HITLER, LENIN, ELIOT, HARPO MARX

"I"
SelF in- dIVIDUALISM SPECIALISM
WILL
GUILT

THERE IS A HIERARCHY OF SENSES WITH SIGHT AT THE TOP, TOUCH AT THE BOTTOM - PLATO

OF ALL THE SENSES, TRUST ONLY THE SENSE OF SIGHT. - ARISTOTLE

SEQUENTIAL MUSIC WITH ALL ELEMENTS SYNCHRONIZED TO SINGLE BEAT

TOUCH

SOUND

TASTE SMELL

SIGHT

96

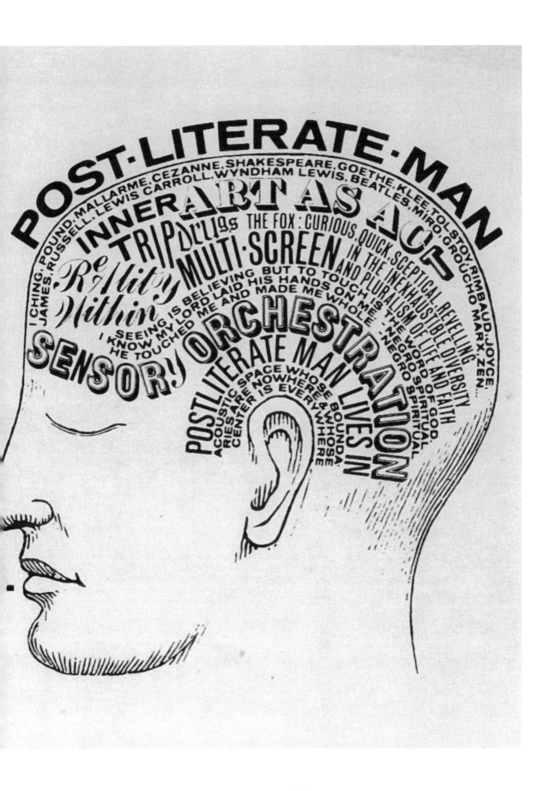

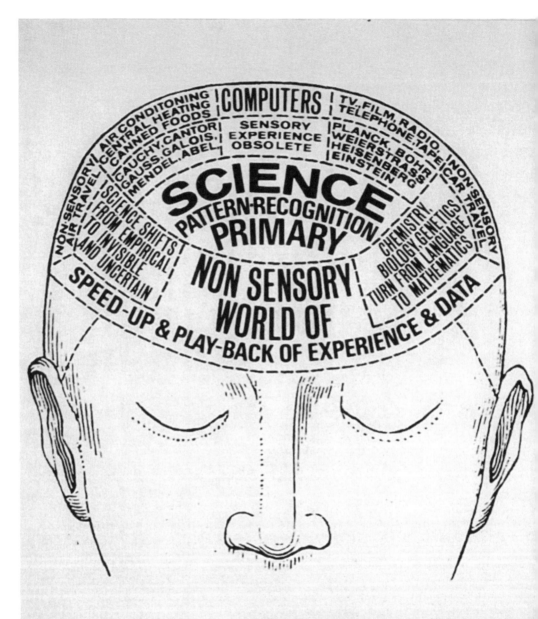

Both images: George Maciunas, 'Contemporary Man',
in *Proposals for Art Education From a Year Long Study
Supported by The Carnegie Corporation of New York, 1968–69*
(San Francisco, 1970), between pages 42 and 43.
Courtesy the G.L. Silverman Fluxus Collection, Detroit.

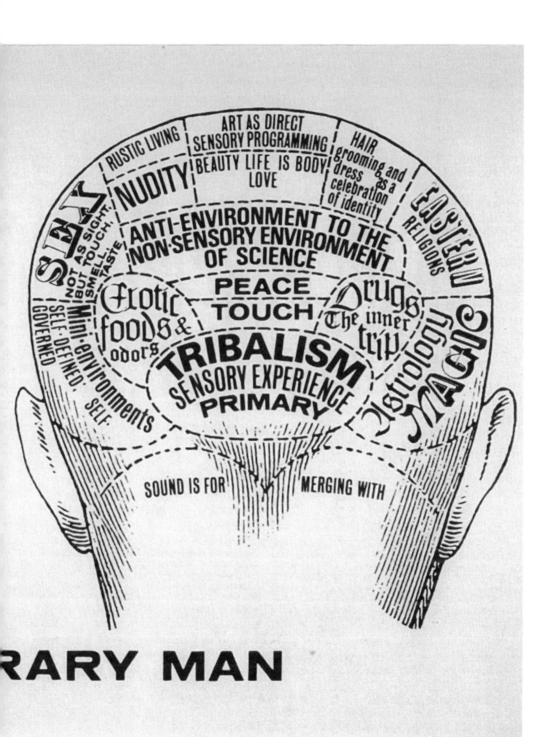

RARY MAN

express themselves, individually, will have a global effect. We, as energies, as spirits, guides, give tools to those who are open to listen. How can you, how can your work, perhaps, serve in opening the eyes of others? That even if you have to stretch it a little bit, not to be fearful of retaliation, or what do they call it? In the theater there is a saying and I forget, I don't know, it was just kind in saying it, in impressing me with, like theatrical.

RM: How is your life as a drag queen? Are you finding high heels, silk stockings, flowing gowns, wigs, corsets, gloves and jewelry to satisfy your hearts desire?[5]

DM: You are talking about now?

RM: Yes, it's a question for George.

DM: Yeah, apparently, he likes this subject! He says, 'Shakespeare says it best: Life is but a stage, and we are all on stage', like to think of it in those terms or not. And to become too serious about our lives is not to give credit to ourselves.

He likes and enjoys these kinds of theories. This man enjoyed thinking about these. So the theater, or yes, drag, in this instance … it's like, you know what it was like? His play-ground. This was where he derived a great deal of enjoyment. There was nothing like it, there was nothing like it … Imitating or taking on those characters and putting a little bounce in your step and pleasing the crowd with a gesture or a comment, or two. And watching them go wild. He obviously has fond memories of these experiences. As he says, 'if you are willing to give it a go, if an individual, if a person, if I were willing to go there with myself. No one forced me to do it. I was fascinated by the exploration and the reaction that it received.' Because, you know, at heart, I always … he always felt alone. Maybe there were many people around him, but at heart he felt alone.

Does that make sense? It's very heady. It's very well thought out. He sees the grand scheme of things in the smallest of things.

RM: Yes, that makes sense.

DM: So, he's got a lot of little things that say a lot.

RM: Is there Starbucks in the afterlife?[6]

DM: Is there Starbucks in the afterlife? There's anything if you would like there to be, there is. However, unfortunately, one of the drawbacks of being out of the body, is that you don't have senses, quite in the same way as you do in a body. The great passion for chocolate is revered all over, in people in the body, out of the body. And when I was in a body I didn't always appreciate that. And now I wish I had. The closest thing that I can come to, to experiencing that is to bring my vibration very near another person who is having that sensation, then it transfers to me. I can enjoy the sensation through that person. Which is often times the way we also communicate. We resonate or vibrate with the soul that is in a body. I think what's happening right here, through that person I can transfer the sensation, the impression. And that individual can then put words to that emotion, to that impression. So it can work both ways.

RM: Do you trust psychic channeling?[7]

DM: All right, it appears to me that his father, or someone, father figure, someone he knew and respected was either a magician or someone who was involved in all of this kind of thing. Having a strong belief, can lead a person into believing anything. Whether knowing or not. There's a difference between belief, which he is pointing out, is more an intellectual understanding, and then there's a knowing, which comes from another place, another sort of intelligence, like the second mind, which is perhaps your soul or your gut feeling. I think what he is pointing out here or bringing me to is: what we think we know is not always what is true. It's our experience and that's really all we really only have.

No one person has all of the answers, but there is an interesting relationship between questions and answers. They are each looking one for another. And they both exist at the same time, perhaps not in the same room. So, to answer your question, that he would say to the skeptics or to the doubters, that if you know in your being that something valid has taken place, something authentic, then it really doesn't matter how it comes through, whether it's a work of art, whether it's Mötley Crüe, or whether it's Barbara Streisand. There is an intellectual truth and there is a knowing truth. And in a way he is saying, you know, people bore him, they bore him. He doesn't have patience for fools, in the true sense.

There is something in the chaos. It's organised chaos. Much like what is going on in the theater or a film. And you don't have to look any further than your own life, or the lives of others, or even perhaps nature, being a force that we are all a part of.

You know, I might add that I was in every situation of this kind. I'll share with you as best as I can the words. But I am not him, and he will only come close to me and impress me, and he will use me and my awareness, my experiences in a way for him to communicate.

Does this make any sense to you? It's like he pulls off the shelf the encyclopedia of my life and says, 'OK, he has this kind of experience, I'll go this way with it.' So, I don't think the words have to be verbatim. I think it is just the idea.

RM: What do you truly think of Yoko Ono?[8]

DM: It is not up to me, to justify or qualify another individual. What he's really pointing out here is, if that … whatever it was, I think he could have done better. That's basically … it's like 'I could have done better, I think I could have done better', lets say. Let's just say that he is handling that question very carefully, apparently. He is talking about a light heart, rather than a heavy heart.

RM: What about art after life?[9]

DM: Art after life. We are all a work of art and a work in progress, at the same time. We have in a physical body an advantage. As a soul not in a body, my way of creating has shifted, or is different, in so far as the way it's easier in one way and more difficult in another. We are our own … we become our own creators. And yet, we are a co-creator. That relationship continues. It's in the way that it is expressed that's different.
Is not as … It's a very immediate thing. If I think it, if I can compose it in my head, if I can, so to speak, arrange it in my mind, it exists. And in a certain way, it exists for you if you can compose it and arrange it in your mind. It's the relationship of building it or creating that it is different. In that sense it is different on this plane than it is on the physical plain. I am not limited by physical. And those physical limitations, the density, the heaviness, is something to be … is useful and at the same time, to answer the question, is more available to me.
The process is the same. It happens, it's arranged or created in your mind, and unlike the physical world, it happens as rapidly as it happens in your own mind. The difference being that I created or we can create a state of mind, a situation, a something and in the physical world in your relationship to it there is a lot more components, there's a lot more parts, it isn't just thinking it. It's like a puzzle.

For instance, I can travel anywhere in the globe in just a split second. I am very fascinated I might add. Like a child in a candy shop. But at the same time, you know, this is a soul that has been around the block. This is an old timer. He has been here before, let's just say.

RM: Do you still play chess with Marcel Duchamp?[10]

DM: Not as often as he'd like. As much as there are certain conditions relating to the physical plane, there are certain conditions relating to the non-physical plane. And one of those conditions relates to the soul's desire to educate, inform, and connect with beings that are very familiar, it's like family. So, he feels, he's not as inclined, at this time, to be involved in playing those kind of things. Marcel is much more connected to, it's almost like he is racing about, it's almost like he doesn't have time, it's almost as if the priority for him has changed, whereby in the physically realm … That as much as you may be together, and have shared many things, that you can be still be worlds apart, be in the same room and be worlds apart. Marcel … is he out of a body?

RM: Yes.

DM: Ok, what he's pointing out here, the gist of it is, that Marcel is racing, chasing after happiness, whereas George is not. Marcel is very disturbed by a lot of things in the word, and angry about injustice. Ohh, really … to the point where … he would break glass.

RM: George, when I join you down there, will I be able to smoke cigars or have you organised things in such a way that I will not be able to?[11]

DM: It's a lot like food, or tasting, or feeling, about tactile. It's close, but it's no cigar. No, you will not be able to smoke.

RM: How many languages exist in the afterlife?[12]

DM: About six thousand, five thousand, seven thousand. There are a lot of different languages. You know, when you study your past lives, you realise that in many instances you have spoken many of them, most of them.

RM: How can we communicate with each other if we speak different languages?

DM: Language is more of a physical thing than it is a spiritual life. The communication that takes place, especially in the higher level is sort of like the difference between kindergarten and twelfth grade, so to speak. It's a telepathic kind of communication. A thought is sent, an idea is sent and received. But he says, it is so useful, again he's fascinated by, it's so useful to speak a language. And that language primarily exists on this level. It is not as used or utilised or as useful or as economical, that's not the word exactly, but, as telepathic, ideas are sent somehow.

RM: Can we ask him who he was in his past life?

DM: There might be a surprise, but he was an athlete, a preacher. He had something to do with the Mormons. I don't know what, I am not familiar, but a religious sect. He is showing me Germany … fascism, and I was saying: 'That doesn't look pretty' and he goes, 'They all aren't all pretty, honey' … that kind of a thing … don't think yours are either.

When he talks about being a preacher, you know, he was, or at least he felt connected to dictators. They were fascinating characters, fascinating character studies for him. He saw himself, many times, and he learned a lot. He observed them a lot. He found it so fascinating that he could find a piece of himself in others. And I can think it's very interesting what Mother Teresa said she found Hitler in herself. Small part, but okay.

And I think, in a certain way, that was one of the reasons why he felt alone. Because, in many cases, I think, he had a few friends, not a lot of friends, a handful, of real close friends. The rest, he didn't have much use for. As a matter of fact, in his eyes, they were like noise, they were static.

Authority figures left a bad taste in his mouth. He recognised the fact that people listened to the so-called authority figures was mind-boggling to him. It was really deeply moving and concerning to him. He felt he wanted to do something

about it. He felt inspired to say: 'Hey, look. Put a mirror up to these people, 'cause, they're fakes, they're not real. They're snake oil. Take a look folks. Take a look at yourselves, take a look at them.' You know? When you do that, you identify yourself, you become a rebel, and one that they can identify. And they're out to squelch you, out to get rid of, because you become noise for them. You become a problem for them.

Anyhow, his lives were, I think, very diverse and very colorful. Very. And some strange things too, or what will be thought of as strange, anyway. Because he is fascinated by the strange and the unusual and what they know. There is an opportunity. And I think, at the same time, your guides or who you are working with and my spirits guides also lent a little help in this. I think initially he is not too wacky about the whole thing. He has said things along the way that were misconstrued and misunderstood, and you know, there is a real resistance on his part anyway to have to explain. Even though he is not in the body anymore, in a way, he doesn't want to involve himself with a lot of people here. It's almost like, someone calling you up and saying: 'You know what? I realised that you broke something in my bathroom ten years ago.' You say: 'What? What are you talking about? It's this small! Get a life, move own, get a life!'

A version of this text was first published in Grady T. Turner & Raimundas Malasauskas, *Looking for Mr Fluxus: In the Footsteps of George Maciunas* (Skuta Helgason/Art in General, NYC, 2002).

NOTES
1. From the call for questions: 'Do you have a question for George Maciunas (1931–1978), artist and the founder of the Fluxus movement? If so, please send it to raimay@hotmail.com. In an attempt to communicate with George Maciunas, we are going to collaborate with an experienced psychic who will deliver your questions (or suggestions, ideas, inquiries, etc.) directly to Maciunas.'
2. Question from Jonathan Monk.
3. Question from Isabel Carlos.
4. Question from Yoko Ono.
5. Question from Geoffrey Hendricks.
6. Question from Jonathan Monk.
7. Question from Jonathan Monk.
8. Question from Yasufumi Nakamori.
9. Question from Christopher Lowery.
10. Question from Charles Dreyfus.
11. Question from Jon Hendricks.
12. Question from Gintaras Makarevicius.

DÉCOR HOLES

by Seth Price

Here is an operation. In 1988 the composer Steve Reich, whom at one point was called a minimalist, used the relatively new technology of the sampler to create a work based around the digitised human voice. The work grew out of phrases and sentences, the cadences of which suggested corresponding musical figures. Double strands laid out like objects upon their shadows. The voice writes the music. Listening through this music, specific language emerges: testimonials from Holocaust survivors, overburdened with meaning, unassailable. Well, a thing only really appears when it's turned into a weapon. Ovens, showers, lampshades, soap: an innocuous group of words, unless we're told that the context is Germany in the 1940s.

Where to locate the power in this operation? First, let us try to assemble some of its recognizable traits. It is an act of writing that does not hesitate to remove material from its native context, a move often seen as inappropriate or even criminal, at least in the realm of pop culture. According to this logic, an original is somehow violated through the creation of its double, a process seen as one more step in the lamentable cultural slide from representation to repetition.

In fact, sampling is not concerned with repetition. Its purpose is the creation of new, discrete events. Each reproduction is an original and a new beginning. Each, in fact, is the first in a potentially infinite sequence, which is to say an infinite sequence. This is where the gesture's violence is to be found, and why it is attended by cultural anxieties. These concerns are often understood to be copyright-related, which means money-motivated, but it's likely that they stem just as much from misgivings about the implications of instrumentalizing human expression. In any case, there's no longer such a thing as a copy.

Artists are universally recognised as experts in the field of human expression. Naturally they have been quick to recognise these issues. I wonder … if sampling may be understood as a process of using stolen documents as raw material for form abuse, might this not be true of all advanced art? Luckily it isn't necessary to answer this question, as a thing doesn't have to be true, merely testable. With this task in mind we turn to the realm of music, a superior place to test artists' reactions to the intrusion of digital techniques, which were introduced to music quite early relative to other art forms.

The notion of 'intellectual property' as regards most written material was codified in Europe in the sixteenth century; a response to the new text-copying technology of print. It was almost a hundred years before this notion really took hold in the world of music and a composer might actually own his composition. Previously, songs were understood to be common property, and, what's more, mutable, much in the way computer programs were initially understood as communal efforts to be shared, altered, and redistributed.

A one-hundred-year lag! Although in this respect music seems to have fallen behind the printed word, it soon leapt ahead. The practice of text copying has aged gracefully since the dawn of intellectual property, and its main exponent remains the printed page, but music has all along been subject to sudden shifts in the controlled reproduction and dissemination of commercial recorded material.

Let us reflect on these changes. To take an example from opera, Toscanini's tenure at La Scala wrought changes that would eventually turn the form into the consummate bourgeois entertainment. Prior to his arrival, the orchestra was seated on the same level as the audience, an audience with none of the docile characteristics of today's opera-goers, rather, a mob of hardy commoners, robust peasant folk, loyal to the toil of the soil, drinking, eating, and jesting in the manner of her C's, U's, and T's: 'Let us meet at the opera and then decide whence we go …', 'Well-met, friend, pray share this flagon …', 'Scubberdegullion', 'Lass', etc.

This is the lumber of life.

It must be emphasised: Toscanini had the luck of good timing. Architecture is the model in Western metaphysics, and as such is a necessary corollary to ritual. At just this moment the bourgeoisie was working itself into a supreme ecstasy of privacy, decorum, and interiority. Built spaces were spaces of fantasy. The opera is such a fantasy, a ritualised repetition of aristocratic tradition. A depletion but also a preservation of forms lacking the vitality to proceed under their own power, delivered in the sorts of patrician packaging necessary to fire

℞

the bourgeois imagination. The emptying gestures of ritual are a force of preservation, just as death is the romanticizing principle in life. In this light, the phenomenon of a proper house for opera can be seen as a secret handshake between the middle classes and the aristocracy. For their part, aristocracies dutifully keep alive those endangered pleasures that repel the bourgeoisie. Now, as then? In our time there is no such thing as a bourgeoisie. Yet … Well, why not? One dreams all day long, just as during the night. It is possible that cultured people are merely the glittering scum that floats upon a deep river of production.

But what results from this? If architecture is the model in Western metaphysics, we are in some sense the inhabitors of older buildings, and ours is the business of living in a ruined house. It's useful to take a hard look at the word *ruin*, a word that splits. On the one hand, it could refer to the sorts of ancient structures cherished in the early nineteenth century: squalid, overgrown, graffiti-covered, surveyed at sunset for best effect. Yet it might also indicate those same ruins today: sandblasted free of graffiti, restored and conserved, made lucrative, seen only in the full daylight of 'open hours'. In the first example, ruin implies benign decay; in the second, active preservation, make-work, and industry.[1] Locating pleasure in benign decay is a perversion, for these structures are useless and wasteful, a spilling of seed, like gay sex, like gay sex.

All that which is not made useful and which serves no profitable function is seen as the unrecuperable waste of a society. This material may be understood as a force that crystallises society's blockages, making visible a sort of cast of its bowels. The Boston Museum of Science features a display of 'petrified lightning', which is merely a lumpy brown rod of sand fused at the instant of extreme heat. The exhibit stands for the operation by which a scientific process is mystified, replaced by a ruin under glass, making a fetish of waste. My anecdotal mention of this exhibit itself belongs to a certain class of artistic vitrine, and one could treat cultural detritus the same way, wringing art from suburban architecture, or ex-urban wasteland.

It is here that our strands come together, for it is in music that one may now locate such fetishes and vitrines. In the era of the picturesquely crumbling abbey or castle, poetry was king of the arts, and it was this form that drew all the radical young dudes. A century later, on the other side of Modernism, in an age when any ancient scrap heap is carefully made over in the image of safety and security, music is the art toward which all the others aspire. It's here you'll find the young romantics. What accounts for this change? As with the adoption of ideas of intellectual property, the schematic shifts in music lag behind those of the written word.

This is the lake of our feeling.

It was not until the affront of the sampler that music really went to work anxiously mapping and itemizing the husks of metropolises constructed by earlier settlers. Seeking a new Classicism. With all the hedonism that follows a period of calamity.[2] The Classical style (if one may be so vain as to label something that exists beyond time) is often said to stretch from Haydn to Beethoven. It might be best understood as a single unbroken lineage in which Brahms writes with Beethoven looking over his shoulder, a carefully organised sequence of events, preserved on paper and embodied in the concert hall. The twentieth century, however, put an end to this careful sequence, substituting a wildly metastasizing growth based on the duplicable recorded signal. The arrival of the digital copy crystallises this development neatly, almost allegorically, almost *too* neatly. One might think that music is in dissolution, heading away from form, increasingly resistant to the physical, and so also to structures of ritual,[3] but this may not, in fact, be the case.

Come what may, everything is reused. Artists rummage through the toolkits of past artists for approaches they may make use of. The task is to take these instruments and fashion new tools. You want a fine-art approach, you borrow the tool from commodity culture. Look for the use, not the meaning! And if it's done wrong, no problem, there is produced a nostalgia for the done-right way. For these reasons, the modern idea of a renovated ruin may be more relevant for art than the nineteenth century model of picturesque decay.

It still eludes me … what is so particular about the sampler? Take a close look at the economic and technological particulars of this tool. In 1979, the first commercial sampler was put on the market for around $25,000. The *Fairlight*. What a name! Ha, ha, ha. The steep price was typical of these early machines, which were consequently purchased by institutions, primarily well-funded university composition labs. In other words, this was a brief period when

fusionne avec au delà

hors l'intérêt
                                                    quant à lui signalé
en général
            selon telle obliquité par telle déclivité
            de feux

                    vers
                ce doit être
                            le Septentrion aussi Nord

UNE CONSTELLATION

                                froide d'oubli et de désuétude
                                        pas tant
                                qu'elle n'énumère
        sur quelque surface vacante et supérieure
                                le heurt successif
                                    sidéralement
                d'un compte total en formation

veillant
        doutant
            roulant
                brillant et méditant

                        avant de s'arrêter
                à quelque point dernier qui le sacre

Toute Pensée émet un Coup de Dés

most of the people exploring sample-based music were classically-trained academic composers, who recognised in the computer a spectacular means of testing their high-flying propositions.[4]

This moment is emblematic of music's Modernist style, which all along had a tendency, as with the abstruse proposals of Schoenberg or Webern, to make advanced theoretical training a pre-requisite for participation. Now it was expected of students that they not only cultivate a familiarity with the usual histories and methodologies, but also rely entirely on the academy for production tools. After all, many middle-class homes featured a piano, but none a computer workstation. It was a natural endpoint to Modernist music's evolutionary chain, which flourished on a delicate diet of technology, money, and control. Hardly characteristic of Modernist music alone, it is true, but this moment so beautifully illustrates it.

But this moment was fleeting. The sampler's arrival upset the balance, and, as often happens with young technologies, the market seeped in, all the strictures slipped, old model of the pyramid, new model of the pancake. Ten years after the introduction of the *Fairlight*, any composer could buy a decent sampler for under one thousand dollars, adding a newly available personal computer to yield a versatile home studio. The same was true of any teenager producing dance music or rap music.[5] All this headlong change left a wake of wreckage and trauma, and, in academic computer music, a unique and peculiar musical period, a curiosity, the equivalent of a geographically isolated evolutionary zone where unique life forms go largely undiscovered. Actions of concealing belong to violence. A bruised music, which seems still to have no name, unsure whether it was the start or the end of something.

Around the same time sampling was introduced, the music industry developed MIDI, a kind of universal machine language that allows electronics to synchronise and exchange information. Packets of information, commands in fact, are relayed from one piece of gear to the next, allowing a synthesiser of one manufacture to get in line with a drum machine of another. These silent commands, such as *start note* and *end note*, are known as events. Arguably a language, and certainly a system of control, destined to be the new coin of the realm, a currency of loins and coins. Because it was intended for swift, industry-wide adoption, the concept had to be widely familiar, rather than

intelligible only to technicians, engineers, and programmers. That meant attaching a friendly front-end to the code. The public happens to be most comfortable with the piano, and this became electronic music's user interface. This is why the events lurking behind most of the music you hear on the radio actually preserve the slight, barely perceptible movement of a fingertip somewhere striking a key. Strike the key and trigger an event, which is immediately sequenced in a series of other events. A chain of control achieved through a simple depression. When I am depressed, there is power at work somewhere.

Many are interested in the idiom of a form, few in the grammar. Personal computers, for example, were originally made so as to be programmable by their owners, but when consumers eventually rejected this aspect it was removed or hidden. Similarly, while the combination of sampled sounds, MIDI, and digital manipulation promised all sorts of possibilities, it turns out that most people don't want to build sounds that have never been heard. They want sounds corresponding to existing phenomena, invocations of reality at the touch of a finger, like paint straight from the tube: brass, woodwinds, car accidents, shrieks, breaking glass. The machine recalls events and dispatches them in a digital relay that is by design simply on or off, making obsolete the weak signal, the half-understood communication. A zero-sum spell.

So, you found the sampler's perfect expression early on, when you hit on the idea of employing sampled human voice as a re-pitchable synthesizer sound. An electronic keyboard simulates a piano, often noting even the force with which the keys are struck: it wants you to believe that it is a percussion instrument. The voice-sample technique, then, is the process of generating limitless copies of a unique and resonant human utterance, refashioned as a sprawling kit of silicon-calibrated fake drums. The voice becomes a structural element under total control, it is made useful, as opposed to evocative or expressive. That which reliably promises communication becomes pure instrumentality, a move based on the notion that instruments give us what we want—predictability, security, control—rather than the confirmation of an accurate representation of the real. It goes to show you that when your desires become reality, you don't need fantasy any longer, nor art.

The technique was immediately popular among academic composers and pop producers

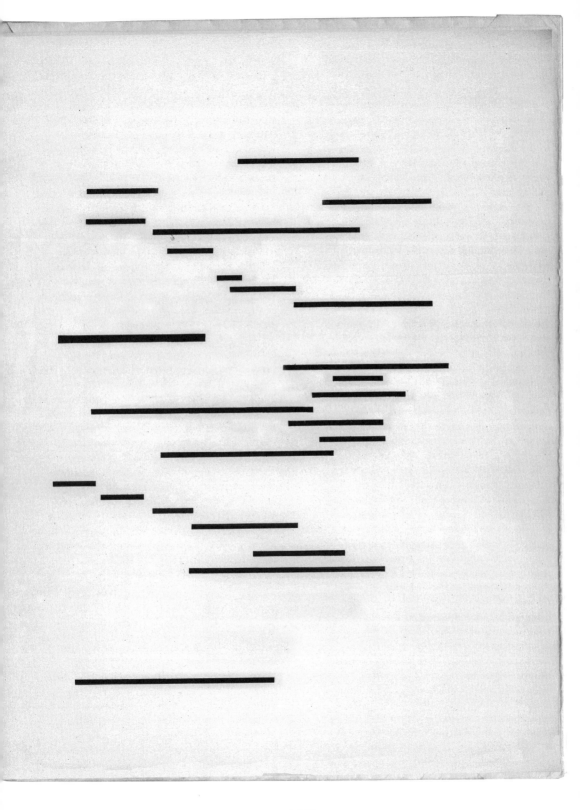

107

alike,[6] but soon disappeared from both realms, possibly because it seemed dated, but more likely because sampled and repitched voice is disturbing, a speech terrible and inhuman, an emulation gone bad. The sampled word is the zero degree of the word, as found in the dictionary, or in poetry. Here the communicative imperative, which depends on repetition and difference, was symbolically short-circuited, and, moreover, from within the cloak of language. It is not surprising that the technique fell into disfavor. Man fall from a tree, that tree be felled, man fall in a well, that well be filled.

Samplers continue to offer one entirely new experience, at least on the level of consumption: the recognition, while listening to an unknown piece of music, of the basis for a sample used in a familiar piece. As you look up with bewildered pleasure, the music charges on, diverging from the repetition you expected. You briefly glimpsed a private, inaccessible field between two disparate experiences, a mental correlate to the phantom step at the top of the stairs. Whatever pleasure you can sustain must rely on simultaneous presence and absence.[7]

Digital duplication was one of the twentieth century's few new schemas. Such developments draw the curtain on older powers, and, by the end of the 1980s, around the time Reich completed his sample-based work, the configuration *avant-garde music* was thoroughly depleted, a constellation made cold from forgetfulness. All forms of depletion are heralded by the degradation of language, and, just as the eclipse of Rome's power was contemporary with the decline of Latin, so the eclipse of avant-garde music was indicated by its wish to transform embodied language into an instrument. A desire to *be*, rather than to *seem*.

You could argue that sampling poisoned the well. On the other hand, it is true that in homeopathic medicine, and sometimes in magic, you put a drop of the bad thing, the thing you fight, into water or some other medium. Sampling may be invasive, negating repetition, disordering us, but then that's the wish of every man: to disorder, to mayhem. You must fight something in order to understand it! Voice sampling, possibly all sampling, gives us a text that is critical of reading.

Graffiti performs a similar operation. The gesture of graffiti must preserve that which it seeks to destroy. Were it to entirely efface its object, its particular critique would vanish.

None, after all, is worse shod than the shoemaker's wife. The work of Marcel Broodthaers occasionally follows this logic, most clearly in his piece *Un Coup de dés jamais n'abolira le hasard*, with its pleasantly incestuous abuse of the Francophone avant-garde. The publication of Mallarmé's poem 'Un Coup de dés jamais n'abolira le hasard', a work distinguished by its typography and disposition of the words upon the page, marked the first time that a poem's conception and meaning was determined through the mechanical printing process. A lyric automation of the design function. In 1969, Broodthaers made a series of pieces that reproduced the exact page layout of Mallarmé's poem, and the layout alone, since he effaced each line of text with a solid black bar. This gesture, while it banished all communicative symbols, retained the striking look and feel of the work.[8] Mallarmé's piece was emptied-out, reduced to seductive packaging. This is a move typical of 'appropriation', which may be considered simply an advanced form of packaging.

These depleted forms were engraved onto aluminum plates, as if prepped for mass production, and presented as fine art. Broodthaers claims and then augments Mallarmé's poem to produce a new, third body, a field between the works. The whole is without novelty, save the spacing of one's reading; the blanks, in effect, assume importance. The madness of the 'a self-annihilating nothing' prescription. But this was only to be expected, since Broodthaers was an imitation artist. It may be that the supreme triumph of such advanced art is to cast doubt on its own validity, mixing a deep scandalous laughter with the religious spirit. There is a violence in this turn, the same violence that attends graffiti: *Don't think, look!*

In regular usage, the word graffiti describes an urban decay-threat, akin to mould, understood as pathology. It may be pathological, but not because it's vandalism, rather because it dreams of total saturation through an open-ended sequence of events, each a slight variation on the last. Such total coverage is a futile and perverse premise, an infinite possibility wedded to perpetual disappointment, a pursuit ripe with frustration. Like the poor man who sells his saucepan to buy something to put in it.

Then again, graffiti, like any human expression, is basically a search to find a style and context that makes further expression possible. Graffiti Culture (and why does it take so long for people to map a 'culture' on to their violence?) represents the anarchic, expressive territory of those who have subverted painterly representation from the standpoint of cool alienation. A person inscribing a coded sign on the side of a bridge piling enacts a ritual repetition: Language is defaced by pictures. Writing that will never have a book. This isn't the business of living in a ruined house; it's the business of representing a ruined house, its interior trappings sketched out for all to see. The art object is seen as an object of contemplation, not to be parsed, but to be puzzled over. Its secrets may have to do with art, but with something else as well, which hovers beyond, with no name forthcoming.

In my view, it's refreshing to watch a form deplete itself: 'Ah, now it becomes easier to see it as not a belief but a historical movement, which is to say a movement of thought. Easier now to trace the social shift and extrapolate out as far as desired: all design, all art, all packaging.'[9] Take vacuum-forming, an industrial process that gives us the ubiquitous polystyrene packaging of batteries, toys, and toothbrushes, as well as of luxury items like boxed candies and cosmetics. Casual research into the use of this process in the plastic arts suggests that the chief instances, including Broodthaers' rectilinear plaques and Öyvind Fahlström's Esso/LSD reliefs, take the logic of the commercial sign as their model. This is congruent with a sustained twentieth-century artistic investigation of advertising and display, from Rudy Burckhardt or Walter Benjamin's interest in the sloughed-off detritus of commodity culture, to a more recent fascination with corporate monograms. What would it mean to employ such a process for the purpose of reproducing not the structures of language and capitalist syntax, but those of the human form? Making a package for conservative statuary and classical figuration, for art itself: a violent cough, as when the human voice is 'repurposed' as an instrument.

What it means is, it shows how far we've come with our packaging. Full circle, the lowest shall be highest. In the evenings, you can stroll out to see how we are coming along with the construction of the temple.

NOTES
1. The French have a saying: 'the consumer has only three basic needs: to be safe, to be loved, to be beautiful.' This is the desire of ruins in our time.
2. Historically, all new forms attack Classicism; it's a move characteristic not only of Romantic poetry, but also of the Neo-Expressionist painting of the 1980s,

for which the darkest place was under the lamp.
3. The sudden shift from wired phones to mobile phones. The telephone is introduced as a wire-bound domestic appliance, a singular site, in fact often attached to the wall, and it serves multiple people, whether through the party line, or later the shared 'phone in the hall', or, ultimately, the family phone. With the introduction of the mobile phone this model is upended, replaced by a roving non-site at the service of one.
4. It's the engineers who strike ground in digital creative arenas. This pattern is apparent not only in early computer music, but also in early computer graphics experiments, and in the earnest, fresh-faced CompSci graduates who are now enabling Hollywood's growing dependence on CGI. Something to do with Leonardo.
5. This raises the question of amateur production. As with all strategies of appropriation, sampling cannot be conceived of in terms of amateur or professional roles. This is part of its violence. Collecting and illegally redistributing material has no professional dimension; the person who compiles a mix tape for a friend is not an amateur. A licit practice that approximates this maneuver is that of a corporation that cheaply purchases rights to *déclassé* cultural material, like bygone dance music, from those now forced to part with it cheaply, thence to repackage these goods for re-consumption, either under the banner of nostalgia (the low-end approach), or for the archiving fetish of the would-be collector (the high end approach).
6. I once recalled someone standing by a keyboard, blurting out 'I don't know what to say!' The phrase belonged to a female character on an early Cosby Show, and was spoken into a new sampling keyboard demonstrated by Stevie Wonder, who appeared as himself. With some deft adjustments he multiplied her apparently random words across the span of the keyboard, repitched appropriately, basso profundo to mezzo-soprano, all subject to easy control through key depression. It was in fact Stevie Wonder, in 1981, who purchased the very first of the famous Emulator samplers, fresh off the assembly line. A quaint memory. What a time I chose to be born!
7. This experience is utterly different from that of recognizing one composer's melodic quotation of another's work, as different as is the scan from the photograph.
8. 'Look and feel,' a term popularised by the computer industry, is often used to describe the overall aesthetic of a particular operating system. Like the shade of seduction used to paint the information architecture. A well-known example is the Macintosh's successful graphic user interface, which was subsequently copied throughout the industry. The term gained notoriety through a series of lawsuits—Xerox against Apple, Apple against Microsoft, and Hewlett-Packard—brought on the basis of whether or not it was legal to appropriate aesthetic qualities crystallised in code. Look and feel, in its current sense, is a notion that did not really exist prior to the personal computer, but one that now affects all consumer realms based on digital technology.
9. Compare emblematic New York graffiti tags of the 1970s, like Zephyr, Futura, or PhaseII, with those of the 1980s such as Sony, Seiko, and Casio, and then with those of the 1990s, by which time the best sense-making letter combinations were used up: Revs, Kuma, Sems, Naers. A graceful arc from poetry to consumer fetish to emptied form. Digital tags such as screen names and internet addresses will not follow this arc, which belongs to the past. Décor Holes.

GUARANTEED DISAPPOINT- MENT

Punk graphic design at the Festival Hall

by Neil Mulholland

The rip-off riff's authentic ring
A singer who can't really sing
Can only mean one fucking thing
Punk rock revival
Affect the look of a man obsessed
Predisposed to the predistressed
Now you know you're properly dressed
Punk rock revival
John Cooper Clarke[1]

Following a stint of trouble-making at Croydon Art School, Jamie Reid began production of the Suburban Press, a publication which resulted from his disillusionment 'at how jargonistic and non-committal left-wing policies had become'[2] during the early 1970s. It was while working on the Suburban Press that Reid made his most significant attempts to break out of the mould of Situationist artiness and the Left's agit-prop in-fighting. Four years later, his 'rip off' graphics and Helen Wallington-Lloyd's 'ransom note' lettering were the benchmarks of 'punk design'. Reid's graphic experiments did not occur in isolation. In general, the 1970s saw a steady growth in 'radical amateurism' as montage techniques were adopted by photoconceptualists, community photographers, feminists, and anti-fascists alike. MINDA's photomontage designs for the Campaign Against Racism and Fascism[3] confronted the rise of Fascism by drawing allusions between the images of the Conservative Party, the National Front and the Nazis. Reid, meanwhile, was carrying out an assault on the iconography of fascism. It would seem that for him, MINDA's strategies were examples of the simplistic propaganda they opposed. From placing a swastika in place of the Queen's eyes ('God Save The Queen') to forming a swastika from marijuana leaves ('Never Trust a Hippy'), Reid ridiculed fascist iconography by striking at its very heart, de-centring its power by problematising the meaning of its imagery.

The curators of Destroy: Punk Graphic Design in Britain—an exhibition of 400 record sleeves, posters and fanzines at the Royal Festival Hall on London's South Bank—have made little concerted effort to locate punk's contributions within a heterodox range of visual practices. However, this exhibition isn't about punk. It's about 'punk graphic design' and their histories are not necessarily identical. Writing in 1980, Peter York noted that the 'main thing that punk introduced was the idea of cut-ups, montage —a bit of Modern Artiness—to an audience who'd never heard of eclecticism. Punk was about changing the meanings of things'[4] a view which has been dusted down to champion the exhibits in Destroy. A problem here might be that such blow-dried approval was clearly intended to celebrate punk's recuperation into the spectacle against which—disciples of its mythical origins cherish to enlighten us—it ought to have rebelled against. Of course, as everyone is also advised, McLaren and Reid recognised from the beginning that delinquent subcultures, since created through the channels of the mass-media, could only simulate revolution.

Perhaps, then, it is reasonable to claim that punk's anti-design stance had always made the whole enterprise peculiarly arty. Not according to another popular myth currently being rehashed, this being that punk designers were untrained, anonymous figures, their designs raw and uncouth, using anything that came to hand—their aim being to deface the designs of happy hippies trained at art school. It is true to say that many designers remain anonymous while designated designers such as Sebastian Conran, who pro-duced promotional material for The Clash, were self-taught. Yet many celebrated punk designers were trained at art school, and for them plagiarism was more of a carnivalesque prank than political art terrorism directed against Western property values. Malcolm Garrett began designing sleeves for the Buzzcocks while still a student at Manchester Polytechnic, where he had developed a taste for International Constructivism: 'I began merging a number of things I liked, the pioneering type of graphic experiments like Futurism and Bauhaus from earlier in the century with stuff from pop art and Andy Warhol.'[5] In the summer of 1977, Garrett's fellow student (and future Assorted Images co-designer) Linder Sterling was finishing her dissertation

γ

on the sanitisation of punk. Her photomontage for the Buzzcocks' 'Orgasm Addict' (1977), while having obvious precedents in dada and surrealism, most closely mirrored the kinds of anti-consumerist montage produced by mail artists and feminist community photographers in the 1970s, satirising imagery from magazines such as *Woman's Own*. Certainly such punk 'designs' were formally chaotic, irregular and harsh, while as 'cultural productions' they appeared subversive in intent. All laudable credentials for any aspiring subculture, but wasn't a very similar 'anti-aesthetic' to be found in the converse Hegelian logic of grunge-formalism which had demarcated 'fine art' from 'design' in most art schools since the late 1960s? *Destroy* is testament to such a view, given that it was not organised by anarcho-syndicalist employees of the Royal Festival Hall, but by Maria Beddoes and Paul Khera, a duet of sentimental graphic designers who, as students, had been inspired by punk to cast aside their airbrushes and set squares in revolutionary ferment: 'This is the *Evening Standard*. This is *Fiesta*. This is a pair of scissors. Now form an advertising consultancy.'

'The idea that you can still go out and do what you want is coming back at last', says Ben Kelly sleeve designer for Godley & Creme, A Certain Ratio, and The Cure among others. 'I still count myself as one of the lucky generation', fortuitously suggesting that some 'punk' designers were luckier than others.[6] If anything, the cult of the individual designer was reinforced by punk's 'version of the *credo quia absurdum est*: you don't like it but you do it anyway; you get used to it and you even like it in the end.'[7] Copyright, an issue previously of little interest to graphic designers, became the hot topic, (battles continue to take place over the attribution of many Pistols graphics): who was the best designer outlaw; who was the least individual? Generating such contradictions, of course, was the whole point. However, given its pedigree, is it still possible to relish the 'irony' of such ambivalence? Adopting a visual vocabulary and style which was entertaining, yet acidly absurd, Reid famously recorded attempts to erase the Pistols from cultural history ('Never Mind the Bans', 1977), before interminably representing their demise in posters and merchandising, much of which is represented in *Destroy*. Yet Reid's fear that 'the posters would end up as decor for trendy lefties' bedroom walls'[8]

was misplaced, for this is one of many times in which they have found their legitimate home in a vinyl sleeved cube, the art-gallery-as-record-fair; legitimate since, according to Reid's version of punk, assaulting the pop scene head on, simply gave the Pistols a lot of publicity, enabling them to make 'Cash out of Chaos'. Khera has an analogous incongruous fable: 'The Pistols were playing on a boat across the river and were banned from coming ashore by the police. We knew that the show would get more of a reaction here and it seems an ironic venue because of punk hating royalty.'[9] One end product of this version of events is Saatchi art. Literally: 'New Labour, New Danger' (1996) saw Reid's Readers' Wives-style letterbox eyes and rip-off style ripped-off by the Right. To complicate matters, Tony Blair's New Labour themselves appear to have heeded McLaren's 10 lessons in how to mask reaction in the cloak of youth and revolt.

Like New Labour, *Destroy* is also about what it excludes, reminding us that cultural history results from a suppression of possibilities. It would have been interesting to have seen Genesis P-Orridge's Paranoia Club business cards here ('E know you don't write back because you hate us'), or perhaps a few posters such as 'Gainsbourgh's Blue Movie Boy', and 'Gary Gilmore Memorial Society'. It seems unfortunate to have missed such an opportunity to have presented Throbbing Gristle's proto-punk work as COUM Transmissions, much of which has far greater appeal than Reid's numerous homages to the Motherfuckers. Unlike many punks who were relatively new to such matters, TG/COUM had been practicing for seven years as performance artists. They had also spent a great deal of time developing punk's deliberately offensive fascination with murderers and criminals, although in this, they were far from alone.[10] TG were particularly adept at arousing an extreme response, leaving people in a dialectical position where they could not switch the situation off as a joke. Many of their record sleeves which are on display, on first inspection seem bland, a banal photograph of an everyday location, but to the initiated the spot is the scene of a crime, usually a rape or grisly murder. Re-presenting the shock effects of sex crime, thought designer Peter 'Sleazy' Christopherson, would provide an effective route to challenge the hegemony of the mass-media's manipulative sensationalism. With a heady mix of urban decay and accounts of the last murder and subsequent apprehension

THROBBING GRISTLE
bring you
20 Jazz Funk Greats

Stereo

UNITED
THROBBING GRISTLE
Industrial Records IR0003

ZYKLON B ZOMBIE
THROBBING GRISTLE
Industrial Records IR0003

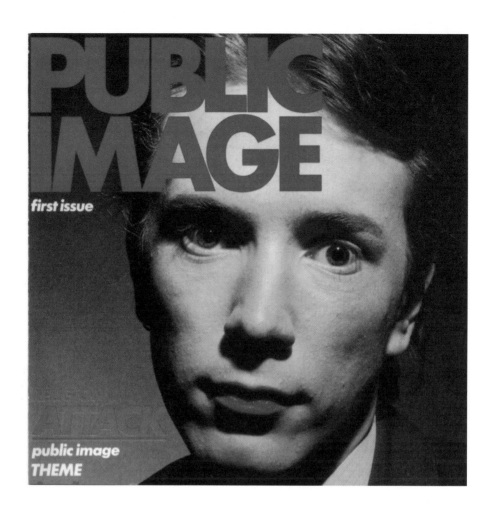

PUBLIC IMAGE

first issue

public image
THEME

ADRENALIN
TG   IR0015
INDUSTRIAL RECORDS LTD.

DISTANT DREAMS (PART TWO)
TG   IR0015
INDUSTRIAL RECORDS LTD.

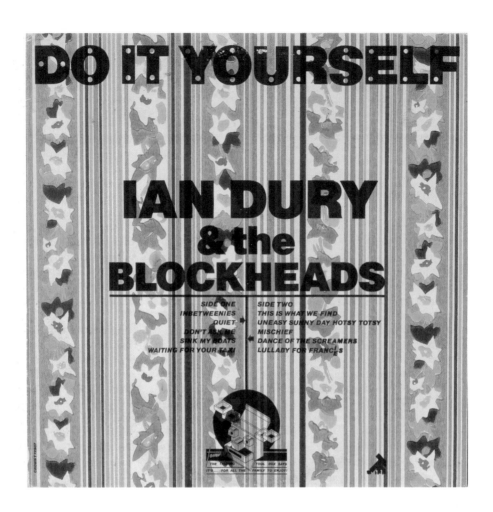

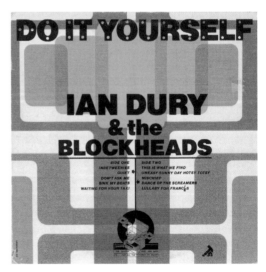

of the Moors Murders,[11] TG pushed sado-masochistic performance to its limits:

> Is it only legality that prevents the artist from slaughter of human beings as performance? … Ian Brady and Myra Hindley photographed landscapes on the Moors in England where they had buried children after sexually assaulting and killing them. Landscapes that only have meaning when perceived through their eyes. Art is perception of the moment. Action. Conscious. Brady as a conceptual performer? … What separates crime from art action? Is crime just unsophisticated or 'naive' performance art? Structurally Brady's photos, Hindley's tapes, documentation.[12]

This 'investigation' into the links between art, sex, prostitution and crime, provoked press malpractice and misinterpretation at a time when most of their short attention span was focused on the Pistols.[13] As a result, P-Orridge received a number of death threats. Satirically exposing the hypocrisy of this situation, 'Death Threats' appeared as a track on *Dead on Arrival: The Third and Final Report of Throbbing Gristle* (1978). The record sleeve dryly alludes to child pornography, involvement with which P-Orridge was also being wrongly accused of at the time.

COUM's feud with the 'straight' artworld was clear, as P-Orridge encouraged the use of text as purely graphic, verbal abstraction, stating that: 'In much contemporary art words are juxtaposed with images and photographs. I do the same in a small exchangeable format. (It amuses me to parody real world/art world).'[14] As for many punk designers, radical amateurism demanded a humorous assault on categorisation and intellectualisation. In many ways this served to challenge the pretensions of semiotic art and rectify the solicitous nature of educational photography by transforming them into humorous forms of insubordination. Early punk graphics derided the vogue for appending abstruse theoretical texts with fetishistic imagery: 'COUM have nothing to say and they're saying it. Make your own theory. COUM have no game to play and they're playing it.'[15]

However, by maintaining a contradictory and absurd stance, much punk design refused to establish the wider contexts in which it might retain a critical stance or challenge viewers to shift the goalposts for themselves. The punk fascination with highly conventional textual and visual cues of crime stories and pornography tended to disallow the ability to manipulate words and images to suggest new meanings:

> To suggest that the prerogative of art is simply to touch on possibilities without comment surely shows an insufficient grasp of visual rhetoric … Surely he must see that no amount of manipulation of context can redeem the use of the gas-chamber logo; in purely artistic terms, which he cannot escape, there are such things as a sense of diminished responsibility and a law of diminishing returns.'[16]

While the arbitrariness of verbal and visual language allowed for graphic artist's manipulation, their control over what was ultimately signified was tenuous at best. For better or worse, punk designers were unwilling to fully manipulate their audience's conclusions, that is, the artist's authority, once the work was in production, was ignored. Yet, even this much was never quite certain with TG. As a riposte to their tarnished image, TG appeared in Arran knit sweaters with Land Rover on an English coastal hillside for *20 Jazz Funk Greats*, one of the highlights of *Destroy*.

Given that playing games is the major design concern here, the emphasis in design of the later 1970s and early 1980s shifts away from 'punk' bands, towards New Wave and New Romantic bands. From the point of view of designers in 1976, such designs would not be 'punk'. This, however, presupposes that punk graphic design was primarily a question of form. It may seem absurd today to think that punk imagery could still be valued for its 'subcultural' status, but it remains clear that it contributed more than a little to changing the social, economic and political topography of Britain. Nonetheless, for many in the late 1970s, regarding record sleeve designs as possible solutions to the problem of the artist's contribution to the perpetuation of an oppressive system, would have made them guilty of the egotism and elitism they deplored: 'If they did anything, they made a lot of people content with being nothing. They certainly didn't inspire the working classes.'[17] Such New Wave sensibilities therefore tend to dominate a great deal of the designs exhibited in *Destroy*.

In all, this seems to have been particularly pressing given that *Destroy* is the third in an annual series of exhibitions at the South Bank Centre entitled *Towards the Millennium*, each of which aim to capture the 'zeitgeist' of a decade through its art or design. Hence, we are given the impression that, from 1978, a greater number of sleeve designs became more absolute, while others look like baroque creations fit to challenge the collection of souvenirs of art history that inspired them. In most cases, however, the carnivalesque and agitational side of punk seems to convert to an emphasis upon record-design-as-commodity. Given that many sleeve designers had quickly abandoned the anti-aesthetic, the emphasis on commodity fetishism was an ingenious means of ensuring that records did not lose their newly acquired art status.

The sleeves selected for the later section of the exhibition explore the ways in which designers sought to correlate style and function when both were in an indeterminate context, producing designs without being preoccupied with the appearance of making or effacing art. The ironic 'Industrial' style which had been initiated by TG in the lead up to the 'Winter of Discontent', was reformulated and taken literally by technological determinists such as Cabaret Voltaire, Brian Eno, and Ben Kelly. Ultra-elegant Industrial sleeves inspired a plethora of designers to lovingly refine the utopian aspirations of ubiquitous modernist schools of design. Drawing on Garrett's successful appropriation of International Constructivist styles, Peter Saville turned his back on felt-tip and photomontage, and injected a melodramatic sentiment of romantic disintegration into the late 1970s by highjacking modernist design for a new generation of 'pale boys' raised on Kraftwerk and Berlin Bowie. Saville elicited a busy abstract sublime, activated by an engaging tension between a mass-produced look and a painstakingly handworked feel to the finished products for Joy Division, New Order and The Durutti Column. The operative tone of Factory designs remained hopeful and visionary, but exuded a powerful lack of meaning and place, creating an look which was neither critical nor nostalgic, but evolutionary.

Prophetically, Peter York once regarded punk designers as a important guides to this new Leisure Class, a new moneyed class which rejected the academic values of the middle-classes, replacing the pedantic rationality of 'good taste' with 'a pluralism of pleasure.'[18] Certainly, Thatcher's emphasis on self-fulfillment, authenticity, and freedom of choice had an obvious appeal to participants in the sixties cultural revolution, many of whom were impresarios. Hence, in liberal post punk design, the consumer was king, driven by the desire to maximise pleasure. New Romantic design was a part of the raw, uncouth, socially, psychologically and sexually insecure new elite who were either unable or unwilling to attain the 'academic

values' associated with Old Labour, values which had secured some members of the excluded a safe path to success since World War II. Such designers were set to take the lead in the corporate image-centred world of the 1980s. New Romantic sleeves openly celebrated the erasure of historical claims to knowledge made by the academic estate, while maligning the nihilism and amateurism of Punk by re-establishing a perfectionist emphasis on image and 'product'. Bow Wow Wow's sources are absurdly eclectic. *See Jungle! See Jungle! Go Join Your Gang, Yeah. City All Over! Go Ape Crazy* (1981, RCA), Nick Egan's translation of Manet's *Luncheon on the Grass*, made the pointed suggestion that style and content were both subservient to the vagaries of fashion, stirring up a superficiality that would often border on neurosis. Following a similar line of reasoning Steve Strange, ex-frontman of punk outfit The Moors Murderers, formed the 'collective studio project' Visage in 1979 with Blitz DJ Rusty Egan, Midge Ure and Billy Currie of Ultravox, and John McGeoch, Dave Formula and Barry Adamson from Magazine. Announcing it 'leisure time for the pleasure boys', they quickly found themselves invited to all the right cosmopolitan parties with rich high profile social termites so despised by punk, and henceforth became the whipping boy of the music press. Robotic beats, banks of varied synthesizers, flattened vocals, and the message of terminally repeated choruses concealed the void between dead-end daily jobs and night time fantasies of The New Darlings of Decadence, who, deriding the conventionality of fashionable outrage, heralded the new order of posing:

> New styles, New shapes
> New modes, they're to roll my fashion tapes
> Oh my visage
> Visuals, magazines, reflex styles
> Past, future, in extreme
> Oh my visage[19]

Strange's desire to substantiate and enrich his own image by depicting his own body as the source of his style was quintessentially New Romantic. The 1982 retrospective album *The Anvil* (Polydor), named after New York's infamous leather 'n' bondage dive, was launched at Strange's very own Paris fashion show. The album cover saw Strange in a Luchino Visconti movie-still photographed by the master of soft porn and presentation incarnate, Helmut Newton. Inevitably, Saville was responsible for the ceremonial graphics.

John Cooper Clarke

This is today's conversation piece!

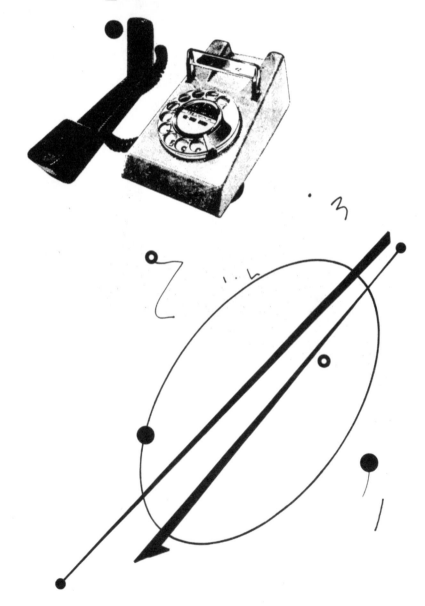

(I MARRIED A) MONSTER FROM OUTER SPACE *(Clarke/Hannett/Hopkins)*

I fell in love with an alien being
Whose skin was jelly, whose teeth were green
She had big bug eyes and the death ray glare
Feet like water wings, purple hair
I was over the moon, I asked her back to my place
And then I married the monster from outer space
The days were numbered the nights were spent
In a rent-free furnished oxygen tent
Where a cyborg chef served up moon beans
Done super-rapid on a laser beam
I needed nutrition to keep up the pace
When I married the monster from outer space
We walked out tentacle in hand
You could sense that the earthlings wouldn't understand
They'd go nudge nudge when we got off the bus
Saying 'It's extra-terestial, not like us'
And 'It's bad enough with another race,
But fuck me a monster from outer space'.
In a cybernetic fit of rage
She pissed off to another age
She lives in 1999
With her new boyfriend, a blob of slime
Each time I see a translucent face
I remember the monster from outer space.

©1977 *Spilt Beans/April Music Ltd*

Despite being responsible for the slick consumer packaging of Public Image Ltd.'s *Public Image* (1978), the typewritten amateurism of punk fanzines such as *South London Stinks* (Anon. 1977) remained in the early issues of Terry Jones' *iD*. This magazine was quickly transformed into a market leader, as the editorial emphasis switched entirely to fashion, its punky credentials distancing it from advocates of the heinous 'graphix' style found in late 1970s fashion journals such as *VIZ: Art, Photography, Fashion*. With Garrett occasionally helping out with design, *iD* succeeded to switch the British Fashion Press's emphasis away from prosaic interviews with 'Them' designers such Zandra Rhodes and the Logan Brothers. Instead was lucid reportage of the outrageous fashions being worn 'on the streets' and at venues such as Blitz, St. Moritz, Hell, Le Kilt and Le Beetroot where nightclubbers had been turning up as living works of art. Here was a sharp, timely contrast to the grubbiness of punk. Theatrical get-ups; swashbuckling pirate clothing, Kabuki masks, make-up, and transvestites were all welcomed. There were sad Pierrot clowns, majorettes, toy soldiers, puritans and Carmen Mirandas. *VIZ* went into receivership, while Strange's Eighties Set took off. Following two entire editions of *The Face* (English for 'Visage') devoted to them,[20] the Now Crowd suddenly became an international movement, 'The Cult with No Name', with an article in *Time*, and lavish spreads in continental magazines from *Stern* to *Vogue*.

Not all New Wave design was as slick and polished as the airbrushed glam that punk rebelled against; nor was it all obsessed with mannerism and the sound of commodities fucking. One direction was the theatrical engagement with 'class' taken in designs such as Barney Bubbles' numerous editions of Ian Dury and the Blockheads' *Do-It-Yourself* (1979, Stiff). Far from being alienated youths, Dury and the Blockheads were ex-art school students (Dury even taught at Canterbury and the RCA) and greatly accomplished musicians. Consequently, Bubbles, another punk designer who had been to art school, took this opportunity to make a humorous jibe at the affected amateurism of de rigeur DIY punk graphics, designing a number of sleeves which resembled schoolbooks covered in scraps of flock wallpaper from the early 1970s. Similarly, John Cooper Clarke, once heralded as the New Wave George Formby, is a poet who, like Ian Dury, had been around for some time but only started to come into his own with the advent of the New Wave:

> You can look at things like Dada and Surrealism and reject it for being a middle-class phenomenon. I think people in the New Wave have done the smart thing and walked into those areas. Now you've got a kind of working class vision of things. I don't think I've ever seen a punk rock group that didn't have something very imaginative about it. It's not being a traitor to your class to go into those areas. It only widens your perspective.[21]

Saville's sleeve for *Snap, Crackle & Bop* (Epic, 1980) represents Clarke's trademark three-piece suit complete with tab collar, shades and JCC punky lapel badges. The 'pocket' comes with Bubbles-designed book of poetry styled like a Telephone Directory, the lyrics overlaid on pages listing the names Cooper or Clarke. With music handled by The Invisible Girls (experienced Mancunian hands Martin 'Zero' Hannett, Pete Shelley, Bill Nelson, and Vinni Reilly) the New Romantic stance as a parody of design, utilising theatrical breaks with 'straight' culture, was both pointedly mocked and cherished:

> Don't doubt your own identity
> Dress down to cool anonymity
> The Pierre Cardin line to infinity
> Clothes to climb in the meritocracy
> The new age of benevolent bureaucracy.[22]

The intellectualisation of youth subculture was one of many targets of Clarke's drollery:

> Twin wheeled existentialists steeped in the sterile excrement of a doomed democracy 'oose post-Nietszchian sensibilities reject the bovine gregariousness of a senile oligarchy.[23]

While *Destroy* is warts and all—including ABC and Duran Duran—it would be unfair to say that the 'punk artifice' parable has been allowed to run unhindered. The curators, perhaps daunted at the number of previous attempts to analyse punk, have settled with displaying everything taxonometrically and in approximate chronological order. This modernist hang was not entirely a contemptible suppression of contingency, given that it gave scope for critical acknowledgment that cultural artifacts are the products of competing value-systems. Hovering in their transparent sleeves, 'punk' graphic designs are bracketed as open verdicts, allowing full

mm

criticism to run as the final, unwritten chapter. Visitors can examine stylistic shifts and provide monolithic theoretical justification for them, or openly consider the indeterminate relationships between the different factions involved without adopting the pretense that anything is capable of resolution. When beginning to consider if Reid's work has been juxtaposed with the first twelve felt-tip pen and typewriter script issues of Glasgow's version of *Sniffin' Glue* to emphasise or undermine punk professionalism, tacit acknowledgment that the hang functions as a reminder that the culture of our age is one that is never finished. Since rules change in accordance with the needs of time and situational modalities, it would seem fair to say that exhibitions such as *Destroy* are one of a series of games played according to undetermined rules. The speculation never ends.

A version of this piece was originally published in *Variant* magazine, no. 5, spring 1998.

NOTES
1. John Cooper Clarke, 'Punk Rock Revival', specially commissioned for *The List* in 1997.
2. Jamie Reid in Jon Savage, *Up They Rise: The Incomplete Works of Jamie Reid* (Faber & Faber, London, 1987), p. 55.
3. MINDA, 'MINDA', in T. Dennett, D. Evans, S. Gohl, & J. Spence, (eds.), *Photography/Politics: One* (Photography Workshop, London, 1979), p. 125.
4. Peter York, 'The Clone Zone (Night of the Living Dead)', in *Style Wars* (Sidgewick & Jackson, London, 1980), p. 47.
5. Malcolm Garrett, quoted in 'Graphics', in *Creative Review*, February 1998, p. 37.
6. Ben Kelly quoted in Domenic Cavendish, 'The Great Rock & Roll Exhibition', in *The Independent* (Style), 31 January–6 February, p. 5.
7. See footnote 10.
8. Jamie Reid in Jon Savage, *Up They Rise: The Incomplete Works of Jamie Reid* (Faber & Faber, London, 1987), p. 43.
9. Ben Khera quoted in *Attitude*, February 1998.
10. 'The passive nihilist compromises with his own lucidity about the collapse of all values. Bandwagon after bandwagon works out its own version of the *credo quia absurdum est*: you don't like it but you do it anyway; you get used to it and you even like it in the end. Passive nihilism is an overture to conformism. [...] Between the two poles stretches a no-mans-land, the waste land of the solitary killer, of the criminal described so aptly by Bettina as the crime of the state. Jack the Ripper is essentially inaccessible. The mechanisms of hierarchical power cannot touch him; he cannot be touched by the revolutionary will.' Raoul Vaneigem, 'Desolation Row' (1967), translated in *King Mob Echo*, No. 1, April 1968, Pygmalion Press, London, p. 7.
11. Throbbing Gristle, 'Introduction' (1:01), 'Very Friendly' (15:54), *Throbbing Gristle Live Volume One 1976–1978* (Mute).
12. Genesis P-Orridge and Peter Christopherson, 'Annihilating Reality', in *Studio International*, July/August 1976, p. 44.
13. Tony Roinson, 'Moors Murder "Art" Storm', in *Sunday Mirror*, 15th August, 1976, p. 9.
14. Genesis P-Orridge, 'Statement by Genesis P-Orridge to his Solicitor April 5th 1976', in *G.P.O. versus G.P-O: A Chronicle of Mail Art on Trial Coumpiled by Genesis P-Orridge* (Ecart, Switzerland, 1976).
15. COUM Transmissions, 'What Has COUM to Mean? : Thee Theory Behind COUM', typewritten statement, undated, COUM Transmissions/ Throbbing Gristle Archive, National Art Library, V&A, London, 1990.
16. Stuart Morgan, 'What the Papers Say', in *Artscribe* 18, July 1979, pp. 18–19.
17. Ian Birch, 'In The Beginning', in *The Book With No Name* (Omnibus, London, 1981) p. 11.
18. Ian Chambers, 'Urban Soundscapes 1976–: The Paradoxes of Crisis', in *Urban Rhythms: Pop Music and Popular Culture* (Macmillan, Hampshire, 1985), p. 199.
19. Visage, 'Visage'.
20. *The Face*, Nos. 7–8.
21. John Cooper Clarke, in *New Musical Express*, January 28th, 1978.
22. John Cooper Clarke, 'Euro Communist / Gucci Socialist', in *Ten Years in an Open Neck Shirt* (Arrow/Arena Books, London, 1983), p. 10.
23. John Cooper Clarke, 'Psycle Sluts, Part 1', *Disguise in Love* (Epic, 1978).

A serialized novel by
Heman Chong
+ Leif Magne Tangen
+ Melissa Lim

CHAPTER ONE

Keller woke up with a start and found himself sprawled on the floor of his bedroom. From the corner of his eyes, he could see a woman stumble onto her feet and move away towards the far side of the room. He tried to place her, but his memory failed him, and he contented himself with merely observing her movements from afar in silence.

He rubbed the sleep away from his eyes and looked around. Keller could see that there was something strange about the configuration of his room, something foreign—as if someone had torn the side of it away and inserted another room. Yet, how could that be possible? It is incredulous. It was just getting too confusing for him. He struggled to get to his feet and peered at the woman again, only to notice her seeming equally as disorientated and begin to weep silently. He turned away and tried to focus his attention on the altered surroundings.

The lines the room were completely distorted, which blurred his immediate view—the lack of straight planes had made it all slightly out of focus. Keller massaged his eyes once more in the hopes that this would dispel the discombobulation.

That did not work.

Keller stood in his place, still bewildered as he tried to regain composure. It took a long time for his eyes to get use to this new geometry. Even then, he could feel a faint, dull throbbing in his head as his mind strained to process this newly imposed space. He tried focusing concentrating on a particular spot; one where he was sure he knew the wall ought to be. There was no longer a single focal point, but thousands, brand new and unfamiliar.

Keller thought of the kaleidoscope he used to fiddle with as a boy. He felt faint at this memory. He shook his head to clear his head, swore silently to himself and tried once again to f-o-c-u-s.

F-O-C-U-S.

No.

Keller sighed. He stood up and climbed over the debris of what used to be his bedroom—or was it? He moved towards the woman, who was cowering at the corner of the room, staring at him with wary eyes. Trying not to catch her gaze, Keller slowly sat himself beside the woman. He could tell that she was slightly afraid of him, yet somewhat comforted that she was not alone in this nightmare.

They sat there for a long time in silence, unable to react to anything in their immediate surroundings, nor what had possibly transpired between them.

'Do you know what the fuck is going on around here?' she asked.

He shook his head, unable to give an answer. He wrestled with possible explanations for this phenomenon while trying to find a way out.

How can there be an exit where architecture itself doesn't exist anymore?

Is architecture predicated on familiarity of form? And if so, is one able to react to a situation only by dint of memory?

The girl tried to stand up once more, but failed. Keller looked intently at the floor, pretending to ignore her discomfort. Strangely enough, at least it was still in one piece, he thought. He kept his eyes focused the floor, braced himself and hoisted his body upwards.

Good. It felt stable enough. He felt an ounce of confidence.

AT LEAST THE FUCKING FLOOR IS STILL THERE.

He inhaled deeply and began to speak.

'Now, listen to me. My name is Keller… I'm going to try and see if there's anyone else here. You have to help me by keeping calm, ok? I promise I'll be back soon.'

He paused and turned to look at her.

The girl nodded mutely.

She looked helpless. She couldn't be complicit with this whole mess.

Keller looked around. To his surprise, he discovered a door latch right beneath his feet. He knelt and undid the latch and lifted the door carefully. After hesitating for a moment, he opened the door, which relented without a creak.

… as if the hinges were well-seasoned and oiled.

Keller peered into the gaping hole, waiting for his eyes to adjust to the new level of illumination, trying not to be surprised even if he see a cheshire cat.

The next room was as distorted as his bedroom, an appearance not unlike some kind of strange pastiche-implosion sick joke. Not only that but he also noticed that the lines demarcating the edges of his bedroom continued seamlessly from his room into the one he was looking at. It was impossible to distinguish the room's form each other. What he saw was a cluster of spaces, all meshed together by something or someone. *Something that spoke of an external force.* As if a gigantic hand had created a flawless lattice of voids. It was as if Keller was balanced on an intersecting series of endless grids. The architectural structure shifted incessantly, as if it enjoyed a freedom and life of its own. This all seemed fresh to him, and in a way, pure. There was an uncanny yet alluring beauty to the visual pattern of this new architecture, and it mesmerised him and confounded him simultaneously.

He found his balance and walked steadily into the next room. Here, he discovered that his feet were planted firmly on the ceiling of the room. But he could feel gravity's pull and checked that he wasn't floating or anything. No. Solid ground. It was just simply that the room had been turned upside down, an inversion of the previous one he had just left. He glanced at the litter of furniture emerging from the floor above—or rather, what used to be 'above'—and smiled knowingly to himself.

Gliding from one room to the next, each resembling a misfit child of post-modern architecture, Keller found himself wondering if this labyrinth was ever going to end. It was fun and novel when it began, but his initial euphoria had died away. In its place, a growing confusion and panic began to seep into his consciousness. He felt exhausted, like a child getting weary of a new toy.

Shaking his head, as if to rid it of negative thoughts, he struggled to move towards another door, which turned out to be a window—a deceptive one though, he soon realised, as it exposed itself to be no more than a photograph of another space. Keller swallowed the lump in his throat and bit his lip. He was angry and could no longer think straight.

In any case, what difference would a thought—let alone thinking straight, make in this situation anyway when the fundamental notions of space no longer conform to basic rules… rules that he, and presumably the rest of the world, were familiar with.

He marched from one room to the next, feeling a mounting sense of frustration and dismay that were becoming uncontrollable.

Just then, he heard a small voice muttering something:

'Hey you. Thanks for coming back.'

Keller whirled around.

There she was, the same girl he had left in his own room only minutes ago—or had it been hours? She was seated on the wall, leaning against the floor.

Never mind that.

He took a deep breath and walked over to her. It was surprisingly easy to convince his mind that a wall could be walked on. He turned his head around, gazing at the way he had came from.

Strange.

Keller took a deep breath, and exhaled in exasperation…

'What's your name?' he asked.

'That sounds like a question I'd like to ask you,' she retorted.

'Don't get tetchy with me. I'm just as…'

'Confused as I am? Of course you are. Now, if you would like to explain how you'd conned me into your room in the first place…'

'That's bullshit! I'm just about to ask you what the fuck you're doing here!' Keller could feel his blood pressure rising. He suddenly noticed that his fingernails were digging into the flesh of his palm.

The woman glared at him and sprung up to her feet. 'There,' she hissed, pointing at the door that Keller had emerged from a moment ago. 'That is my bedroom. And this,' she gestured towards Keller's bedroom. 'This is my living room. Or rather, it used to be my living room until you decided to take up residence here…'

'Look, I don't want to kick up a fuss here, but I'd seriously appreciate it if you just took your leave now,' Keller said behind gritted teeth. 'As far as I am concerned, you have bloody crashed into my world, and I don't need this to start the day off.'

The woman glowered at Keller for a moment. Then her shoulders loosened and hunched slightly, and she slid her back down against the wall. Keller ran his clammy fingers through his disheveled hair as he watched her body quiver gently with sobs.

'I don't understand,' they both echoed at the same time.

Keller turned his attention back to the structure of the room. The lines continued to relocate themselves, converging and diverging intermittently, whilst maintaining that bewildering seamlessness from one room to the next. He let his eyes trace a path along one particular shifting line that stretched onto the next space, halting only at a sharp corner of the room.

That was when that sense of realization which struck him earlier as he explored the myriad spaces reiterated itself.

'That next room... you said that's your bedroom?' he queried the woman cautiously.

He was aware of her nodding slightly. He found himself bopping his head in time with hers, as if in concurrence.

'Now... it... it kind of looks more like mine,' Keller said haltingly.

'I'm sure it's mine. I have no idea who you are or what you want or what is happening, but I AM SURE THAT THIS IS MY APARTMENT!' she screamed.

Truth is, Keller couldn't tell one from the other anymore. If anything, the desperation and futility he felt within him and the sense of panic he was trying to conceal echoed in the demeanor of the woman.

He walked into the next room, opened a window and jumped out.

To be continued
(www.dot-dot-dot.nl)

REVIEW[1]

For every forgetting seems to have its price[2]

… is one of the most fascinating artists of the last ten years, and at the same time one of the most difficult to understand. As a student, … encountered Guy Debord's Situation Theory, the Structuralism of Lacan, Levi-Strauss, Barthes and Foucault, and Post-structuralism of Baudrillard and Derrida.[3] …'s knowledge of visual culture was derived from television.[4] However, in the last few years … has refused to identify his/her sources, claiming that knowledge of these would only restrict interpretation of …'s work.[5]

Throughout the 20th century, many ordinary objects were called art.[6] The principle of appropriation was originally developed by Marcel Duchamp at the beginning of the 20th century, reaching a climax in the 1960s with Pop Art. At the end of the 1970s it came back into fashion and, even more so than in Pop Art, pictures from advertising or television were adopted wholesale by artists for use in their own work.[7] The world is packed with information, … seems to suggest. Before experiences come, one has already learnt all about them, so what is there to get excited about?[8]

Solutions and final conclusions are never on offer. …'s works function in precisely the same way: they are never complete, always undergoing a process of alteration. Their validity is a short duration, but in this brief time, they hit the viewer's feelings exactly.[9] … demonstrates that artistic concern with the present can be handled not only in photography, film, Conceptual and installation art, painting but also in …[10].

… operates suggestively with our perception of the outside world, its association-laden structures, colours, forms, illusions and clichés.[11] A complex world needs rules in order to function, but these should always demonstrate their purpose in an atmosphere of tolerance and reason. This idealistic sense of social concord is a constant theme in …'s artworks. Thus … presents something in context of art that is only too often counteracted in everyday life.[12] …'s installations, photographs and objects emphasise, in an unpretentious and yet precise way, moments of displacement and the disappearance of space and time.

… emphasises this aspect in the pieces *Ohne Titel (Untitled)*.[13] They reveal, both in their triviality and their vitality, the intimate and mundane nature of the passage of time. This breathtaking amassing of production touches on the deeper meaning of an art that is totally synchronised with the duration of life as it is lived.[14] A network of allusions is the result, which mixes biographical components with historical and mythological narrative threads in a typically Postmodern style.[15] Works have different realities. Thus … presents overlays in time. Diverse things happen at diverse moments, even with the same material or in the same place. Witnessing this process, the viewer begins to realise that reality eludes every kind of documentation.[16]

An unorthodox conception of history emerges. This is not cut and dried, but shifts with the perspective selected. …'s compositional openness is therefore more than a principle of style: he/she opposes the desire for order and control that is often visible in architecture and the organisation of interiors.[17] …'s work seems unfinished, both in terms of presentation and of content.[18] His/her open-handedness in fact challenges the mechanisms of art presentation, creating a crossover between the visual arts and other artistic activities.[19] Among them is his/her presentation or imitation of natural phenomena as art, while at the same time obviously revealing the technique used to recreate it without diminishing the impressively subtle effect. … is not primarily interested in the distinction between nature and machine but in the viewer's relationship to both.[20]

Just when one has been taking in by his/her aesthetic offerings, they turn out to be tricks. It is for instance impossible for the reader of this book not to touch the following two pages ('as the concept of this article, … would like the following two pages not to be touched'), because he/she has to turn them over before can carry on reading.[21] He/she is also concerned with social consequences of intervention in the ecosystem and their relationship to financial and symbolic values.[22]

Subsequently, his/her concepts became more complex.[23] …'s protagonists are often linked with social or political events. …'s theme is the moulding of individual behaviour through the mass media and social structures.[24] … conjures up independent worlds in which his memories and inventions intermingle.[25] … subtly combined personal experiences and ideas from art theory with political points of view. … often reflects aspects of this particular position as a gay artist from Cuba, but without falling into banal clichés.[26] Why, for instance, are pictures of black actresses usually underexposed while white men are brightly lit? But for all the political rhetoric, the work is also fascinating because of its occasionally sentimental nostalgia—the objective of all battles is simply 'winning back beauty'.[27] … is not concerned here with ironic exposure of his subject, but with analytical observation.[28] The works do not encourage direct identification with their subjects, for he keeps them in a distant perspective.[29] Advertising, propaganda and missionary appeals work like magnets. If they are successful, they catch the masses by the throat, draw the close and do not let them go again.[30]

Subsequent developments are normally left unresolved.[31] The works may seem skittish at first sight, but after a few moments one senses their profoundity.[32] Their boundaries become visible but also open.[33] They reflect the conditions of the perception, the peculiarities of his/her medium and the (implicit) political dimension of its use.[34] But what might seem like amateur mistakes actually represent a detailed examination of the medium.[35] Within these works, we don't know whether the she-wolf is standing in front of us or behind us; whether the herd of horses is stamping about above or below us.[36] …'s theme is the ordinary day, the public space, presented so subtly that no information gets lost.[37] Always being watched—this was true not only in the GDR, but also characterises the reality of the Postmodern network.[38]

In many of his works, … refers in multifarious ways to the works of other artists.[39] From time to time, artist friends help to produce …'s works. This enables … to defy the romantic myth of the autonomous artistic genius, and to widen his/her work with additional facets of content and style.[40] No comment is made. The participants all have their own ideas and perceptions, but they keep them to themselves.[41]

NOTES
1. By Valentinas Klimašauskas; all subsequent sentences are taken from Burkhard Riemschneider & Uta Grosenick (eds.), *Icons, Art Now* (Taschen, Köln, 2001).
2. Astrid Wege on Mike Kelley, p. 85.
3. Jean-Michel Ribettes on Peter Halley, p. 65.
4. Raimar Stange on Tracey Moffatt, p. 108.
5. Susanne Titz on Thomas Demand, p. 34.
6. Cristoph Blasé on Katharina Fritsch, p. 50.
7. Cristoph Blasé on Richard Prince, p. 134.
8. Cristoph Blasé on Eija-Liisa Ahtila, p. 13.
9. Cristoph Blasé on Liam Gillick, pp. 54–55.
10. Susanne Titz on Franz Ackermann, p. 10.
11. Susanne Titz on Franz Ackermann, p. 10.
12. Cristoph Blasé on Angela Bulloch, p. 24.
13. Astrid Wege on Andreas Gursky, p. 62.
14. Jean-Michel Ribettes on Nobuyoshi Araki, p. 17.
15. Raimar Stange on Keith Edmier, p. 40.
16. Cristoph Blasé on Pierre Huyghe, p. 80.
17. Astrid Wege on Candida Hofer, p. 70.
18. Cristoph Blasé on Liam Gillick, pp. 54–55.
19. Yilmaz Dziewior on Cosima von Bonin, p. 22.
20. Yilmaz Dziewior on Olafur Eliasson, p. 42.
21. Raimar Stange on Andreas Slominski, p. 152.
22. Yilmaz Dziewior on Dan Peterman, p. 125.
23. Susanne Titz on Gillian Wearing, p. 170.
24. Astrid Wege on Paul McCarthy, p. 106.
25. Yilmaz Dziewior on Kai Althoff, p. 14.
26. Yilmaz Dziewior on Felix Gonzalez-Torrez, p. 58.
27. Raimar Stange on Zoe Leonard, p. 96.
28. Yilmaz Dziewior on John Currin, p. 30.
29. Susanne Titz on Rineke Dijkstra, p. 36.
30. Susanne Titz on Barbara Kruger, p. 91.
31. Astrid Wege on Jeff Wall, p. 169.
32. Cristoph Blasé on Philippe Parreno, p. 120.
33. Astrid Wege. on Gerwald Rockenshaub, p. 145.
34. Astrid Wege on Thomas Ruff, p. 146.
35. Cristoph Blasé on Diana Thater, p. 158.
36. Cristoph Blasé on Diana Thater, p. 158.
37. Cristoph Blasé on Thomas Struth, p. 154.
38. Raimar Stange on Jane and Louise Wilson, p. 176.
39. Yilmaz Dziewior on Georg Herold, p. 66.
40. Yilmaz Dziewior on Franz West, pp. 172–173.
41. Cristoph Blasé on Vanessa Beecroft, p. 20.

Tourette Syndrome: Instantaneously Present John Russell

Stretched across the surface like a squirrel pegged out on the grass, my head is clamped and I am instantaneously presented (both theatrically and un-theatrically) to the aesthetics of my own stinking bourgeois mor(t)ality.

You dirty bastards, don't you realise there are real women and children dying out there? You bloodless, Socratised, cock-sucking, Plato-junky wankers! Come behind this red rock and I will show you *real* terror in a handful of cultural studies, sociology and stylised politics!

I will show you real terror but more of that later. I guess … I guess I come from the wrong side of town but I'm going back there as soon as possible. But as you say 'I see very well what this cover of *Paris Match* means to me'. **You lying bastard!** – no, you don't – you don't see – you can't see – that's the point – you can't see – you're blinded! You fucking cunt! This is a screen of screaming heads!

I'm blind! I'm blind! I'm cracked – like a used cyanide capsule! I'm trapped – like a *screaming monkey!* I'm pinned from behind, with my eye blown out in front, splattered across the surface – slipping across the surface in a further play of signification and visuality, the process overlapping and underlapping in the microscopy of figure, skin, pore, atom – searching for intelligibility and unintelligibility alike in the shine and sweat of the paint.

This is a glutinous coming-to-be – oscillating and repeating across the liquid slick of gore and slime, with the movement of maggots swarming and bulging beneath the swilling surface; with the germs fucking and procreating above and the torso swollen and bursting to expose the jellied organs within – pinks and gay reds *… and then there are the mauves!*

Oh yes, *always* there are the mauves but I am pinned – pinned in the instantaneously present, so I can't see them – nailed like a fucking grape – reality is reflected in my eye *and now who is going to tell me London is owned by the big corporations?*

Ah yes … the big corporations … with the big paintings in their foyers … I remember them, but now as I watch, I feel bluebottle flies (Calliphora) laying their eggs in my eyes and mouth – and I see the green and orange stains of putrefaction creeping up my abdomen like a sunset; distension is visible; observable swelling of the body and blebbing, with purple transudate widespread; eyes bulging, organs and cavities bursting, veins marbling and the spread of putrefaction stains to neck and limbs. And you say: 'Put your hand into that pot of boiling water and tell me nothing can exist outside language'. Fuck off!

From a pamphlet accompanying the exhibition
Abstract Painting by Fabianne Audéoud & John Russell
at The International 3, Manchester, 2001.

SEMANTIC POETRY TRANSLATION[†] OF 'TOURETTE'S SYNDROME'

★

Being
made
taut & caused
        to
        extend so as
                to
                cross
                from   of said object
                        one side   boundary
                the   topmost
        of material constituting the
            layer
                                to
                                the other

Possessing   tail
the   bushy
traits   flexible
of   long
arboreal   a
rodents having
of
the genus Sciurus and related genera
of the family Sciuridae

Fastened with slender
                usually
                cylindrical
                pieces
                of
                wood
                or
                metal

† See: De Boer, 'You are, therefore I think:
the considerate iconicity of Stefan Themerson's
Semantic Poetry', in DDD9.

for holding
    parts
    together or serving as a
                    support
                    for
                    suspending
                    one
                    thing
                    from
                    another
        To

an expanse of ground covered with narrow-leaved green herbage or similar plants

        uppermost
The part of my body
        containing the brain
                &
            the eyes
                ears
                nose
                mouth
                &
                jaws
Is fastened
as if with a tool
            with opposing
            & often adjustable parts
                        for bracing objects

And   I   (by means suitable for
without   am   dramatic performance as well
perceptible offered   by means not suited to the stage)
delay   for
            observation, examination & consideration

An
underlying
set of principles
manifested by outward   or   style
              appearances   of
                                  behaviour

Of the highly offensive & abhorrent
        conformation to the standards & conventions
                            of
                            a middle class system
                                        of ideas of
                                        right & wrong
                                        conduct
                        belonging to myself

You malicious
        scandalous
        unethical
        corrupt offensive
                disagreeable people

Do you not perceive
              mentally outside
                        of the
                        position
                        of your
                        self
              the   young
              verifiable   adult   persons
              existence of female   between
                            humans   &   infancy
                                          &
                                          youth
              passing from physical life?

You people   who
are devoid   are indoctrinated   draw   are
of   in   male   so
human   the   copulatory ardently
emotion   beliefs   organs   devoted
or   of   into   to
feeling   Socrates   your   Plato
!   !   mouths   that
                                 by   the
                                 creating   devotion
                                 a   resembles
                                 practical   a
                                 vacuum   mastur-
                                 in   batory
                                 their   addiction
                                 mouths   !
                                 !

Advance to where I stand on
                          the
                          other
                          side of   this
                                    large body
                                    having the hue of
                                    the long-wave end of
                                    the visible spectrum
                                    evoked in the human
                                    observer by radiant
                                    energy with wavelengths
                                    of approx 630–750
                                    nanometers & made of
                                    hard, naturally formed
                                        petrified matter

And I will allow you to see intense
                          overpowering
                          fear

Contained in a small quantity of:		&
a	the	the methods
department	systematic	or tactics
of	study	involved
learning	of the	in
of the	development	managing
shared	structure	a state
knowledge	interaction	or government
&	&	using
values	collective	artistic forms
of a	behaviour	&
society	of	conventions
	organised	to
	groups	create
	of	effects
	human	!
	beings	

I will allow you to see intense
                overpowering
                fear that has verifiable
                        existence
On the other hand
a greater quantity of the idea
                of the previously expressed words
                will follow subsequently

Which is my opinion based on incomplete evidence …

              ★   ★

I form an opinion from little or no outward signs
I move toward something from a run-down
                    compactly settled area
      as distinguished from surrounding rural territory
but I'm moving on a course into the past
without undue time lapse
      within the limits of ability

But as you say
        'I perceive exactly as stated the faculty
        of intellectual
        or aesthetic perception
        or appreciation by
                the nearly spherical hollow organ that
                        is lined with a sensitive retina
                        is lodged in a bony orbit in the skull
                        is normally paired
                        is the vertebrate organ of sight
        what this front of a binding of *Paris Match*
        means to me'

You, marked by falsehoods
        born of parents not married to each other!
– no, you don't –
        you don't have the faculty of the organ
        lodged in a bony orbit in the skull
– that's the most distinguishing detail –
        you don't have the faculty of the organ
        lodged in a bony orbit in the skull

you have less than 1/10 of normal vision
in the more efficient organ of sight
        (20/200 or less on the Snellen test)
You engaged female pudenda
        that leads from the uterus to the external office
        of the genital canal
                engaged in physical union of
                male & female genitalia
                accompanied by rhythmic movements
                        (usually leading to the ejaculation
                        of semen from the penis
                        into the female reproductive tract)!

This is a protective device
        of upper or anterior division of the animal body
        producing harsh high tones!

I have less than 1/10 of normal vision in
the more efficient organ of sight!

I have less than 1/10 of normal vision in
the more efficient organ of sight!

I am broken into parts with suddenness & violence
        like a used gelatin packaging shell containing
        a compound of cyanogen,
                a univalent group
                    – CN with a more electropositive element!

I'm placed in a restricted position
        like a nonhuman primate mammal voicing
        sudden sharp loud cries in harsh high tones!

I'm held fast, immobile from toward the back
        with my nearly spherical hollow organ
                lined with a photosensitive retina
                from which nerve impulses
                are sent to the brain
        burst by explosion in front

spurt forth in
        scattered
        drops
        from one side
                    to the other
                    of the exterior boundary

moving with a smooth sliding motion from one side
to the other of the exterior boundary

an opportunity for action
        at a considerable distance in space
                to show by conventional token
                or other symbolic means
                and relating to a method of instruction
                involving sight

a continuous operation extending over
                & under
                occupying the same area in part
in the investigation
with an optical instrument consisting of
      a lens or combination of lenses for making
           enlarged images of minute objects
           of bodily shape or form
           external limiting tissue layer of body
           a minute opening by which matter passes
                through a membrane
           a unit of matter
           the smallest unit of an element
           having all the characteristics of that element
           and consisting of a dense, central
           positively charged nucleus
           surrounded by a system of

```
e         e         s
  l       l       n
    e     e     o
        c c r
e l e c t r o n s
        c r r
      e   o   o
  l       n       n
e         s         s
```

Thoroughly in an effort to find comprehension
      by the power of knowing
    & by not knowing
      in the same manner
in the bright by reflection of light
& to emit or exclude moisture
      in beads as a result of condensation
of a mixture of a pigment
      & a suitable liquid to form
      a closely adherent coating
      when spread on a surface in a thin coat

*   *   *

This is an entering
    or assuming of a condition
        an objective existence
        a reality that
          is   &
          to   gaining   likely
          be   in   to
          in   import-   advance
          the   ance   or
          future   succeed

Having the appearance
    of the hard protein substance
        resembling jelly
    that absorbs water to form a viscous solution
    with strong adhesive properties
 & that is obtained by cooking down materials
                  such as bones
                  or hides

Swinging backwards
     &   like a body suspended from a fixed point
     forwards   under the action of gravity
freely   & commonly used
          to regulate movements
             (as of clockwork)

& appearing again from
    &   one side to the opposite side
    again   of the smooth
    &   slippery
    again   surface
           of clotted blood
          & viscous mud
          flowing like water

With the changing of posture
                & position
                & place of soft-bodied
                        legless grubs   assembling
                        that are   in a crowd
                        the larvae   &
                        of dipterous   becoming
                        insects   protuberant

In a lower position than
the surface soaked thoroughly with that fluid
        having no independent shape
but having a definite volume
        not expanding indefinitely
&   being only slightly compressible;

With the small masses of living substance
                capable of developing into organisms
                engaging   (or one of their parts)
                in coitus
                with each other   in a higher position
                & bringing forth offspring

And the human body   expanded   &   broken
                apart   in size   open
                from   & volume   from
                the head   beyond   pressure
                &   a normal   within
                appendages limit
To
cause the differentiated structures within
to   consisting of cells & tissues
be   (the consistency of jelly)
open   & performing some specific function
to   in an organism
view –
        colours bluish red to red in hue
        of medium lightness
        & low to moderate saturation

&
bright
lively reds (resembling that of blood
                                     or the ruby)

...   &   between
                        about   blue
            moderate colors that fall midway &   in hue
                                               red
in addition
occupying their position in that place!

Oh yes   between
at all times   about   blue
the moderate colors that fall midway &   in hue
                                      red
occupy their position in that place

But I am held fast –
            held fast in the present
                        of this particular instant
so I can not perceive them –
            with my paired
                    hollow
                    nearly spherical
                    vertebrate organs of sight
                    that are lined with a senstive retina
                        & lodged in a bony orbit
                                    in my skull
Fastened like an
as   extremely obscene
if   contemptuous
with   disgusting
a   smooth-skinned
nail   juicy
            white with a tinge of
            berry   a colour midway yellow
                             between &   in hue
                                        blue

to deep red
or a colour midway   blue
between   &   in hue
red

(eaten dried or fresh as a fruit
or fermented to produce wine)

And what person is going to emphatically
or   express
which persons are   assurance to me at this
                           in   present
                           words   moment
                                           in
                                           time

The city & port in S.E. England
that is the capital of the United Kingdom
comprised of The City & 32 other boroughs
of an area of 632 square miles
        (or 1637 square kilometers)
& with a population of 6,377,900
      is held as property
      by the big bodies formed & authorized by law
                    to act as a single person
                    although constituted by
                            1 or more persons
                            & legally endowed
                            with rights & duties
                            including
                                the capacity
                                    of succession
                                        ?

        ★   ★   ★   ★

Ah yes …

The public bodies
of considerable magnitude
who are granted charters
        recognizing them as   separate
                           legal entities
        having their own   rights
                           privileges
                           & liabilities

              distinct from   those of
                           their members
…
                               lines
With products formed through application of &
    large in   with   colours
    dimensions   pigments
    bulk
    or extent   on a surface
                    for artistic effect
    positioned within
        the
    bounds of their entrance
              or reception rooms
        but
        in
        the
        momentary
        present
        as
… With effort I   I   I
    summon   observe   am conscious
    knowledge attentively of the physical
    of them   sensation
    from   coming from
    my memory   my discrete
                         end organs

Of blowflies
  with abdomens
        or   iridescent blue in colour
      whole bodies
                  who   &
                  breed   make
                  in   a
                  decaying loud   flight
                  organic   buzzing
                  matter   noise   in

Bring forth &
deposit
their animal reproductive bodies
      consisting of ovae
      together with   a
      their nutritive & protective envelopes   new
      each with the capacity to develop into   individual
                                            capable
                                            of
                                            independent
                                            existence

  into the pair of
hollow structures each with a lens
  located in bony   capable of focusing
  sockets of my   incident light
      skull   on an internal
                             photosensitive retina
                                            from which
              brain   nerve
                    the   impulses
                        to   sent are

as well as the cavity bounded inside   &   outside
          lying   by the   by the
          at   oropharynx lips
          the
          upper   containing
          end   tongue
          of   gums
          my alimentary canal   &
                                  teeth

& with my organs of sight
I apprehend discoloured spots
                      the colour of
      a hue   both   a hue between
      resembling   that   that
      that of   resembling   resembling
      fresh grass   the petals   blood
      or   of an   or
      the emerald   eponymous   the ruby
                           flower

Caused by the
          decomposition of   (typically anaerobic)
          organic matter by the splitting of proteins
                            by bacteria & fungi
        with the formation of foul-smelling
                            incompletely-oxidized
                            products

                opposite
Advancing in a direction along the part of my body
by   to   that lies between
slow   the   the thorax & the pelvis
imperceptible centre   which encloses
degrees   of   the stomach
                the   pancrea
                earth   liver
                            & spleen

                    normal dimensions
                    beyond
The process of being expanded is apparent
                    by pressure
                    from within

d i f f u s e d   o v e r   a   c o n s i d e r a b l e   e x t e n t

It is possible to observe
                    the organized physical substance
                    of my person
                    becoming puffy
                    as from internal bleeding
                              or accumulation of other fluid
                    & assuming the appearance
                                        (flaccid)
                              of a large blister

& a substance produced by the process
        with a hue   of passing through a
            between   membrane
        that   &   that   pore
        resembling   resembling   or interstice
        the petals   blood   in the
        of an   or   manner of
        eponymous   the ruby   perspira-
        flower   tion

        swelling up
Organs curving outward
of   protruding
sight

Bodily parts   each   or
        consisting performing cooperating
        of   a   in
        cells   different   an
        &   specific   activity
        tissues   function

                                                    apart
& other (hollow) areas breaking   open   flying
                        from   suddenly
                        internal   &
                        pressure   violently

Membranous
tubular
branching   mottled
vessels that carry blood acquiring a streaked effect
            from   resembling
            the   a metamorphic rock
            capillaries   formed by alteration
            toward   of limestone
            the   or dolomite
            heart   irregularly coloured
                                    by impurities

&
now   discoloured
the broader distribution of the spots
                            caused by the decay
                            of organic matter
                            (accompanied by
                            an offensive odour)

to the part of the body that joins the head
                            to the shoulders
& to the projecting
            paired   movement
        appendages used for &
                            grasping

        (sometimes modified into sensory or sexual organs)

&
you make a statement
the   by expressing in words
reader   the following opinion
                        belief
                        judgement
                        or determination of fact:

"Cause the terminal
            part of
            your arm   grasping
            generally used for &
                            holding
            consisting of a wrist
                        palm
                        4 fingers
                        & an
                        opposable
                thumb

                to be in the specific interior of
                a designated round fairly deep
                domestic container typically made of
                pottery metal or glass containing a clear
                odorless & tasteless liquid essential for
                most plant & animal life in the process
                of changing from a liquid to a vapour
                by the application of
                            heat

```
& communicate to me
    by          that
    speech      in
    or          the space
    writing     outside
                the boundary
                or limit                    thoughts
                of the communication of &
                        through         feelings
                        a
                        system      (including its rules
                        of          for combining
                        arbitrary   its components)
                        signals
                        such as voice sounds
                                gestures
                                or written symbols
                        usually used by a nation
                                        people
                                        or other community
```

The notion that *no thing is able to have actual being* ”

🙏 Go forth & multiply!

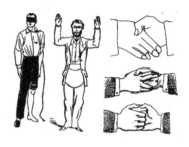

INAUGURATING THE PLEASUREDOME

Compiled by Jan Verwoert

'We know the scene: there is a gathering, and someone is telling a story. We do not yet know whether these people gathered together form an assembly, if they are a horde or a tribe. But we call them brothers and sisters because they are gathered together and because they are listening to the same story.

We do not yet know whether the one speaking is from among them or if he is an outsider. We say that he is one of them, but different from them because he has the gift, or simply the right—or else it is his duty —to tell the story.

They were not assembled like this before the story; the recitation has gathered them together. Before, they were dispersed (at least this is what the story tells us at times), shoulder to shoulder, working with and confronting one another without recognizing one another. But one day, one of them stood still, or perhaps he turned up, as though returning from a long absence or mysterious exile. He stopped at a particular place, to the side of but in view of the others, on a hillock or by a tree that had been struck by lightning, and he started the narrative that brought together the others.

He recounts to them their history, or his own, a story that they all know, but that he alone has the gift, the right, or the duty to tell. It is the story of their origin, of where they came from, or of how they come from the Origin itself—them, or their mates, or their names, or the authority figure among them. And so

156

 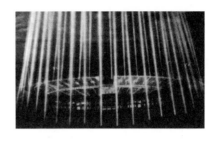

at the same time it is also the story of the beginning of the world, of the beginning of their assembling together, or of the beginning of the narrative itself (and the narrative recounts, on occasion, who taught the story to the teller, and how he came to have the gift, the right, or the duty to tell it).

He speaks, he recites, sometimes he sings, or he mimes. He is his own hero, and they, by turns, are the heroes of the tale and the ones who have the right to hear it and the duty to learn it. In the speech of the narrator, their language for the first time serves no other purpose than that of presenting the narrative and of keeping it going. It is no longer the language of their exchanges, but of their reunion—the sacred language of a foundation and an oath. The teller shares it with them and among them.'

Jean-Luc Nancy, *The Inoperative Community*

'We are first of all, as friends, the friends of solitude, and we are calling on you to share what cannot be shared: solitude. We are friends of an entirely different kind, inaccessible friends, friends who are alone because they are incomparable and without common measure, reciprocity of equality. Therefore, without a horizon of recognition. Without a familial bond, without proximity, without *oikeiótes*. [...]

How many of us are there? Does that count? And how do you calculate?

Thus is announced the anchoritic community of those who love in separation. The invitation comes to you from those who can love only at a distance, in separation. This is not all they love, but they love; they love lovence, they love to love—in love or in friendship—providing there is this withdrawal. Those who love only in cutting ties are the

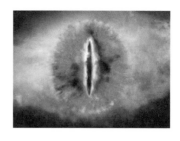

uncompromising friends of solitary singularity. They invite you to enter into this community of social disaggregation, which is not necessarily a secret society, a conjuration, the occult sharing of esoteric or crypto-poetic knowledge. The classical concept of the secret belongs to a thought of the community, solidarity of the sect—initiation or private space which represents the very thing the friend who speaks to you as a friend of solitude has rebelled against.

In the meantime, in the course of the first avowal's moment, which still belongs to the community of compassion, you had better keep silence to preserve what remains of friendship. And as the friends know this truth of truth (the custody of what cannot be kept), they had better keep silent together. As in mutual agreement. A tacit agreement, however, whereby those who are separated come together without ceasing to be what they are destined to be—and undoubtedly what they more than ever are: are destined to be—and undoubtedly what they more than ever are: dissociated, 'solitarised', singularised, constituted into monadic alterities; […] they are solitary, but they ally them-selves in silence within the necessity of keeping silent together—each, however, in his own corner. This is perhaps a social bond, a contemporaneity, but in the common affirmation of being unbounded, an untimely being-alone and, silmultaneously, in joint acquiescence to disjunction. How can you be together to bear witness to secrecy, separation and singularity? You would have to testify where testimony remains impossible. You would have to witness the absence of attestation, and testify in behalf of that absence.'

Jacques Derrida, *The Politics of Friendship*

 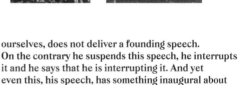

'It is each time the voice of one alone, and to the side, who speaks, who recites, who sometimes sings. He speaks of an origin and an end—the end of the origin, in truth—he stages them and puts himself on stage along with them. But he comes to the edge of the stage, to its outer edge, and he speaks at the softest limit of his voice. Or rather, it is we who stand at the furthermost extreme and who barely hear him from this limit. Everything is a matter of one's practical, ethical, political—and why not add spiritual?—positioning around this singular eruption of a voice. You can always make a myth of it again. But this voice, or another, will always begin interrupting the myth again— sending us back to the limit.

On this limit, the one who exposes himself and to whom—if we listen, if we read, if our ethical and political condition is one listening or reading—we expose ourselves, does not deliver a founding speech. On the contrary he suspends this speech, he interrupts it and he says that he is interrupting it. And yet even this, his speech, has something inaugural about it. Each writer, each work inaugurates a community.

There is therefore an unimpeachable and irre- pressible literary communism, to which belongs anyone who writes (or reads), or tries to write (or read) by exposing himself—not by imposing himself (and anyone who imposes himself without in any way exposing himself is no longer writing, no longer reading, no longer thinking, no longer communicating). But the communism here is inaugural, not final. It is not finished; on the contrary, it is made up of the interruption of mythic communion and communal myth.'

Jean-Luc Nancy, *The Inoperative Community*

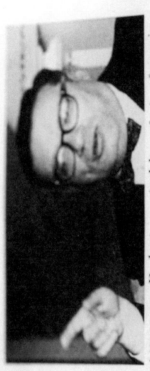

ASIMOV: Robots capable of performing manual tasks more efficiently than human laborers will render the lower grades of human being rather obsolete.

...ested also that genetic selection and manipulation will be used to breed human beings of exceptional intelligence, creative imagination, physical strength and resistance to disease; but ...t expressed grave doubts about our ...bility to decide wisely which individuals ...powered to select who should be ...ll be allowed to breed — and for what ...cific traits. In appraising the impact ...n enforced genetic control on the func-...n and status of the family in 1984, ...ion was divided between those who ... that marriage will become obsole-...t in an era of test-tube babies bred ... raised by the state; and those who ...e convinced that the institution ...ld continue to flourish because the ...ly-security drive is in the nature of ...n and not of society. Part One of our ...ussion ended as we introduced the ...ct of nonmatrimonial changes in ... relationship between the sexes.

Budrys responded with the proph-...at "the concept of a social or sexual ... will become nearly meaningless" ...iler of ... special free-

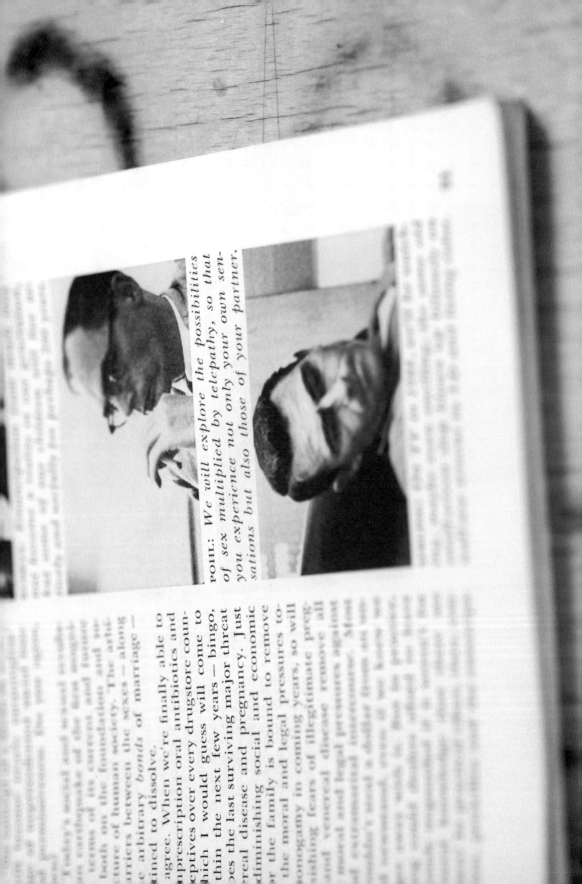

Today's moral and sexual revolu-
... earthquake of the first magni-
... terms of its current and future
... both on the foundations and su-
... ture of human society. The arbi-
... rriers between the sexes — along
... e arbitrary bonds of marriage —
... ined to dissolve.

... agree. When we're finally able to
... nprescription oral antibiotics and
... eptives over every drugstore coun-
... hich I would guess will come to
... thin the next few years — bingo,
... es the last surviving major threat
... real disease and pregnancy. Just
... diminishing social and economic
... r the family is bound to remove
... the moral and legal pressures to-
... onogamy in coming years, so will
... nishing fears of illegitimate preg-
... and venereal disease remove all
... ral and legal pressures against
... and extramarital intercourse. Most

POHL: *We will explore the possibilities of sex multiplied by telepathy, so that you experience not only your own sensations but also those of your partner.*

BLISH: *It's possible that some sort of faster-than-light interstellar propulsion will be discovered before we get manned rockets any farther out than Jupiter.*

already get a lot of people — and terribly hopeful for ... Rats wired up so that on the current in their ... re centers will forgo ... ay after day — sex, sleep, ... st to keep pushing that ... them to the point of ... rs to starvation. And it ... e same sort of effect on ... se I know of, a terminal

writers, have long dreamt of this movement and cannot help but be exhilarated.

HEINLEIN: *What will our children accomplish? Take the wildest speculation, square
it, cube the result, and the answer still
won't be big enough to match the truth.*

t man is a kind
a in a laboratory
to me that all
ctions between
l worthlessness,
to the twin cri-
. We can expect
e in, therefore,
of sensuality
n ever-new re-
and electronics
ry phenomena
ffect will move
V set and into
This will be-
when pleasure
e point of in-
pose to these
tions and raw

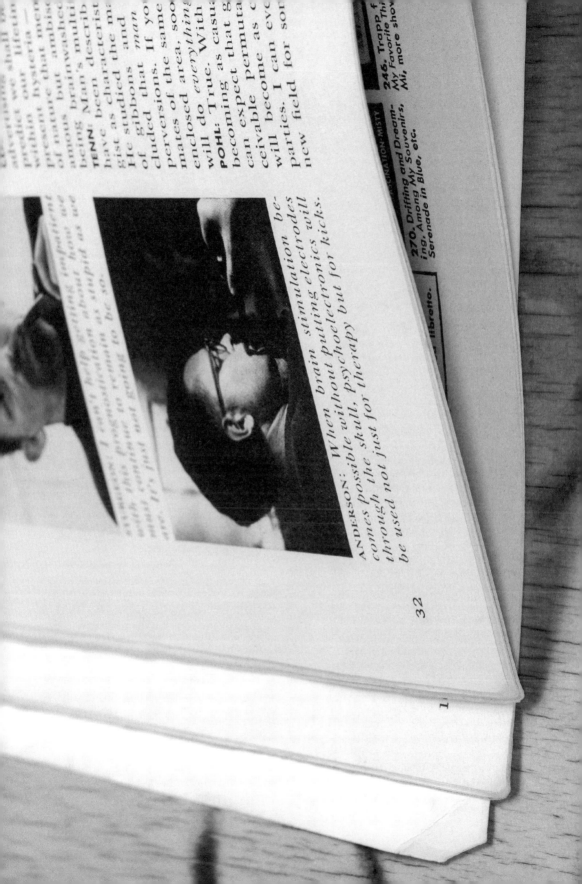

ANDERSON: When brain stimulation becomes possible without putting electrodes
through the skull, psychoelectronics will
be used not just for therapy.

... advertise we shall lifetim ...
... predict our lifetim ...
... within hysteria ...
... present that ambise ...
... of nature but ...
... amos brainwashed ...
... being Man's multi ...

TENN: Man's describ ...
... have been characteristi ...
... gist as character the ma ...
... He studied the ...
... of gibbons man ...
... cluded that If yo ...
... perversions. the same ...
... mates area, soo ...
... enclosed everythin ...
... will do everythin ...

POHL: True. With ...
... becoming as casua ...
... can expect that g ...
... ceivable permuta ...
... will become as c ...
... parties. I can ev ...
... new field for so ...

I can't help feeling impatient we
at when people about how as
human progression to be so
with this fine to remain as so
and continue gains
one mission as stupid as to

32

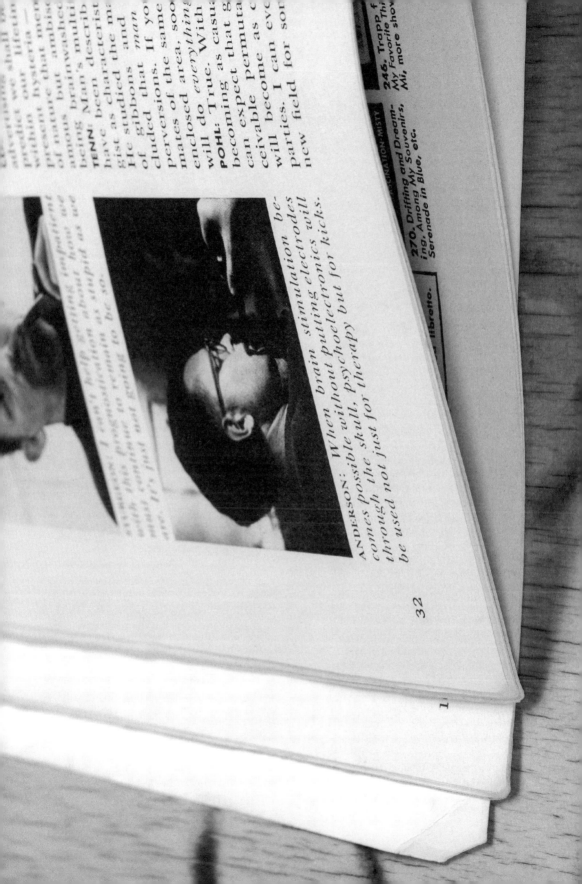

246. Trapp F
My Favorite Thi
Mi, more show

270. Drifting and Dream-
ing. Among My Souvenirs,
Serenade in Blue, etc.

libretto.

ON 1984 AND BEYOND

by Emily Pethick

We Earth-bound men, we have had it, the next
century belongs to the space-farers.
Algis Budrys, '1984 and Beyond',
Playboy magazine, July–August, 1963

Published in 1963 across two issues of *Playboy*'s
interview section '1984 and Beyond' invited
12 science fiction writers—including Arthur C.
Clark (a regular contributor to *Playboy*'s fiction
section) Robert Heinlein (author of *Starship
Troopers*) and Rod Serling (creator of *The Twilight
Zone*)—to talk about their visions of the future of
society circa 1984. Forty-two years later, Gerard
Byrne resurrected this article, editing it into a
screenplay and re-enacting it with a group of
actors in the Netherlands, reworking the piece in
two stages, beginning with a live reading, which
was developed into a subsequent film.

Where George Orwell's 1949 vision of the
future sees a dystopian totalitarian regime,
Playboy's group of writers see immanent sexual,
scientific and social liberation. At the same
time they appear steeped in political tensions
and social and ideological anxieties surrounding
the cold war, their visions of the future simultaneously unfold fears of the present. Opening
with a discussion about the Russian-American
race for the moon (Clark predicts a moon landing
circa 1970, and Venus circa 1980) the writers
debate the likelihood of the Russians not only
capturing the moon, but the 'entire orb', before
proceeding to imagine its commercial potential,
and to speculate over lunar real estate and
tourist travel. Ideological fears of Communism
and discussions of racial issues only too easily
translate into imagined alien presences, as the
writers gauge how their appearance might
'horrify humanity', however they conclude that
'few aliens are apt to be more startling than
man himself.'

What kind of race will inhabit the moon is
also debated, both as a place for the elite or alter-
natively for social minorities and disadvantaged,
as well as a site for a new race of 'lunarians'.

In science, narcotics are predicted to intensify
sexual gratification and the elimination of disease.
The need for sleep and the secret of eternal life
are also key developments seen to be upon the
horizon, as well as population growth problems,
Algis Budrys predicts that some of their children
would live 'actively and usefully for perhaps
200 years.' When asked their predictions for
'the life of an affluent city-dwelling bachelor at
the turn of the coming century', their subject is
a white collar worker whose possession of 'the
commodity in great demand on the labour market
of the 21st Century: originality and freshness of
thought' is a prediction that was not far wrong
considering the 'knowledge economy' of today,
although his working week of four days per week,
unlimited sick leave and three month vacation,
was a little far fetched for the contemporary
subject that would ultimately become caught in
the clutches of high-capitalism.

Although the discussion reveals how politi-
cally and scientifically in tune the writers
were, some moments of wonderfully far-flung
speculation reveal that they are after all
in the business of creating fantasy fiction.
The conversation does, however, come back
down to earth, as it ends with a discussion about
whether man really has the capacity for such
change. With the benefit of hindsight one sees
the speed of human and scientific development
was somewhat slower than this group had
imagined, and if it had taken place after the first
moon landing they might not have envisaged
it as such an attractive place to be. Future
developments that were not addressed in the
conversation are also striking, most notably
the civil rights movement and the effects of
feminism, which were already well underway by
this point in time (perhaps not that surprising
given the fact that at this time, science fiction
was a notoriously white-male-dominated
genre), and the extremity of the effects of
high-capitalism and climate change.

The future that the writers imagine is of course
the one we are living out today, and through the
process of re-enaction Byrne inverts the text by
imagining the past, re-activating it in the here-
and-now by re-introducing bodies, voices, objects
and surroundings, in order to create a sense of
reality out of textual material. Editing down the
original interview without adding any extra words,
Byrne's reconstruction is by no means seamless, it
contains numerous discontinuities that

166

disrupt the linearity of the article—itself an edited version of the original conversation, of course. Furthermore, by the siting of the work in the Netherlands, and working with Dutch actors, a dislocation in time and space occurs that acknowledges the impossibility of faithful representation. The script also becomes a vehicle to test out different genealogies of performance, both through live spoken word and in film, the work becomes as much about the process and implications of the act of re-enaction as the end result.

The first stage of Byrne's production took the form of a public reading before a present audience with eleven actors arranged in a row of armchairs, heavily lit by stage lights. Through the very act of restaging it, small details were introduced, such as clothes, mannerisms, tones of voice and their relationships to one another, the actors developing their characters from the given facts, venturing beyond the borders of the documentary. Where stage performances in their very nature simplify and over-exaggerate details and gestures in order to resonate before a present audience, the film developed this into a more complex and layered interpretation of the script, the camera penetrating tiny movements, the fragmentation of the scenes leading to a further loss of linearity, moving further into the realm of fiction.

While the original article was most probably sandwiched between bountiful soft-focus images of nude women, in Byrne's film the writers are set against the cold, stark architecture of Hugh Maaskant's Provinciehuis in 's-Hertogenbosch, and Gerrit Rietveld's sculpture pavilion in the garden of the Kröller-Müller Museum in Otterlo, shifting the discussion from the context of *Playboy* to equate the writers' ideas with the futuristic, utopian visions of contemporaneous avant-garde architects. The latter site is itself a posthumous reconstruction of Rietveld's temporary Sonsbeek Pavilion, and is an entirely open structure, which Byrne sees as kind of ruin, both in its structural configuration and in the use of pierced blocks (evocative of Arabic structures), and in its function as a memorial to the architect. Byrne cites these two locations as reflecting the different aspects of attitudes present in the text; the more American-looking Provincie-huis summoning a sense of the white-collar 'Organisational Man' (a term coined by William White in 1954) and the Rietveld Pavilion

effectively as a pre-meditated ruin complete with it's monumental effigy-like sculptures by Barbara Hepworth, giving a sense of how contemporary man might have wanted to be perceived in the future.

The conversation unfolds over various spaces both inside and outside of the buildings, merging two distinctive sites into one. The men loiter in the transitional areas of vast lobbies, stairwells and porches as well as outside in the pavilion. In the original publication and in Byrne's orchestration of a live public reading, there was no clear articulation of breaks, or the passing of time. In the film, however, the characters are brought together in different constellations, which are announced at the beginning of each section, although there is no clear indication of who is who, and some of the characters barely enter into the conversation. These breaks and long silences become a noticeable departure from the stage play, playing with what one can see and not hear, with characters talking in the background, on the telephone, and outside windows creating the sense that more than one conversation is taking place at the same time. On the other hand, fervent discussion is frequently interjected with jovial laughter that cements the characters' lively relationships to one another.

As with the Modernist architecture, Byrne introduces a series of almost incidental-looking objects into the background of the film, which add a further sense of continuum from the time that the article was produced, honing a strongly Modernist aesthetic sensibility that enhances the performance of the actors and the text itself. When the writers stand around in the Rietveld Pavilion deliberating the possibility of extra-terrestrial beings in the universe, the looming Barbara Hepworth sculptures in the background cast a silent presence, appearing almost as alien in form as the strange beings discussed by the writers. Byrne points out a kind of forwards-and-backwards vision that is encapsulated by these sculptures and their positioning in the pavilion: their futuristic form is simultaneously combined with the fact that sculpture at that time was often understood in relation to archaeology, with the idea of how a civilisation might leave itself for the future to interpret. Standing face to face with one of Hepworth's large rounded bronzes, Bradbury remarks that, 'the study of aesthetics, I think, will be essential to the task of comprehending the bizarre life forms we are going to be encountering, just as aesthetics has a lot to do with the problem of assimilating the various coloured races here on earth,' thus equating the shock of the avant-garde forms with notions of social acceptance, pointing to the intrinsic conservatism of society that fears difference and change.

Further on in the film the smooth progress of the conversation is punctuated by a lone saxophone player giving a rendition of Gerry Mulligan's 1959 'Take Five' at the side of the street with the writers circled around him. At the time this was a breakthrough in the popular embrace of Jazz, effectively mediating it for the middle classes, however it has now become more associated with elevator music and buskers. Other objects also have an invisible presence, such as the frequent mentions of the writers' books, and, of course, *Playboy* itself. In the very act of mining old issues of a mainstream magazine without an intended lifespan, Byrne not only resurfaces a significant text, but also re-addresses *Playboy*'s history as a publication that, in this period, actively engaged in liberal politics and in the practice of defining the present as well as envisioning the future. In fact, the very nature of magazines is that their aim is to be of their moment, to represent the current, so that they quickly become out-of-date and disposable. When aligning these more ephemeral artefacts alongside avant-garde art and architecture Byrne highlights differing sets of cultural values, showing objects which are deemed worthy of preservation alongside those that have fallen by the wayside as a way of rescuing their historical plight.

Thus Byrne's *1984 and Beyond* is by no means a simple reconstruction of a document, but a collection of multiple narratives and parallel histories that lead tangentially outwards, forming connections between three time periods, 1963, 1984, and 2005, as well as forming loose associations between isolated cultural events. Viewed with the benefit of hindsight there is an element of pathos in the sense of optimism found in the reconstruction of a conversation that imagined what our contemporary condition became. Through the process of acting this out, Byrne builds what he describes as 'a provocative model of how all representation work', forming a speculative, multivalent, and compelling image of how an unremarkable moment from the recent past, now only half remembered, was imagined as a future by a slightly more distant past. Simultaneously looking backwards and forwards, Byrne's piece reflects upon the role of the imaginary in the way in which we position ourselves between past and future, and the place of the subjective viewpoint in the process of historical reconstruction.

Gerard Byrne's *1984 and Beyond* was produced by 'If I Can't Dance, I Don't Want To Be Part Of Your Revolution' (The Netherlands) and 'Momentum', the Nordic Biennial of Contemporary Art (Norway). The first edition of 'If I Can't Dance …' in 2005 was curated by Frederique Bergholtz, Annie Fletcher and Tanja Elstgeest. A version of this text appeared in an accompanying publication.

GET THE NEW YORKER
FOR $1 AN ISSUE
AND SAVE YOUR MONEY FOR THE GOINGS ON ABOUT TOWN.

❑ **YES!** Please send me a year of *The New Yorker* (46 issues) for only $46.00.
I'll save 76% off the cover price!

Name

Address   Apt. No

City   State   Zip

Email

❑ Please send me two years (92 issues) for only $76.00.
❑ Payment enclosed   ❑ Bill me later

G5FS2A

Canadian annual price is $90.00 U.S. including GST and HST where applicable.
First issue mails within 6 weeks. The one year newsstand cost of *The New Yorker* is $193.70.

THE NEW YORKER

GIVE THE NEW YORKER
FOR $1 AN ISSUE
AND BE THE TALK OF THE TOWN.

❑ **YES!** Please send a Gift Subscription of *The New Yorker* (46 issues) to the
person listed below for only $46.00. I'll save 76% off the cover price.

GIFT TO: GIFT FROM:

Name   Name

Address   Apt. No   Address   Apt. No

City   State   Zip   City   State   Zip

Email   Email

G5FS2A

❑ Payment enclosed   ❑ Bill me later

Canadian annual price is $90.00 U.S. including GST and HST where applicable.
First issue mails within 6 weeks. The one year newsstand cost of *The New Yorker* is $193.70.

THE NEW YORKER

169

FORM-GIVING

by Rob Giampietro

1. Basket

The Gift came, as gifts often do, without my asking
for it. Its cover flashed up on my computer screen
by way of an Amazon.com server that drew upon a
collective memory of what customers like me had
already purchased when I logged in one afternoon
looking for a particular book on Shaker design.
The cover, probably designed in part by *The Gift*'s
author, Lewis Hyde, caught my eye because it
featured a drawing that Hyde, who is an English
professor at Kenyon College, credits inside as
'Basket of Apples'. The drawing, however, is
more properly credited as 'A Little Basket Full
of Beautiful Apples' and was made 150 years ago
by a self-taught Shaker woman named Hannah
Cohoon, who would have called it a 'gift drawing'.
I had first seen it several days before, in an article
from *The New Yorker* by Adam Gopnik on the
Shakers titled 'Shining Tree of Life', where he
describes both the drawing and the circumstances
of its making:

> Visions and ghosts came down, and the
> Shakers, chiefly women and young girls,
> made 'gift drawings': the drawings were gifts
> from above, not gifts to another. [...] One of
> them, 'A Little Basket Full of Apples' (1856),
> is among the key drawings in American art,
> with a tonic sense of abundance—all the
> apples just alike, each with its rub-on of
> rouge, like blush applied by an adolescent
> girl—allied to obsessive order.

A few weeks earlier, I'd become interested in
gifts after having a vision of my own (or perhaps
it was something more like a dream). Waking
suddenly one night, I scrawled the following
assignment for my students on the back of a
New Yorker subscription card by my bed:

> Form small groups and spend time together
> this week. For next week's class, give a gift to
> a group member that will evoke an emotional
> response when given.

I clicked on *The Gift*'s cover and placed it in
my cart. About ten days later, a brown padded
envelope arrived in my mailbox at work.
Unwrapping it, I found myself facing Hannah
Cohoon's apple basket once again.

2. Spirit

Hyde's book is an inquiry into both the meaning
of gifts and the place of creative artists in a
commercial society. His first essay begins with an
examination of book covers. He writes

> At the corner drugstore my neighbours and
> I can now buy a line of romantic novels written
> according to a formula developed through
> market research. An advertising agency
> polled a group of readers. What age should
> the heroine be? (She should be between 19
> and 27.) Should the man she meets be married
> or single? (Recently widowed is best.) [...]
> Each novel is 192 pages long. Even the name
> of the series and the design of the cover has
> been tailored to the demands of the market.
> (The name Silhouette was preferred over
> Belladonna, Surrender, Tiffany, and Magnolia;
> gold curlicues were chosen to frame the
> cover.)

Then comes Hyde's insightful question 'Why do
we suspect that Silhouette romances will not be
enduring works of art?', to which he responds

> It is the assumption of this book that a work
> of art is a gift, not a commodity. Or, to
> state the modern case with more precision,
> that works of art exist simultaneously in
> two 'economies,' a market economy and a
> gift economy. Only one of these is essential,
> however: a work of art can survive without
> the market, but where there is no gift there
> is no art.

What is a gift, and how are gifts distinguished
from commodities? Hyde clarifies this:
'[A] gift is a thing we do not get by our own efforts.
We cannot buy it; we cannot acquire it through
an act of will. It is bestowed upon us.' Hyde then
invokes the word 'gifted', reminding us that it
can be used to describe an individual's talents,
and he explains that talent is also a kind of gift.
Intuition and inspiration fall into this category,
too, following Hyde's insight that

> As the artist works, some portion of his
> creation is bestowed upon him. [...] Usually, in
> fact, the artist does not find himself engaged
> or exhilarated by the work, nor does it seem
> authentic, until this gratuitous element has
> appeared, so that along with any true creation
> comes the uncanny sense that 'I', the artist,
> did not make the work.

This is the drip, the wrinkle, the tiny imperfection
or hiccup in techonology that snaps the
whole artwork into place. It reminds me of the
increasingly popular practice of leaving—or even
aestheticizing—mistakes in order to 'open up'

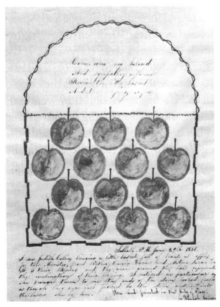

Left: cupboard with drawers (c.1825-1850). This page: "The Tree of Light or Blazing Tree" (1845) and "A Little Basket Full of Beautiful Apples" (1856), by Hannah Cohoon.

poor and unhoused, chaste roof to shelter r, though, that a cross-erican population, rich etween, joined them, ure of reasons. And a phans and abandoned Shaker colonies the g appearance of fam-egular intake, as well, dered in for food and times—"winter Shak-ed.)

early followers shared was a reborn Christ. he fulfilled and com-er presence made the ually complete, both Her latter-day follow-wn her messianic pre- were clear, and out-1827 letter (published J. Stein, a Shaker his-entucky Shaker, Wil-liam S. Byrd, of the famous Virginia Byrds, admits that many "scof at the idea of Christs making his second appearance in Ann Lee" but then adds defiantly, "The same Christ that dwelt in Jesus of Nazareth, appeared the second time in this female, the spiritual Mother of all the new creation of God." Much as St. Augustine lent some of his sense of guilt and morbidity to early Christianity, Ann gave her neurasthenic desire for order and hyper-organization to all the later Shakers. Crowded poor people learn to hate disorder with a passion that for the wealthy is only a pastime; Groucho Marx, to take another important American spiritual leader, was so appalled by the chaos of his tenement childhood that, it was said, for the rest of his life he hated to have one kind of food on his plate touch another. (Whenever we see a fanatic appetite for order, there were probably once six kids in one room.)

Ann Lee became wildly controver-

a piece of work. By admitting the artifice of an artwork, the indefiniteness of a 'finished' piece, the artist also admits his own humanity, and, in so doing, empathy may form between the artist and audience. The work of the audience completes the work of the artist, and each is grateful for the participation of the other.

Hyde explains, 'Even if we have paid a fee at the door of a museum or concert hall, when we are touched by a work of art something comes to us which has nothing to do with the price.' Often we talk about the 'spirit' of a gift—similar to the Shakers' ghosts and visions—and this spirit passes from the artist through the work of art to society. 'The spirit of a gift is kept alive by its constant donation,' says Hyde, adding, 'a gift that cannot be given away ceases to be a gift.' So what was once a gift can suddenly become a commodity simply by ceasing to give it away? Yes, says Hyde, warning that 'the way we treat a thing can sometimes change its nature.' Art may enter the world through the economy of gifts, but it may also soon change into a commodity. Rather than spreading from one person to the next, the artwork is now confined, corralled, and cordoned-off. It belongs to one person and not another. Removed from circulation, its social power fades to equal that of any other privately-owned good. This is why the most sought-after buyers of art among galleries and dealers are those most willing to lend, showcase, and ultimately give away their prized collections.

3. Present

For a short essay in *Tibor Kalman: Perverse Optimist* titled 'The Joy of Getting', Michael Bierut provides a first-hand account of receiving Christmas gifts from Kalman's renowned New York design firm M&Co:

> They seemed to arrive on the same day all over town. Usually, some of the younger designers in my office would see the package with the M&Co mailing label as it arrived, and personally carry it back into the studio. The opening of the package, inevitably an event in itself, was something no one wanted to miss.

The gifts, given annually between 1979 and 1990, became increasingly complex as the years went on, as well as increasingly consistent with Hyde's formulation of gifts as community-defining objects in constant circulation. As he tries to sum them up, Bierut jokes, 'I can't imagine that any of them

resulted in getting business for M&Co', and, in a literal sense, he is probably right.

The gifts were sometimes banal (cookies and chocolates), sometimes ironic (a plastic paperweight in the shape of a crumpled sheet of paper), sometimes functional (a desk set), and sometimes elemental (space represented by rulers of wood and steel, time by a wall calendar and clock). The gift from 1986, a dictionary, included with it that classic symbol of education, an apple, looking in the photographs like it was plucked from Hannah Cohoon's basket or maybe off the tree of knowledge in the Garden of Eden itself. Knowledge, like food, is a gift that circulates freely, brings us together, and is, in the best of times, ever-flourishing.

Knowledge is also the frame for M&Co's penultimate gift, dubbed 'the $26 book', a lesson on the nature of giving itself. According to Kalman, following the toppling of the Berlin Wall in 1989, M&Co had 'a change of heart over holiday gift-giving. Instead of trying to outdo the previous year's present, this year's bounty would deflate all expectations'. Though he was always a provocateur, I doubt Kalman intended this 'deflation' to be as jarring as it sounds. Rather, I suspect, in the light of such a revolutionary, community-restoring global event, Kalman understood that the wall's destruction was the ultimate gift, not an object of desire but an action that made the world a better place. This is the 'deflation' he had in mind: there was great beauty in the destruction of an ugly old wall.

M&Co's gift followed suit, getting its audience to literally judge a book by its cover. What appeared at first like a dirty second-hand hardcover book had been bookmarked with notes and dollar bills totalling $26, a number that, according to Kalman, was purposely set at $1 over the federal limit on gifts. Since accepting the full amount was essentially a crime, M&Co suggested that recipients give some or all of their bounty away. Kalman observed that

> The entire transaction took place inside the individual's conscience; it was a completely private experience. It was like finding five dollars in the back of a cab and deciding to keep it, or getting too much change in a store. We were interested in exploring those feelings.

Bierut describes the experience of receiving the $26 book this way:

VINTAGE BOOKS

The Gift

Imagination and the Erotic Life of Property

Lewis Hyde

It was transcendent: not just a gift but an experience, combining surprise, humor, pathos, and guilt in an astonishingly controlled sequence. Everyone who received it was invited to feel not just the joy of getting but the joy of giving.

Bierut concludes by observing that Kalman is 'the person who has given me more gifts than anyone else outside my immediate family'.

4. Landmark
From design critic Steven Heller's biography of the designer Paul Rand:

> Various designers failed to redesign the UPS logo satisfactorily. Rand decided to retain the shield believing that it had symbolic significance for the men who wore it. He replaced the type face and added the 'gift' box atop the shield. Before showing his proposal to UPS, he asked his young daughter Catherine, for her opinion —according to Rand, she said: 'That's a present, Daddy.'

While designers churn out new designs every day for clients and seldom get sentimental over them, the disposal of Rand's 1961 UPS logo in 2003 triggered a reaction throughout the design community—and the culture as a whole—that can only be described as loss. The old UPS logo, in its quiet way, had become something that was almost universally beloved. Writing of this kind of passing, Hyde observes, 'The gift is property that perishes. […] The gift that is not used will be lost, while the one that is passed along remains abundant.' Once removed from circulation, Rand's old UPS logo inevitably wilted and passed away, just like a painting stuffed in the attic.

'It's sad that this little package couldn't have survived', wrote Scott Stowell, a former M&Co designer himself, for *Metropolis* magazine. In the year following the UPS logo's demise, Stowell was prompted to write 'The First Report of the (Unofficial) Graphic Design Landmarks Preservation Commission', which put forward the radical idea that certain design icons have reached such a point of cultural recognition and affection that they have ceased to belong to their owners, and should, like beloved buildings, be somehow independently preserved. Many of the designs he recommends for preservation are already in the public domain; only five of Stowell's recommendations represent private businesses. They are the logos of ABC, NBC, CBS, and UPS, and the former AT&T bell. Not by coincidence,

all of these companies are built on communities of ordinary people and are often a fundamental part of our everyday lives. We are the nodes on these companies' networks, so invariably we feel a sense of ownership over their identities. In allowing them to move through us, we have, even temporarily, made their identities our own, witnessing television signals, phone calls, and packages as they spread from one person to the next, all over the globe.

5. Catalog
A new image of the globe in 1966 was part of what sparked Stewart Brand to create *The Whole Earth Catalog*.* After launching a public campaign aimed at getting NASA to release their then-rumored satellite image of the earth as seen from space into the public domain, Brand's liberated globe became a symbol for a publication that Brand described to the *Catalog*'s young designer J. Baldwin as something 'so that anyone on Earth can pick up a telephone and find out the complete information on anything. […] That's my goal.'

Lecturing at Stanford 40 years later, Apple CEO Steve Jobs described the *Catalog* as 'Google in paperback form, 35 years before Google came along: it was idealistic, and overflowing with neat tools and great notions.' What merited an item for inclusion in the *Catalog* was its usefulness and accessibility, or, as Brand wrote in his introduction from 1969,

> An item is listed in the CATALOG
> if it is deemed:
> 1. Useful as a tool,
> 2. Relevant to independent education,
> 3. High quality or low cost,
> 4. Easily available by mail.

Always being updated and improved, *The Whole Earth Catalog* was in a constant state of evolution, much like today's open-source technologies, passing round and round among its issuers and its audience for improvement. It cost $4. When the Catalog ceased operations in 1971, Brand held a 'demise party' at the new San Francisco Exploratorium, giving away $20,000 in cash to promote the extension of the Catalog's mission. Among the recipients were the then-fledgling Homebrew Computer Club whose early members included young Apple founders Steve Jobs and Steve Wozniak. To Hyde, giving to fill a need makes sense not just emotionally but formally. When we give to charity, we do not expect anything directly in return. Again, rather than a

* See: Reinfurt, *Global Branding*, DDD9.

The assembly line came together, as usual, a few weeks before Christmas, when staff, interns, friends and friends of friends were called into the studio for a weekend of inserting money into the pages of 500 old books.

linear exchange, a one-for-one, gift exchanges move in a circle, broadening the reach of a community's resources by seeking recipients for whom gifts have not yet been bestowed. 'Where does the gift move?' asks Hyde. 'The gift moves toward the empty place.'

6. Ceremony

The idea of filling an empty place, or celebrating the end of something with a generous gift back to the community, is something intrinsic to gift economies, a kind of giving that Hyde names the 'threshold gift' or the 'gift of passage', and we see it with great clarity in the Native American tradition of the potlatch, which is described by that great contemporary Open Source technology, Wikipedia, as follows:

> Originally the potlatch was held to commemorate an important event such as the death of a high-status person, [...] Sponsors of a potlatch give away many useful items such as food, blankets, worked ornamental mediums of exchange called 'coppers', and many other various items.

What these sponsors got back was prestige among their peers. Those that gave a potalch enjoyed increased reputation and a more highly prized social rank. The more gifts that were given, the more valuable these gifts became and the more respected their givers became. Hyde restates this in terms of commodity markets by saying that 'Capital earns profit and the sale of a commodity turns a profit, but gifts that remain gifts do not *earn* profit they *give* increase.'

We earn something by our own effort, and earnings cannot be given to others. Profits, too, are generally kept by their earner and any gain in value to profits returns to the earner. The gift economy is the opposite. We cannot earn a gift through our own efforts, it must be given to us. And once we have it, it gains value only when we give it to another member of our community. Value follows the gift rather than remaining with the individual, and an increase in value comes only to the community as a whole. Hyde compares the rise of value in a gift economy to a mathematical vector, defined by its movement and direction. Commodities, on the other hand, stay put.

In terms of the potalch, the prodigious amount of goods given back and forth between neighbouring tribes became a great asset in helping those less fortunate. To borrow from economic terminology, it was a case of 'spillover benefits'.

Hyde writes an entire chapter on the potlatch, contrasting its rituals to those of a market economy by pointing out that in terms of the potlatch,

> Virtue rests in publicly disposing of wealth, not mere acquisition or accumulation. Accumulation in any quantity by borrowing or otherwise, is, in fact, unthinkable [in a gift economy] unless it be for the purpose of redistribution.

In terms of the potlatch, a consequence of this redistributory imperative is the fact that the 'coppers'—whose function is purely aesthetic—gain in value as they crack and break with use. A copper that has broken in two is treated not as one but two precious objects, because breaking the gift both represents its past and imagines its future. Once perfect and singular, it has worn through time and constant circulation and, in breaking, its spirit is released and allowed to spread even farther.

7. Bond

An analogue to the community dynamics of the potlatch is those of the scientific community, which circulates knowledge in journals that generally do not pay for their articles. In fact, these articles, Hyde reminds us, are referred to as 'contributions', and the payment for them is recognition, or credit. Among other things, this practice ultimately preserves the structure and collaborative potential of the group.

The more a scientist gives, the more his community knows. The more prestige they give him in return, the more ambitious his work is able to become. We've seen that giving a gift creates a bond between two people, and that the obligation of the gift is to give it in turn to another person, and so on. In the process a community is established around the gift, and the very structure of this community guards against the use of the gift for an individual's financial gain. The individual may receive credit, prestige, notoriety, or power within the community as a result of his gift, but monetary income is out of the question, for it converts the community's gift into the individual's profit. We can take our cash elsewhere—Hyde calls it a 'medium of foreign exchange'—but prestige has currency only

he different
, as was his
de the most
al way of
yself as a
ot experts,
ght-year-old
"Catherine,
present,
uldn't have

in currency
te his offer
that had
would
ut of the

er did. The
e was that it
ut I prefer
the time,
ody could
t; I just
t juncture."⁶²

within our professional group. 'It is the cardinal difference between gift and commodity exchange that a gift establishes a feeling-bond between two people, while the sale of a commodity establishes no necessary connection', Hyde notes.

Within the community, Hyde explains that 'gifts carry an identity with them and to accept the gift amounts to incorporating a new identity'. He uses 'teachings' as his primary example of this, and by 'teachings' he means lessons that have a transformative power on us, forcing us to see ourselves afresh. This is because gratitude for a gift, as Hyde points out, can only be felt once we have laboured to receive it. '[W]ith gifts that are agents of change,' like the recognition of a young artist's talents by a master,

> it is only when the gift has worked in us, only when we have come up to its level, as it were, that we can give it away again. Passing the gift along is the act of gratitude that finishes the labour. The transformation is not accomplished until we have the power to give the gift on our own terms.

To understand this labour in terms of a conventional gift, consider being given a camera for your birthday. If it sits in a drawer, it's not a gift you may be very grateful for. Only with the investment of your time and energy—your labour—does the camera gain significance to you. The gift of a camera becomes your gift for photography, a gift you might someday share with others. The labour or gratitude applies to any significant gift you've been given, from a birthday present to a second chance at life.

8. Call
An example from Malcolm Gladwell's *The Tipping Point* underscores the similarity between the 'labour of gratitude' and the communication technique of known as the 'call to action'. Writing of Howard Levinthal's experiments at Yale University in the 1960s, Gladwell explains that Levinthal wanted to test the degree to which fear could work as a motivating tool. Levinthal's experiment involved printing up several booklets about the dangers of tetanus that ranged from a 'low fear' version featuring a pleasant, text-only explanation of the disease and its effect, to a 'high fear' version, featuring gruesome color photos and a litany of indescribable case studies. While the 'high fear' booklets may have convinced more students of the dangers of tetanus, only 3% of the students in the entire study got a tetanus shot. When Levinthal did the study a second time, redesigning each booklet to include a map to the campus health clinic, vaccination rates jumped up to 28% of the entire group. The students had learned about something potentially life-saving, and now they were being asked to act on this knowledge. Even more interesting is the fact that the students that got vaccinated came in equal parts from 'high fear' and 'low fear' groups. Fear had nothing to do with their decision to get vaccinated, but the map did.

Think about booklets like Levinthal's that you've been given at your own doctor's office. Like so many objects presented to make us act, these booklets are commonly given free of charge. If we don't receive something through market exchange, is it possible to think we've received it through a gift transaction instead? In being made to 'look its best', there's arguably a ceremonial aspect involved, but when you're given something you haven't asked for in a certain way (like in an elegant box) or by a certain person (like your girlfriend), *what* you've been given carries with it an obligation to at least consider *why* it's been given to you. Much is written about how objects are best made, but we've thought less about they are best given. How does an object enter into the world? What are our rituals for giving it? What are the responsibilities that commonly come with accepting it?

9. Dilemma
Rather than call these kinds of responsibilities 'work', Hyde opts to call them 'labour', distinguishing between them by defining 'work' as 'what we do by the hour', whereas 'labour sets its own pace. 'We may get paid for it,' Hyde continues, 'but it's harder to quantify.' Gifts resist quantification, both in terms of profit made and time expended. 'The growth [of a gift] is in the sentiment. It can't be put on a scale.' Hyde quickly demonstrates that this argument has very serious implications. 'If a thing is to have market value,' he continues, 'it must be detachable and alienable so that it can be put on the scale and compared.' Now, Hyde asks,

> Consider the old ethics-class dilemma in which you are in a lifeboat with your spouse and child and grandmother and you must choose who is to be thrown overboard to keep the craft afloat. [...] [This is] stressful precisely because we tend not to assign comparative values to those things to which we are emotionally connected.

WHOLE EARTH CATALOG

access to tools

Hyde follows this hypothetical situation with an actual 1971 cost-benefit analysis by the Ford Motor Company involving the Pinto, where the core equation was 'cost of safety parts vs cost of lives lost'. According to Ford estimates, the cost of letting 2,100 cars blow up, creating 180 unnecessary deaths and another 180 injuries was 64% cheaper than fixing an $11 auto part.

The reason the part needed to be switched in the first place—the fuel tank of the Pinto was badly engineered—is a design problem, and calls to mind the 11th of Milton Glaser's '12 Steps on the Graphic Designer's Road to Hell', a collection of hypotheticals intended to serve as a primer on design ethics and morality. The 11th Step asks us to consider, 'Designing a brochure for an SUV that flips over frequently in emergency conditions and is known to have killed 150 people.' While we can assume that Ford's engineers didn't intentionally design the Pinto's fuel tank to rupture, once the hazard has been discovered it seems, morally speaking, like it's Ford's obligation to fix it. Likewise, while we can assume that most designers wouldn't knowingly promote a car that was unsafe. Glaser's hypothetical asks us what we would do once we have that knowledge. The commercialist might be willing to use design to sell the Pinto anyway. But if we consider the offering of such information to be giftlike, then we might regard our own talents for communication as giftlike, too; and therefore we might feel responsible for both labouring toward the gratitude of our own gifts and for our community's responsible use of them.

At the 45th International Design Conference in Aspen in 1995, Milton Glaser began a speech by arguing that the axiom 'good design is good business' may no longer be useful to designers in explaining the value of their creativity to clients. He returned to the idea of 'good design' in his conclusion:

> We may be facing the most significant design problem of our lives—how to restore the 'good' in good design. Or, put another way, how to create a new narrative for our work that restores its moral center, creates a new sense of community, and re-establishes the continuity of generous humanism that is our heritage.

I now realise, though it scarcely mentions the word 'design', that *The Gift* is one of the most significant books about design that I have ever read. If the narrative that Glaser requires is one that allows for the community, generosity, and morality of what we do to be restored, I can see no better narrative to use than the only one where the object itself is the mechanism for those connections to be made. I have come to believe that the most powerful economy our profession can come to understand is the economy of gifts, and the most important stories we can tell are those of how our objects travel. Hyde teaches us that gifts must move. The next move is yours.

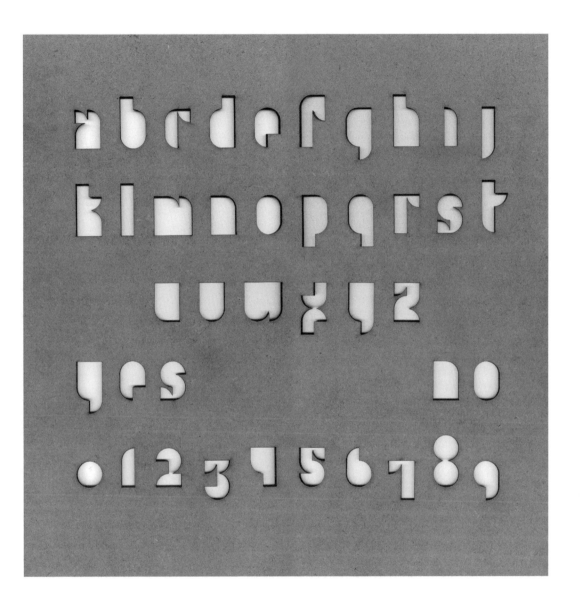

(party)
per
bend
sinister

A–Z, 0–9, YES/NO

by Paul Elliman

A few years ago a friend of mine in the art history department at Yale told me she had just been introduced to Albers at a college fellows lunch. I said to her What? That's impossible. She said No, no, it was definitely him; very old German guy with silver hair, Josef Albers. I said No, you don't understand. He's been dead for 25 years—look I'll show you a picture of him. I found an old catalogue with his portrait on the back page. She said Yes, that's him, Josef Albers. He was very friendly and it was definitely him.

The idea that he was or is somehow still around seems compelling enough. I started thinking about Albers and his work in a more grounded sort of way—not as someone whose presence can only be transmitted through the pages of a book, the medium of writing, or audio recordings. Artists have always tried to keep in historical contact through works from the past. I thought fuck it, why not just make contact with Albers directly?

I was curious about the stencil typeface he'd designed in 1926, while he was at the Bauhaus. In a famous example of the work, Albers cut the letters out of a large square of glass. Adding the words YES and NO would turn it into a kind of Ouija keyboard. I was thinking of using glass, but hardboard is fine for a Ouija board, and it's also an Albers material—his square paintings were made on this board, in 16, 24 and 40 inch sizes.

The séance itself was an odd and, I suppose, inconclusive event, though no more solemnly ridiculous than any good history seminar should be. It may have been a bit too conventional in the sense of a professor, head stuck in the past, fumbling with the technology of the presentation. In fact, I was never sure how to make the pointer for the board. The planchette, they call it. I'd spoken to a spiritualist, who told me not to worry about it, just use a glass or something that can move around easily enough. She thought I didn't even need the board, I could just write the letters on the table. Basically, that it wasn't the thing, an object, but something less tangible—a kind of energy or faith.

HYPHEN PRESS

WWW.LINETO.COM

Lorem ipsum dolor sit amet, consectetur
adipisicing elit, sed do eiusmod tempor
incididunt ut labore et dolore magna aliqua.
Ut enim ad minim veniam, quis nostrud
exercitation ullamco laboris nisi ut aliquip
ex ea commodo consequat. Duis aute irure
dolor in reprehenderit in voluptate velit
esse cillum dolore eu fugiat nulla pariatur.
Excepteur sint occaecat cupidatat non
proident, sunt in culpa qui officia deserunt
mollit anim id est laborum.

CALARTS
GRAPHIC DESIGN
PROGRAM

WHICH FONT?

Ask FontBook.
FontBook.com

ARTS COUNCIL: MANHATTAN

CASCO

OFFICE FOR ART, DESIGN AND THEORY